THE FOUR DIMENSIONS OF PRINCIPAL LEADERSHIP

A FRAMEWORK FOR LEADING 21ST-CENTURY SCHOOLS

Reginald Leon Green
University of Memphis

Allyn & Bacon

Boston   New York   San Francisco
Mexico City   Montreal   Toronto   London   Madrid   Munich   Paris
Hong Kong   Singapore   Tokyo   Cape Town   Sydney

Library of Congress Cataloging-in-Publication Data

Green, Reginald Leon.
    The four dimensions of principal leadership: a framework for leading
21st-century schools/Reginald Leon Green.
        p. cm.
    ISBN-13: 978-0-13-112686-2
    ISBN-10: 0-13-112686-5
    1. School principals.   2. School management and organization.   I. Title.
    LB2831.9.G745 2010
    371.2'012—dc22

                                                        2008045152

Executive Editor: Stephen D. Dragin
Editorial Assistant: Anne Whittaker
Marketing Manager: Jared Brueckner
Production Manager: Wanda Rockwell
Creative Director: Jayne Conte
Cover Designer: Lisbeth Axell
Cover Image: Getty Images Inc.

For related titles and support materials, visit our online catalog at www.pearsonhighered.com.

Between the time website information is gathered and then published, it is not unusual for
some sites to have closed. Also, the transcription of URLs can result in typographical errors.
The publisher would appreciate notification where these errors occur so that they may be
corrected in subsequent editions.

CCSSO Copyrighted Material
The Interstate School Leaders Licensure Consortium (ISLLC) Standards were developed by the
Council of Chief State School Officers (CCSSO) and member states. Copies may be
downloaded from the Council's website at www.ccsso.org.
Council of Chief State School Officers. (1996). *Interstate School Leaders Licensure Consortium
(ISLLC) standards for school leaders*. Washington, DC: Author.

Allyn & Bacon
is an imprint of

10   9   8   7   6   5   4   3   2   1
ISBN-10:   0-13-112686-5
ISBN-13: 978-0-13-112686-2

PREFACE

Providing the leadership for 21st-century schools is a challenging endeavor for any individual who assumes the role. *The Four Dimensions of Principal Leadership: A Framework for Leading 21st-Century Schools* characterizes those challenges and outlines the functions that individuals must perform if they are to be effective in the role. We are in a new era that requires school leaders to know themselves and the individuals with whom they work and serve. They have to understand the complexities of organizational life, build bridges through relationships, and utilize best practices to enhance teaching and learning. Additionally, they must have a vision that is communicated to all stakeholders, be able to build trust among colleagues, and be skilled in distributing leadership roles throughout the organization.

In my first publication, *Practicing the Art of Leadership: A Problem-Based Approach to Implementing the ISLLC Standards*, the challenges of the current era were approached by presenting a series of theories that inform leadership best practices. The content of that text offered readers an opportunity to acquire an in-depth understanding of the practical application of those theories by analyzing scenarios depicting real school situations. This work confronts the challenges of the era, using a multi-dimensional focus. It addresses the nature and complexities of leadership in 21st-century schools relative to the behavior of leaders, their influence on followers, the structure of the organization, and other factors that influence the academic achievement of students. My goal is to divide school leadership into four dimensions, providing readers an opportunity to analyze and engage in leadership practices from four perspectives: (1) *understanding self and others*; (2) *understanding the complexities of organizational life*; (3) *building bridges through relationships*, and (4) *engaging in leadership best practices*. There will be instances when the reader will find the content of the first work helpful, especially the theoretical framework it provides in the areas of communication, decision making, conflict management, and change.

The essence of the four dimensions is woven into a tapestry of excellence that identifies a balance between opposing forces and informs leadership practices that foster effectiveness in 21st-century schools. They provide school leaders with more than knowledge of leadership theories and their application–additionally, they provide them with an integrated approach to working collaboratively with others to solve complex school problems in a manner that will enable all students to achieve academically.

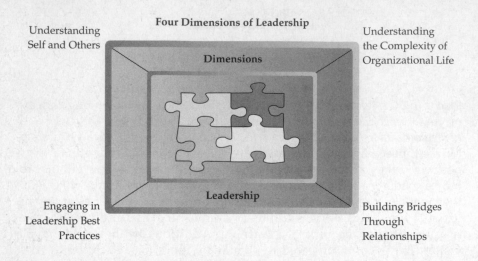

Four Dimensions of Leadership

THE COMPOSITION OF THE DIMENSIONS

Embedded in the four dimensions are the concepts, theories, and proposi-
tions being espoused by today's foremost leadership theorists and writers.
Whereas each dimension is significant in its own right, they build on one another. Accordingly, the essence of leadership effectiveness clearly emerges
when all four are working simultaneously. If any one of the four is missing,
leadership effectiveness is challenged.

THE USE OF DICHOTOMIES

Dichotomies are used in introducing and exploring the content of each dimension. The basic premise for use of dichotomies is quite straightforward. A review of contemporary leadership literature reveals that many theories offering
principles and practices of leadership for 21st-century schools are explained,
using some type of dichotomy (Green, 2005; Hoy & Sweetland, 2001;
Lunenburg & Ornstein, 1996). There is tremendous power in using dichotomies to illustrate that theories informing leadership have two extremes.
In this work, as we discuss the principles of leadership theories, the two extremes are explored. We illustrate, through the use of practical school situations, that effective leadership is the result of an individual's ability to find the
balance between the two extremes. For example, leaders must find a balance
between exhibiting task behavior and exhibiting relationship behavior; controlling followers or acquiring a commitment from followers, or distinguish-
ing between enabling forces and hindering forces. The critical factor is the
leader's ability to assess a given situation and match leader behavior with that
situation.

THE VALUE OF ACQUIRING THE DELICATE BALANCE

A balance between the style and behavior of the leader and the situation must be found. For, it is the acquisition of this delicate balance that is likely to make the difference between effective and ineffective leadership in schools. This balance, of course, is situational, requiring the individual to have knowledge of the inner workings of an open social system and to become skilled in adapting to various environmental influences. Therefore, a key concept embedded in this work is adaptability. Discussing leadership in this manner offers insight into leadership as a combination of understanding self and others, adapting to various organizational structures, building relationships with other individuals, and preparing for the impact of environmental influences.

CONTENT OF THE TEXT

The text is divided into five sections. Section I provides readers with a general overview of the principalship which is used interchangeably throughout the text with the term school leader. Each of the remaining four sections is devoted to an exploration of a dimension of leadership. In the chapters contained in those sections, each dimension is extensively explored, and the interrelationship and interdependency relative to leadership are probed in an in-depth manner. Examples are presented that illustrate how effective leaders communicate, implement a vision, establish goals, assume responsibility for their attainment, structure schools for effective teaching and learning, empower people, and lead in a manner that enables all students to reach their full potential. In some instances, content may appear to be repetitious. However, concepts are necessarily repeated, as they overlap in a number of instances, further illustrating their importance.

In 21st-century schools, actions of school leaders should be informed by purpose, process, and a desired outcome. Chapter 1 is particularly devoted to this concept. It provides a general overview of school leadership delineating what leaders of 21st-century schools need to know and be able to do, describing the purpose, process, and desired outcome. Chapters 2 and 3 proceed to allow readers an opportunity to develop a foundation for leading a school by understanding self and other individuals. Having read Chapters 2 and 3 and having discerned how effective school leaders establish a foundation for leading, the other three dimensions are presented in the remaining chapters, allowing readers to focus their attention on structuring the organization for effective teaching and learning, leading with compassion, and utilizing best practices to meet the needs of students and stakeholders.

Reginald Leon Green

Dedication

I dedicate this book to the true leaders in my life who made its writing possible. First, my brother, the late Mr. Charles D. Green who demonstrated that graduation from college was possible for the Green boys; Mr. B. T. Dozier, the man who made college possible by providing me with work aid at Tennessee State University; the late Mr. Oliver Johnson, Principal of Lincoln Junior High School who mentored me into school leadership; the late Dr. Neil Aslin, my doctoral advisor at the University of Missouri-Columbia, who modeled the true meaning of leadership; Dr. Willie Herenton who fostered my entrance into the Rockefeller Foundation Superintendent's Preparation Program; Mr. Earnest Grayson who gave me my first top-level administrative position as deputy superintendent of the Jefferson County Schools (Louisville, Kentucky); Dr. Frederick Gies who introduced me to the world of higher education and the professorial ranks, and last, but not least, Dr. John Goodlad, who inspired me with his depth of knowledge, creativity, and wisdom.

To these individuals, I say thanks for a very rewarding professional experience. Because of your leadership, "I am me."

ABOUT THE AUTHOR

Reginald Leon Green is Professor of Educational Leadership at the University of Memphis. He received the Ed. D. in Educational Administration and Supervision from the University of Missouri-Columbia. He has served at the teacher, principal, deputy superintendent, and superintendent levels of K-12 education, and has been in higher education for Sixteen (16) years. In 1977, Dr. Green was one of five educators chosen nationally to participate in the Rockefeller Foundation's Superintendency Preparation Program, and in 1996, he was selected as an associate to the Institute for Educational Renewal, under the leadership of Dr. John Goodlad.

Dr. Green has published books on inner-city education, educational leadership, and articles on educational restructuring, primary grade restructuring, gang violence, and other contemporary educational issues. He has completed national inquiries into nurturing characteristics that exist in schools, as well as standards and assessment measures being established as a part of the national school reform movement. This work led to the publication of the book entitled *Practicing the Art of Leadership: A Problem-Based Approach to Implementing the ISLLC Standards* and development of the Center for Urban School Leadership at the University of Memphis, where Dr. Green administered programs to prepare principals for roles in urban school leadership, using a nontraditional approach. Dr. Green teaches courses in educational leadership with a focus on instructional leadership and participatory governance and change.

ACKNOWLEDGMENTS

Many creative individuals must be acknowledged for the content of this book. First, I am grateful to Jean, my wife, who spent countless hours alone while I worked to complete this book. She was my strongest supporter and my best, critical friend. Without her, none of my work would be possible. Thanks, Jean, for all you do and most of all for being the lady you are. Next, I express my appreciation to Dr. Sharen Cypress, Associate Professor at Freed-Hardeman University, who served as my writing partner and spent countless hours researching topics, reviewing sections of chapters, and designing many of the exhibits that appear throughout the book. Also, appreciation is expressed to Dr. Glynda Cryer, retired educator (Memphis, Tennessee), who read and edited many drafts of chapters and advised me on their structure and content.

In addition, I would like to thank Ms. Courtney Fee for her contributions to *Understanding Self and Others* and the many other individuals who have completed work in the Center for Urban School Leadership and tested many of the concepts as they practice leadership in schools across West Tennessee. I am also grateful to the many school leaders who allowed me to interview them. I give special thanks to my students who were members of the Memphis Leadership Scholars, Cohort 2.

Members of Memphis Leadership Scholars
Cohort 2

Adriane M. Allen	Stephanie Kelly	Rita Matheny
Brenda Williams-Diaz	Jennifer M. Donald	Kiva Taylor
Margaret Gilmore	Carmen Y. Gregory	LeAndrea Taylor
Shaneka Lopez	Sabrina Sneed-Matthews	Charlene Thornton
Valerie Eskeridge-Matthews	Linda McClora	Kimberly N. Shaw

I also thank the reviewers of this book: Ira E. Bogotch, Florida Atlantic University; Rose Mary Newton, University of Alabama; and Larry W. Hughes, University of Houston.

INTRODUCTION

THE ROLE OF 21ST-CENTURY SCHOOL LEADERS: PURPOSE, PROCESS, AND OUTCOME

The new definition for leaders of 21st-century schools centers on purpose, process, and outcome. One of the most important aspects contributing to the effectiveness of 21st-century school leaders is their ability to identify and articulate the purpose, process, and desired outcome for all school programs, projects, and activities. The importance of each of these components is briefly discussed.

Purpose

The purpose of all school-related programs, projects, and activities should be student achievement, providing focus, and offering directions to a faculty. People in the organization need to know and understand the purpose of the work. With knowledge of the purpose, all individuals can set priorities, focus on the desired outcomes, and reflect on their behavior in route to those outcomes. It provides meaning and establishes directions for action. It fosters commitment and hope. It answers the question, "What is the meaning of our work?" To acquire the purpose, leaders must analyze each situation, for purpose is embedded in the data regarding each situation.

Process

Process denotes the methods, procedures, and techniques that a faculty can use to achieve the identified purpose. People in school organizations have to be able to identify processes that can be used to achieve the stated purpose. In some instances, this might pose a challenge, as individuals might have to abandon old behaviors in favor of new skills that meet the needs of today's students. To be effective, school leaders must be astute in recognizing when the existing skills of individuals fall short of those needed to enhance the academic achievement of students. With this understanding, they can identify a clear process to be used in achieving organizational goals.

In some instances, people become complacent and are content with current conditions, thus, they fall short of their potential. In these instances, it becomes necessary for the leadership to expose them to new and different processes. These processes are embedded in theories, as theories inform practice. They provide directions regarding processes that can be used to achieve the purpose.

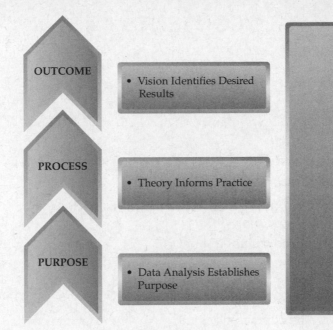

EXHIBIT F.1 Purpose, Process, and Outcome

Outcome

Outcome is the result of the efforts contributed to achieving the desired purpose—enhanced student achievement. Therefore, to be effective, school leaders need to facilitate the establishment of a shared vision, for the outcome is embedded in the vision. Once a shared vision is established, a clearly defined process can be used to achieve the desired outcome, responding to the question, "How will the positive results of our work make a difference in the academic achievement of students?"

More often than not, it is the lack of a clearly defined process for use in obtaining the identified purpose that becomes a stumbling block, hindering leadership effectiveness. Therefore, one might conclude that having a clearly defined process to use in pursuing the school's purpose is tantamount to achieving the desired outcome. A graphic description of this concept appears in Exhibit F.1.

When leaders begin with the outcome in mind and conceptualize and internalize processes that can be used to achieve their purpose, they build a capacity to lead. In building that capacity, three significant elements should be evident. The style of leadership should be facilitative, and, in that process, leadership should be distributed throughout the organization. Finally, freedom should be extended to individuals who are willing to assume responsibility for their behavior. Through these essential elements, the importance of purpose, process, and outcomes is evident, and it is these elements that are discussed throughout the text.

CONTENTS

1

Preparing Leaders for 21st-Century Schools

(Standards 1 through 6)

"The difficulty lies not so much in developing new ideas as in escaping from the old ones."

JOHN MAYNARD KEYNES

"The strength of any organization is a direct result of the strength of its leaders. Weak leaders equal weak organizations. Strong leaders equal strong organizations. Everything rises and falls on leadership."

JOHN C. MAXWELL

Variance and Disparities in Student Achievement

Standards, Competencies, and Accountability Measures

INTRODUCTION

Over the past century, we have progressed through many educational reform eras. During each of those eras, the role of school leaders has been redefined. With each new definition, a number of books, articles, and publications, written by various authors representing different paradigms, offer processes and procedures to clarify the roles and responsibilities advocated by the new definition. Yet, schools continue to struggle, and some writers and researchers believe that it is because today's school leaders are ill-equipped to manage the challenges that they face (Hoachlander, Alt, & Beltranena, 2001; Levine, 2005). They proffer that the leadership being provided is not sufficient to enable all students to achieve a level of excellence that will afford them an opportunity to live and work in a social and political democracy. Therefore, once again, school leadership is being redefined.

For leaders of 21st-century schools, the definition is being informed by standards, competencies, and accountability measures. This movement is permeating the field of school leadership, forging a connection between school leaders and student achievement (see Exhibit 1.1). The fundamental principles underlying the movement are high expectations for all children and the accountability of individuals accepting responsibility for their education (Marzano, Waters, & McNulty, 2005; Riley, 2002). As the focus of the previously mentioned connection intensifies, the role of school leaders has escalated to include visionary leadership, instructional leadership, data analysis, public relations, curriculum design, building professional learning communities, and a staggering array of other professional responsibilities.

This chapter contains five areas and has, as a purpose, the establishment of a foundation for the remainder of the text. The first area presents a definition of 21st-century school leadership as defined by the new standards, competencies, and accountability movement. The next area examines standards that inform the behavior of 21st-century school leaders. In area three, the focus is on competencies that school leaders should master, and area four

EXHIBIT 1.1   The New Accountability Movement

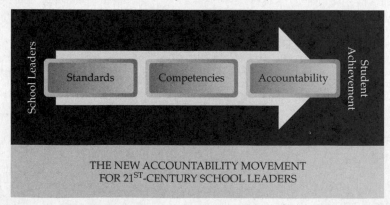

School Leaders

Standards   Competencies   Accountability

Student Achievement

THE NEW ACCOUNTABILITY MOVEMENT
FOR 21ST-CENTURY SCHOOL LEADERS

presents some of the accountability measures that are being used to assess the performance of school leaders. The chapter concludes with an overview of the content of the remaining chapters in the text.

21ST-CENTURY SCHOOL LEADERSHIP DEFINED

The 21st-century school leader is the "chief learning officer" of the school, an individual with a vision for the future of the school who can articulate that vision to all stakeholders. Leaders collaborate with other individuals and groups to create, manage, and implement an instructional program that meets the needs of all students.

This new definition emphasizes that 21st-century school leaders are instructional leaders responsible for developing and supporting a collaborative school culture focused on teaching and learning. It is a shift from the definition offered in the previous era which presented managerial functions as the major focus of school leadership. In the current era, managerial functions remain important; however, the major focus has shifted to instructional leadership. Nevertheless, the need for school leaders to perform managerial functions cannot be minimized. Even though the functions are different, effective leaders are also effective managers, requiring them to divide their functions into two parts. To illustrate the point, a description of the functions 21st-century school leaders perform in an instructional leadership role and in a managerial role is presented in the following section.

Instructional Leadership Roles and Functions of School Leaders

Although instructional leadership has been identified as vital for effectiveness in schools, at least since the 1970s, the current accountability movement has given it a renewed focus (ISLLC Standards 1–6, 2008; NAESP, 2004; Stricherz, 2001). Some of the specific functions of the new role are:

- ✔ Providing instructional leadership through the establishment, articulation, and implementation of a vision of learning that is supported by all stakeholders.
- ✔ Creating and sustaining a community of learners (a team) that makes student and adult learning the center focus, and then, collaborating for goal attainment.
- ✔ Facilitating the creation of a school culture and climate based on high expectations for students, faculty, and community stakeholders.
- ✔ Advocating, nurturing, and sustaining a school culture that is conducive to student learning and staff professional growth.
- ✔ Leading the school improvement process in a manner that addresses the needs of all students.
- ✔ Engaging the community in activities to create shared responsibilities for students and school success.

✔ Utilizing multiple sources of data to assess, identify, and foster instructional improvement.

In fulfilling this new role, school leaders must have a vision of a desirable future for the school. Then, they have to communicate that vision to all stakeholders and place a "relentless focus" on the academic achievement of students. In addition, they have to align assessments with standards and accountability systems and make an intensive effort to assist teachers in improving their practice. They must provide extra instruction for students who need it (NAESP, 2004).

Managerial Roles and Functions of School Leaders

By tradition, school leaders functioning in managerial roles were primarily concerned with organizational maintenance, attempting to coordinate and control organizational activities. In order to accomplish this, they established and followed a predetermined set of rules and regulations. As complex issues surfaced, they addressed them with the short-range objective of maintaining order and consistency.

Today, as leaders seek to improve instruction, thus enhancing student achievement, they perform managerial functions in every step of the process; school improvement requires school leaders to manage the organization, operations, and resources in an efficient and effective manner (ISLLC Standard 3, 2008). Quite clearly, in addition to having effective leadership skills, enhancing student performance requires school leaders to have effective managerial skills. Although there are many variations of management, 21st-century school leaders will most likely be engaged in planning, organizing, staffing, coordinating, directing, reporting, and budgeting. Following are some examples of such tasks:

✔ *Planning*—Many states and school districts require school leaders to develop a school improvement plan. Development of the plan requires the assessment of student progress, the establishment of goals, identification of budgetary resources, and the assignment of faculty and staff to perform various tasks.

✔ *Coordinating*—People, programs, and activities have to be coordinated, and community resources have to be mobilized to ensure that the school mission is supported and goals of the school improvement plan are achieved.

✔ *Budgeting*—School leaders have to prepare and manage an annual operating budget, as well as various student activity accounts. This function requires the school leader to have detailed knowledge of fiscal operations and business management procedures, and it should be completed with a focus on meeting the goals and objectives of the school improvement plan.

✔ *Directing*—Effective school leaders manage the school operation to ensure organizational efficiency and effectiveness. In some instances, individuals have to be motivated and/or influenced to perform assigned tasks. When school leaders understand the level of readiness of faculty and staff members, they are positioned to use the power of influence to ensure that organizational tasks are completed in a timely, efficient, and effective manner.

✔ *Staffing*—School leaders have to be skilled in recruiting, selecting, placing, and retaining quality faculty and staff. In addition, once employed, these individuals have to be provided focused professional development to assist them in fulfilling their assigned responsibilities.

✔ *Reporting*—Effective school leaders complete various reports that illustrate accountability for the effective and efficient use of resources. They also establish plans to respond to and influence the political, social, economic, legal, and cultural context of the school. This will allow them to maintain positive relationships in the external school community.

✔ *Organizing*—To maximize teaching and learning time, school leaders have to develop an organizational structure that focuses daily operations on the academic achievement of students. This function includes such activities as scheduling and dividing work assignments to ensure that the learning environment is safe and that work is assigned and performed in an ethical manner (ISLLC Standards, 2008; NAESP, 2004; NASSP, 2004).

Leaders are different from managers in that they build relationships and use the power of influence to gain the commitment of followers. They empower followers and encourage them to be creative and to take initiative in their area of assignment, and, when necessary, they are willing to subordinate their position for the good of the school community. A hallmark of their leadership style is helping others grow so they build capacity to contribute to school goal attainment.

Without question, effective school leaders manage the organization; however, they manage using principles of leadership that influence collaboration and cooperation, and they continuously seek practices and procedures that can be used to enhance teaching and learning. Management and leadership must be balanced, as a structure must be in place, and the actions ongoing in that structure must be coordinated and monitored to ensure organizational efficiency and effectiveness.

STANDARDS, COMPETENCIES, AND ACCOUNTABILITY MEASURES

Supporters of the standards, competencies, and accountability era advocate the new definition for 21st-century school leadership (Lashway, 2003; Reeves, 2002; Riley 2002). In this era, leaders are faced with challenges of meeting standards, becoming effective instructional leaders, and assuming responsibility for managing the organization in a manner that facilitates the academic achievement of all students in attendance. The Interstate School Leader Licensure Consortium (ISLLC, 2008), a leader in the movement, developed and presented to the education community six standards that inform the behavior of 21st-century school leaders. As a result of their actions, states across the nation have been motivated to adopt some form of standards and accountability measures in order to inform leadership preparation and practices in their state. The ISLLC Standards, as well as other standards, are being used to build an infrastructure to ensure that school leaders acquire the knowledge, disposition, and skills necessary to understand existing school conditions. The standards also provide a structure to create collaborative environments and build the capacity to prepare all students to become productive citizens, able to live and work in a social and political democracy. The six ISLLC Standards leading the movement, as well as practices that can be used to meet these standards, are listed in the next section.

THE SIX ISLLC STANDARDS

Standard 1: An education leader promotes the success of every student by facilitating the development, articulation, implementation, and stewardship of a vision of learning that is shared and supported by all stakeholders.

Functions:
  A. Collaboratively develop and implement a shared vision and mission
  B. Collect and use data to identify goals, assess organizational effectiveness, and promote organizational learning
  C. Create and implement plans to achieve goals
  D. Promote continuous and sustainable improvement
  E. Monitor and evaluate progress and revise plans

> **Meeting Standard 1:** Readers can engage in activities that require them to describe approaches that they would use to bring an underachieving school up to and above the established standard. They can also engage in persuasive conversation, model behavior that they would use to communicate, influence commitment, and develop plans to share ideas and programs to members of a faculty and the community. In addition, they might engage in meaningful role-play activities. Role-playing is a useful activity in preparing to meet this standard, as it provides readers an opportunity to convey the goal they want to achieve as a school leader and describe a process of achieving that goal.

Standard 2: An education leader promotes the success of every student by advocating, nurturing, and sustaining a school culture and instructional program conducive to student learning and staff professional growth.

Functions:
  A. Nurture and sustain a culture of collaboration, trust, learning, and high expectations
  B. Create a comprehensive, rigorous, and coherent curricular program
  C. Create a personalized and motivating learning environment for students

D. Supervise instruction
E. Develop assessment and accountability systems to monitor student progress
F. Develop the instructional and leadership capacity of staff
G. Maximize time spent on quality instruction
H. Promote the use of the most effective and appropriate technologies to support teaching and learning
I. Monitor and evaluate the impact of the instructional program

Meeting Standard 2: Both the internal and external climate of schools influence the teaching and learning process and must be a major concern of school leaders while they strive to establish an effective school program. This requires school leaders to be sensitive to their leadership style, as well as the style that others bring to the schoolhouse. There must be a connection between leaders and followers.

In analyzing this standard, we visited 18 schools and identified the internal and external climate of those schools. In collaborative dialogue with the principals of those schools, the hindering and enabling forces of both the internal and external climates were identified, and approaches that were used to transform the hindering forces into enabling forces were discussed. Identifying the type of climate that best supports an instructional program is important, but schools differ; therefore, the most appropriate climate for teaching and learning will differ, from school to school. Consequently, school leaders must be skilled in analyzing the internal and external forces of a particular school in order that leader behavior that best supports instruction in that school can be exhibited.

Standard 3: An education leader promotes the success of every student by ensuring management of the organization, operation, and resources for a safe, efficient, and effective learning environment.

Functions:
A. Monitor and evaluate the management and operational systems
B. Obtain, allocate, align, and efficiently utilize human, fiscal, and technological resources
C. Promote and protect the welfare and safety of students and staff
D. Develop the capacity for distributed leadership
E. Ensure that teacher and organizational time is focused to support quality instruction and student learning

Meeting Standard 3: Schools have to be structured for success, as structure establishes roles and functions, governs organizational behavior, and brings order to the organization. To a large extent, the structure of the school will determine the extent to which individuals participate in the decision-making process, the use of resources, instructional effectiveness, and the safety of instructional and pupil personnel.

To meet this standard, readers might consider conducting inquiry into various school structures and designing operational procedures that effectively align those structures with the vision they have for a school. They might also use problem-based case studies to analyze behavior aligned with various structures, establish role expectations, and outline evaluative standards for different structures. It is important for school leaders to understand the values and beliefs that individuals in school organizations have about the nature of their situation. These values and beliefs form the culture of a school and influence the structure that school leaders put into practice.

Standard 4: An education leader promotes the success of every student by collaborating with faculty and community members, responding to diverse community interests and needs, and mobilizing community resources.

Functions:
- A. Collect and analyze data and information pertinent to the educational environment
- B. Promote understanding, appreciation, and use of the community's diverse cultural, social, and intellectual resources
- C. Build and sustain positive relationships with families and caregivers
- D. Build and sustain productive relationships with community partners

Meeting Standard 4: School leaders cannot always address every situation. Consequently, they must be able to acquire the support of individuals inside and outside of the schoolhouse. In acquiring this support, the art of collaboration is a critical factor. It is easy to say, "Let us collaborate," but collaboration is difficult to put into practice. Therefore, to meet this standard, readers might consider practicing the art of collaboration. They can pinpoint challenging school situations and engage other individuals to assist them in meeting those challenges. They can also participate in activities where they experience taking risks and removing obstacles that inhibit success. In addition, they might design a plan that requires trusting people and their judgment and influencing individuals to accept responsibility for school organizational goal attainment. The 21st-century school leader realizes that the involvement of stakeholders is of primary importance, and it is a skill that is acquired through practice.

Standard 5: An education leader promotes the success of every student by acting with integrity, fairness, and in an ethical manner.

Functions:
- A. Ensure a system of accountability for every student's academic and social success
- B. Model principles of self-awareness, reflective practice, transparency, and ethical behavior
- C. Safeguard the values of democracy, equity, and diversity
- D. Consider and evaluate the potential moral and legal consequences of decision making
- E. Promote social justice and ensure that individual student needs inform all aspects of schooling

Meeting Standard 5: Schools are very diverse, and the make-up of that diversity is multifaceted. There are racial, cultural, religious, socio-economic, and gender diversities, just to mention a few of the readily identifiable differences that exist in today's schools. To meet this standard, readers can visit schools where the student population is highly diverse. We have found in discussing the subject with principals that exposure to a diverse population is very important. One can talk about diversity, but to bring the concept into focus, one must be exposed to it and embrace it. Thus, the dichotomy is talk and action. In addition, readers can log experiences and identify strategies that they would use to recognize and respond to students of diverse cultures. Also, they might analyze scenarios that are laden with diverse issues. One such scenario appears in Chapter 2. The leader behaviors that are frequently exhibited in terms of strategies to use in diverse school settings are fairness, sensitivity, consistency, respect, reliability, and acceptance of differences.

Standard 6: An education leader promotes the success of every student by understanding, responding to, and influencing the political, social, economic, legal, and cultural context.

Functions:
   A. Advocate for children, families, and caregivers
   B. Act to influence local, district, state, and national decisions affecting student learning
   C. Assess, analyze, and anticipate emerging trends and initiatives in order to adapt leadership strategies

Meeting Standard 6: An effective school leader should know the community and be knowledgeable of the social, political, economic, and academic barriers that impact education. The school leader should collaborate with the faculty, staff, and community leaders to develop a plan of action to identify these barriers, eradicate them, and move students to continuous academic and social improvement. To address this standard, readers may tour communities, attend parent/teacher meetings, attend board of education meetings, and develop school community relations plans that they can implement. These plans should address factors that affect schools as they recognize a variety of ideas, values, and cultures, and include models and strategies of change and conflict resolution.

Standards are the heart of 21st-century school leadership, as they inform what school leaders should know and be able to do. Although opinions vary in this area, there are commonalities in much of the literature relative to the leader behavior informed by the standard's movement (Fullan, 2001; Hughes, 2005; IEL, 2000; ISLLC, 2008; NAESP, 2004; Sergiovanni, 1996; SREB, 2001). These sources agree that 21st-century school leaders need to be future-focused, able to develop, communicate, and implement a shared vision, and able to create true learning communities. They should also be purpose and value-driven and able to lead instructional change, placing student and adult learning at the center. In summary, they understand self and others, are knowledgeable of the complexities of school organizational life, can build bridges to goal attainment through relationships, and utilize best practices to address the needs of all students. The ISLLC Standards which have these behaviors embedded in them should be exhibited by 21st-century school leaders. We turn now to the school leader's ability to conduct activities to meet the advocated standards through an examination of thirteen (13) core competencies.

THE COMPETENCIES

In leading 21st-century schools, it is important for school leaders to be competent in several areas. From a preponderance of the literature, describing what effective school leaders should be able to do, 13 core competencies have been identified. These competencies inform the type of skills and attributes that the new reform movement is requiring of school leaders.

The 13 Core Competencies

- *Visionary Leadership*—Effective leaders demonstrate energy, commitment, and an entrepreneurial spirit. They communicate values and a conviction that all children will learn at high levels, and they inspire others with that vision. These leaders are able to influence a faculty to display faith and trust in their decisions and to assist in the transformation process. They elevate people to a place they have never been.

- *Unity of Purpose*—Effective leaders develop unity of purpose with all stakeholders and keep the school focused on student learning. They are able to acquire the commitment of faculty members around a single focus and align their behavior with activities that foster goal attainment. These leaders realize that beginning with the end in mind and providing positive directions for faculty and staff are critical to leadership effectiveness.

- *Learning Community*—Effective leaders create empowering environments that support innovation, involvement in decision making, and continuous professional development. They distribute leadership throughout the organization and influence individuals to display mutual support for goal attainment.

- *Instructional Leadership (Teaching and Learning)*—Effective leaders facilitate the application of current knowledge in learning and human development. They are able to use data to make instructional program decisions that meet the needs of all students.

- *Curriculum and Instruction*—Effective leaders understand the relationships among curriculum coherence, student success, and pedagogical leadership. They keep the school focused on student learning and are able to put a curriculum that contains research-based strategies sufficient to meet the needs of all students into practice.

- *Professional Development*—Effective leaders are lifelong learners who demonstrate commitment to their own professional development and renewal. They also ensure that all faculty and staff members are engaged in programs and activities that keep them motivated, energized, and inspired to perform at their maximum level of effectiveness.

- *Organizational Management*—Effective leaders continuously improve the culture of the school by utilizing the principles and practices of effective organizational management. They structure the school organization in a manner that conveys high expectations for students and adults and the effective use of material resources.

- *Assessment*—Effective leaders facilitate the use of a variety of strategies to monitor student performance and continuous learner development. The process they use contains a built-in plan for improving student achievement.

- *Reflection*—Effective leaders reflect on practices and evaluate results for the purpose of modifying future practices as warranted. They acquire and analyze knowledge about themselves to achieve self-understanding, as they realize the ability to self-assess and initiate action for self-improvement is a critical aspect of being an effective leader.

- *Collaboration*—Effective leaders engage all stakeholders in the creation of a caring, safe community that values self-motivation, active inquiry, and positive social interaction. They are able to work in a multicultural environment and can enhance student achievement, working with individuals who have diverse views and interests.
- *Diversity*—Effective leaders create an environment in which the ethical and moral imperatives of schooling in a democratic society are valued. Unfair treatment and inequalities are recognized and eliminated.
- *Inquiry*—Effective leaders create an environment in which inquiry guides the continuous improvement of the school organization. They are concerned with identifying proven practices and acquiring information that can be aligned with instructional needs.
- *Professionalism*—Effective leaders demonstrate ethical and moral leadership and a commitment to the development of the profession. They display behavior that conforms to the ethical standards of the profession and put a system in place that influences all members of the school organization to behave in a similar manner.

These competencies speak to the depth of leadership and the power of leaders who exhibit the behavior they describe. Green (2006) developed *The Leadership Behavior Inventory* which measures the extent to which school leaders exhibit the behaviors informed by these competencies in a school setting and their relationship to school effectiveness. Results from these measures and other scholarly works referencing the behaviors that these competencies inform suggest that school leaders who become skilled in these competencies and exhibit the behavior informed by them are likely to meet and exceed the standards advocated for 21st-century school leaders (DuFour & Eaker, 1998; Mai, 2004; Marzano, 2003; SREB, 2006).

STYLES OF LEADERSHIP FOR 21ST-CENTURY SCHOOLS

The increased responsibility on 21st-century school leaders brings still another element into the equation. Having acquired the competence necessary to lead, one must consider the style of leadership that will foster effectiveness in the schoolhouse. Today's school leaders are expected to move the school organization from its current condition to a vision that is shared by all stakeholders. In order to meet this expectation, tasks have to be completed. Thus, individuals are employed and assigned specific responsibility for the completion of those tasks. Of equal concern, the individuals employed have specific goals and objectives that they are attempting to achieve. Both the organizational tasks and the goals and objectives of the individuals employed have to receive consideration from the school leader. Thus, a dual situation emerges, the organizational tasks that are to be completed and the manner in which the leader interacts with followers considering their goals. In essence, the behavior school leaders display in directing an individual or group of individuals to complete tasks for the purpose of achieving school goals and/or outcomes is classified as their style of leadership (Stogdill & Coons, 1957).

Over the years, school leaders have used various styles to achieve the goals and objectives of the school. Different schools and situations offer different challenges, and different leadership styles have different effects on followers. Therefore, being able to identify the appropriate leadership style to use in a given situation is a valuable quality. What leaders must keep in the forefront are the two-dimensional phenomenon, organizational tasks to be completed and the behavior of the leader.

Studies of leaders and the manner in which they achieve desired results in organizations have revealed a great deal about the styles of leaders and which styles tend to be favored by followers. The results of a study of three different styles of leadership, autocratic, democratic, and laissez-faire, conducted at the University of Iowa by Lewin, Lippitt, and White (1939) revealed that followers preferred leaders who placed emphasis on shared decision making and viewed followers as equals. Another well-known study conducted at The Ohio State University characterized leader behavior as initiating structure or giving consideration. This study revealed that followers were highly satisfied when leaders used a combination of highly structured and highly considerate behavior (Stogdill & Coons, 1957). Still another study conducted at the University of Michigan revealed that effective leaders were generally task-oriented, set high performance goals, and focused on such administrative functions as planning, coordinating, and facilitating work (Likert, 1967).

A number of other studies have been conducted on leader behavior in an attempt to determine the style of behavior that is most effective in reaching organizational goals. In one way or another, the results of most of those studies reveal data regarding the two-dimensional phenomenon of autocratic task-oriented behavior and humanistic relationship-oriented behavior. For a detailed discussion of the aforementioned studies and a number of others, refer to Chapters 1 and 2 of the companion text, *Practicing the Art of Leadership: A Problem-Based Approach to Implementing the ISLLC Standards (3rd. ed.)*.

Transactional vs. Transformational Leadership

A noteworthy study for consideration by 21st-century school leaders is the examination of leadership behavior conducted by Burns (1978). Burns also characterized leader behavior in two dimensions; one set of behaviors was characterized as transactional and another transformational.

TRANSACTIONAL LEADERSHIP   In contrasting the two types of behavior, transactional leadership behavior can be described as behavior of a contractual nature. The leader engages followers in an exchange to gain cooperation and ensure task completion. It is a power-based, rewards and punishment relationship; leaders get tasks completed by providing rewards to followers who complete tasks in a specified and desired manner. In addition, followers may be subjected to some type of punishment if tasks are not completed as specified and/or desired. Transactional leadership is a managerial style of leadership, a way of maintaining the workflow of the organization; both leader and follower achieve their objective (Bass, 1985). One might relate such behavior to the work of Getzels and Guba (1957) who theorized that leaders should seek congruence between two dimensions, the organizational dimension (normative) and the individual dimension (idiographic). They offered that with congruence of the two dimensions, organizational effectiveness would be increased (Green, 2009).

TRANSFORMATIONAL LEADERSHIP In contrast, transformational leaders lead with knowledge of individuals inside and outside of the schoolhouse. They have a vision of the future of the organization, can effectively communicate that vision to followers, and are able to get them to understand the importance of its attainment. In addition, transformational leaders are able to inspire followers to deeply commit to the vision and work in an interdependent manner toward its attainment. Consistent with the behavior informed by ISLLC Standard 5, they subordinate their own interests and are able to inspire followers to behave in a similar manner.

The transformational leader has a vision of the future, and their followers are bound together around a set of common beliefs, values, and norms that foster attainment of that vision. They develop partnerships with followers inside and outside of the schoolhouse and enroute to vision and goal attainment, they empower followers to make decisions and create a culture that enables them to participate in a collaborative manner. In essence, they share their power, distribute leadership tasks, and inspire others to lead.

The standards of this educational reform era have specifically identified the behavior that 21st-century school leaders should exhibit. Those behaviors are immersed in the definition of transformational leadership as defined by Burns (1978) and Bass (1985). Consequently, for the purpose of this work, we advocate that 21st-century school leaders consider transformational leadership as their primary style. In doing so, they should consider the following practices:

Facilitative Leaders Transformational leaders are facilitators. They exhibit behaviors that enhance the collective abilities of a school faculty. They use their position to support professionalism and the free exchange of information. As a result, the faculty feels empowered and performs effectively, adapts to change, and solves problems in a manner that improves the overall performance of the school. It is through this non-directive, collaborative behavior that school leaders foster a learning community wherein individuals participate in collaborative dialogue, create a shared vision, and coordinate resources to achieve that vision.

The critical factor is the behavior of school leaders as they interact with members of the faculty. By interacting with one another, faculty members build relationships; they raise the faculty to a level of productivity higher than is likely to exist when members of the faculty or the leader function independently. This professionalism and free exchange foster mutual respect and synergy; leaders gain the commitment of stakeholders and can be confident in distributing leadership throughout the organization.

Distributive and Responsible Leaders   Another essential characteristic of transformational leaders is their willingness to distribute power and authority. This is an important characteristic since many scholars and practitioners assert that the challenges of leading a 21st-century school far exceed the capabilities of any one individual (AACTE, 2001; Elmore, 2000; Levine, 2005; Peterson, 2002). Therefore, to a large extent, leadership effectiveness lies in the ability of school leaders to select appropriate people and assign them to perform roles and functions that are within their ability (Collins, 2001). As school leaders share the leadership role, they must give consideration to preparation, ability, and interest levels of the individuals selected. They must also encourage individuals to conduct inquiries into best practices and to function in a trust-based culture.

Sharing the Leadership Role   Assigning proficient faculty and staff to roles and functions is critical. If individuals are not assigned to fulfill roles which they are capable of performing, major tasks in the organization could go unattended, negatively affecting the entire school operation. Thus, school leaders have to have an understanding of themselves, as well as all individuals who work in the schoolhouse. With this understanding, leadership can be effectively distributed throughout the school organization. For example, if the principal is proficient in the area of instructional leadership and spends considerable time in that area, it would be prudent for him/her to employ an assistant principal who is highly capable of fulfilling the functions of organizational management. In that way, assignments can be separated; duplication can be avoided, and the school can benefit from the expertise and talents of both individuals. This concept is fully explored in Chapters 2 and 3.

The Preparation, Ability, and Interest of Followers   Other key factors to be considered in distributing leadership throughout the school organization are the preparation, ability, and interest of individual faculty members who accept and fulfill leadership roles and responsibilities to which they are assigned. Not only must they be willing and able to fulfill assigned roles and responsibilities, but they need to have an understanding of how their roles and functions fit into the school's master plan—the overall purpose, process, and desired outcome.

When leadership is distributed throughout the school organization, it is important for each individual to bring a skill set to the table. The school is an open social system. Individuals in the system function as a part of a whole, and the actions that they take affect the whole. Thus, when individuals do not or cannot fulfill their assigned responsibility, they can cause disconnect in the organization, and that disconnect can inhibit goal attainment. Realizing that, in some instances, skill sets have to be developed, school leaders must assist individuals in recognizing and accepting the fact that a void exists in their preparation. In such instances, school leaders must create or identify a professional development program that fulfills that void. Professional development will be explored in greater depth in Chapters 8 and 9.

Conducting Inquiry into Best Practices   Having accepted responsibility for an assigned area of the school program, individuals must conduct inquiry into best practices and procedures for leading the part of the program for which they are assigned. When individuals conduct inquiry to identify proven practices for use in their assigned area, they are placing themselves in a position to actively participate in discussions and make quality decisions that positively affect the entire school organization.

Functioning in a Trust-Based Culture   The environment of the school must foster within individuals a commitment to achieve the outlined purpose. Consequently, if distributive leadership is to be effective, school leaders must create a trust-based culture wherein teachers are satisfied to the point that they collaborate with the school leader and assume leadership roles and responsibilities for enhanced student achievement. Earlier in the chapter, 13 competencies that inform the behavior of 21st-century school leaders were presented. Of those 13 competencies, five (5) describe the skills necessary for use by school leaders in developing that trust-based culture. Those five are as follows:

1. Visionary Leadership
2. Unity of Purpose
3. Establishing Professional Learning Communities
4. Organizational Management
5. Instructional Leadership

When school leaders are proficient in these five leadership competencies, there is a greater potential for the development of a professional learning community (Ivy, 2007). In such a community, the type of trust-based culture exists wherein teachers and other individuals are receptive to assuming a leadership role.

Quite clearly, for distributive leadership to be a positive force in the school organization, individuals have to function in dual roles; they have to be independent thinkers, as well as a part of a group. Once they accept this dual role, they are positioned to achieve greatness functioning as individuals who influence greatness for the entire school.

Freedom with Responsibility

Transformational leaders believe in, value, and are committed to recognizing and utilizing the knowledge, talents, and skills of everyone in the organization. However, in general, school effectiveness and the academic performance of students are the primary responsibilities of the school leader. Thus, in granting individuals freedom to perform tasks in the organization, those individuals have to be willing to assume responsibility for the outcome of the tasks assigned. One cannot expect to have freedom to make decisions that affect the organization if they are not willing to assume responsibility for the outcome of those decisions. Given that school leaders are directly responsible and accountable for total school effectiveness, freedom for other individuals to share organizational leadership has to be commensurate with the level of responsibility they are willing to assume. The more responsibility an individual is willing to assume, the more freedom and latitude school leaders can afford them.

ACCOUNTABILITY MEASURES

With the passage of the *No Child Left Behind* legislation, the connection between student achievement and school leaders has been strengthened. As it strengthens, there is renewed interest in the performance of school leaders and the methods used by school districts to evaluate their performance. Increasingly, school district administrators and practitioners are turning to comprehensive national standards, such as those developed by the Interstate School Leadership Licensure Consortium (ISLLC) for the purpose of developing instruments to use in assessing the performance of school leaders (Lashway, 2003). Given that these standards inform the behavior of school leaders, it seems reasonable to use them to design assessment tools to determine the extent to which school leaders are exhibiting those behaviors.

The Performance Appraisal of School Leaders

The performance appraisal of school leaders often takes different formats. Some of the most common ones are checklists based on indicators from the ISLLC standards, checklist of behaviors based on state standards, predetermined goals developed by school districts, self-assessments by school leaders, parental observations, and portfolios. Assessments using these tools are being conducted by central office personnel, parents, teachers, and principals themselves (Doud & Keller, 1998). For example, in the state of Illinois, one form of assessment being used is the Principal's Monthly Report. This form contains such information as student test scores, the number of student discipline referrals, student attendance data, and teacher attendance data. A similar system of self-assessment is used in North Carolina; however, that state has additional steps in its process, which requires school leaders to rate themselves and to provide evidence to support the rating given. A rubric scale aligned with state and national standards for school leaders allows principals to be rated exemplary, adequate, or needs improvement. Once the rating is given, a discussion ensues between the principal and his/her supervisor resulting in a professional plan containing goals that address deficient areas and strategies for the removal of the deficiencies. Follow-up conferences between the principal and supervisor allow for monitoring and adjustment of the plan.

Portfolios are another tool being used to record the performance of school leaders. In this process, a goal is identified and becomes the focus of the principal's activities. The principal collects evidence to demonstrate progress toward goal attainment. Similar to the process in Illinois, school leaders might include in their portfolios such items as handbooks, test scores, attendance records, and dropout rates (Hackney, 1999).

Regardless of which form is used, involvement of the principal is necessary. Principals need to have a clear understanding of the expectations of their roles, ratings to be applied through the appraisal system, what the ratings mean, and the consequences, if any, should they need to enhance their effectiveness. According to Reeves (2002), the instrument used should rate the performance of principals using four categories: (1) exemplary; (2) proficient; (3) progressing; and (4) not meeting standards. In the state of Tennessee, a similar form will be used, as of 2008; legislation was passed requiring principal candidates and practicing principals to progress through four levels during their career. The levels required are aspiring, beginning, professional, and exemplary. At each level, there are indicators that inform the behavior of the principal, and those indicators are directly related to state standards.

MAKING THE CONNECTION: THE REMAINING CHAPTERS

Our experience serving at every level of K–12 education influenced the remaining chapters of the text. Of equal influence were five years of research, during which time an extensive review of the literature was conducted, and the findings from various sources were integrated into the contents of the text. These sources included interviews with superintendents, central office administrators, association presidents, teachers, and community stakeholders, using a protocol to solicit responses concerning the practices of school principals. Our goals were to identify leadership practices that are most effective in school districts and to determine if any common trends existed among those districts.

Finally, for five years, while leading a principal preparation program at the University of Memphis in Memphis, Tennessee, we conducted research on principal preparation and logged experiences of emerging and practicing principals. Working with stellar principals at the university and observing them practice the art of leadership in schools further informed the discussion of the roles of principals and the functions they perform on a daily basis. Those roles and functions cluster into four dimensions. Thus, the remaining chapters of the text are organized in four parts, each exploring, to some extent, what 21st-century principals need to know and be able to do in order to effectively lead a school.

Using the terms principal and school leader interchangeably, the four sections emphasize the principal functioning as an instructional leader. The approach has been to focus on instructional leadership and instructional issues that lead to excellence in student achievement. Aspects of the principalship, such as budgeting, business management, and other technical areas, are mentioned, but not fully addressed. The importance of these technical areas is recognized; however, our intent was to present a textbook that approaches the principal as the lead learner and to discuss issues in a manner consistent with the reality of what is occurring instructionally in today's schools. Consequently, our focus highlights the principal as instructional leader, a person responsible and accountable for designing, developing, and implementing a curriculum that meets the needs of all students, and enhances their academic achievement.

Part I: Preparing Leaders for 21st-Century Schools establishes the framework for the text as it describes the standards that inform the behavior of school leaders of today, the competencies that describe the level of proficiency school leaders must acquire, and the accountability measures by which their effectiveness is assessed. We conclude this first section with a discussion of the roles of principals, the functions they perform, and the style of leadership that tends to be most effective in today's schools.

Part II: Dimension 1 establishes a foundation for leading 21st-century schools. The focus is on school leaders understanding self and the individuals with whom they work and serve. The content addresses the beliefs, values, strengths, and other personal aspects of leaders and followers. From reading the combined chapters, readers can develop an understanding of how school leaders position themselves to suspend assumptions, refrain from making broad generalizations, and adapt their leadership style to various situations as might be necessary to enhance their leadership effectiveness.

Part III: Dimension 2 explores schools as open social systems. The climate, culture, and structure of the school organization, as well as the interaction of people, are discussed with the intent of providing readers an opportunity to acquire an in-depth understanding of school life and to assist them in understanding how school leaders build a capacity to lead. The dimension concludes with an investigation of how effective school leaders employ and retain quality teachers.

Part IV: Dimension 3 addresses the humanistic side of leadership, which includes developing and sustaining relationships in the internal and external environment of the schoolhouse. Building teams that share accountability for school goal attainment is a major part of this dimension as it establishes a framework for distributive leadership, fostering a learning community that addresses the special needs of students.

Part V: Dimension 4 examines the basic processes school leaders use in instructional renewal and describes what school leaders should do to improve instruction. It explores how instructional leaders bring about organizational change utilizing best practices. The last chapter in Section V presents a school improvement model that readers might utilize.

Collectively, these chapters address the instructional roles and functions of 21st-century school leaders answering the following five questions:

1. How do standards, competencies, and accountability measures inform the behavior of 21st-century school leaders?

2. How do 21st-century school leaders build a foundation for effective school leadership?
3. How should principals structure schools for effective teaching and learning?
4. What types of relationships must a principal have to effectively lead a school that meets the need of all students?
5. What factors should school leaders consider in program planning, design, development, implementation, and change?

Finally, to assist readers with the application of the four dimensions, throughout the text, we refer them to sections in the companion text, *Practicing the Art of Leadership: A Problem-Based Approach to Implementing the ISLLC Standards (3rd. ed.)*. That text provides a theoretical framework for each of the aforementioned sections through an investigation of theories and presentations of practical examples of the basic administrative processes of communication, decision making, conflict management, and change.

■ ■ ■

Implications for Leadership

- We are currently in an era where school leaders are under intense pressure to improve their schools.
- School leaders are being asked to meet new demands and complete tasks in a wide variety of areas.
- The standards, competencies, and accountability movement have ushered in school leadership requirements that necessitate a new type of leader for 21st-century schools.
- The requirements for leading 21st-century schools are multi-dimensional; thus, school leaders must be prepared to use a multi-dimensional approach.
- Researchers and writers supporting the needed change criticize traditional school leadership preparation programs for having failed to adequately prepare school leaders to meet these new mandates (Hoachlander, Alt, & Beltranena, 2001; Levine, 2005).
- Universities across the nation are redesigning their leadership preparation programs to prepare principals to meet the challenge of leading a 21st-century school.
- There is widespread agreement that for instructional change to be effective, programs must be structured in a manner that facilitates collaborative activities between universities and school districts.
- Participants are entering leadership preparation programs through a rigorous selection process and receive instruction that is research-based and focused heavily on instructional leadership.

• Program participants are functioning in cohort groups that have mentors who provide experiences in authentic contexts and settings. In these groups, they seek solutions to real-world problems and dilemmas, tending to form bonds that enhance their effectiveness as school leaders (IEL, 2000; Murphy & Hawley, 2003; Wilson, 2006).

Reflective Practice

1. What are some challenges you would face in implementing the standards?
2. Which competencies would challenge you most in providing the leadership in 21st-century schools?
3. What approaches do you use to assess your level of accountability in a leadership role?
4. Which of the approaches described in this chapter would you utilize to enhance your leadership capacity? Explain.

Chapter Essentials

Interstate School Leaders Licensure Consortium Standards and Core Competencies

The six ISLLC Standards and the 13 leadership core competencies combine to inform leadership behavior for 21st-century school leaders.

The Role of 21st-Century School Leaders

The role of school leaders has expanded to include a larger focus on teaching and learning, professional development, data-driven decision making, and accountability for student learning. The shift is from school leaders taking an authoritative top-down role to a transformational facilitative role with teachers, parents, and other stakeholders participating in making decisions that affect the school and student achievement.

Principle

By building leadership capacity in others, school leaders can foster the attainment of a shared vision.

Dichotomy

From variance and disparities in student achievement to standards, competencies, and accountability measures for student achievement

The leadership paradigm is shifting; it is no longer effective to threaten people into compliance. Our society, through its laws and practices, is emphasizing the human element—the worth of the individual.

References

American Association of Colleges for Teacher Education (AACTE). (2001, March). PK-12 *Educational Leadership and Administration.* Washington: D.C.

Bass, B. (1985). *Leadership and performance beyond expectations.* New York, Free Press.

Burns, J. M. (1978). *Leadership.* New York: Harper Torchbooks.

Collins, J. (2001). *Good to great: Why some companies make the leap . . . and others don't.* New York: Harper Collins Publishers, Inc.

DuFour, R. & Eaker, R. (1998). *Professional learning communities at work.* Alexandria, VA: Association of Supervision and Curriculum Development.

Doud, J. L., & Keller, E. P. (1998). *The K-8 principal in 1998: A ten-year study.* Alexandria, Virginia: National Association of Elementary School Principals.

Elmore, R. F. (2000, Winter). *Building a new structure for school leadership.* Washington, D.C.: The Albert Shanker Institute.

Fullan, M. (2001). *Leading in a culture of change.* San Francisco, CA: Jossey-Bass.

Getzels, J. W., & Guba, E. G. (1957). Social behavior and the administrative process. *School Review, 65,* 423–441.

Green, R. L. (2006). *Leadership behavior inventory.* Memphis, TN: University of Memphis.

Green, R. L. (2009). *Practicing the art of leadership: A problem-based approach to implementing the ISLLC standards.* (3rd ed.) Boston, MA: Pearson Education, Inc.

Hackney, C. E. (1999, May). *Three models for portfolio evaluation of principals.* The School Administrator. Arlington, VA: American Association of School Administrators.

Hoachlander, G., Alt, M., & Beltranena, R. (2001). *Leading school improvement: What research says.* Atlanta, GA: Southern Regional Education Board.

Hughes, R. (2005). Creating a new approach to principal leadership. *Principal, 84*(5), 34–39.

Institute for Educational Leadership, Inc (IEL). (2000). *Leadership for student learning: Reinventing the principalship.* Washington, D.C.: Author.

Interstate School Leader Licensure Consortium (ISLLC). (2008). *Educational leadership policy standards.* Washington, D.C.: Council of Chief School Officers.

Ivy, S. (2007). *School leaders' behavior informed by thirteen core leadership competencies and the relation to teacher job satisfaction.* (Unpublished Dissertation). Memphis, TN: University of Memphis.

Keynes, J. M. (1963). *The general theory of employment: Interest & more.* McMillan (reprinted, 2007). Retrieved from Web site: cepa.newschool.edu/het/essays/Keynes/general.html

Lashway, L. (2003). *Improving principal evaluation.* Retrieved from Web site: Eric.uoregon.edu/publication/digests/digest172.html

Lewin, K., Lippitt, R., & White, R. K. (1939). Patterns of aggressive behavior in experimentally created "social climates." *Journal of Science Psychology, 10,* 271–299.

Levine, A. (2005). *Enhancing school leaders.* Washington, D.C.: The Education Schools Project.

Likert, R. (1967). *The human organization: Its management and value.* New York: McGraw-Hill.

Marzano, R. J., Waters, T., & McNulty, B. A. (2005). *School leadership that works: From research to practice.* Alexandria, VA: Association for Supervision and Curriculum Development.

Maxwell, J. C. (2003). *Thinking for a change: Eleven ways highly successful people approach life and work.* Nashville, TN: Center Street.

Mai, R. (2004, Spring). *Leadership for school improvement: Cues from organizational learning and renewal efforts.* Educational Forum, *68*(3), 211–221.

Marzano, R. J. (2003). *What works in schools: Translating research into action.* Alexandria. VA: Association for Supervision and Curriculum Development.

Marzano, R. J., Waters, T. & McNulty, B.A. (2005). *School leadership that works: From research to results.* Alexandria, VA: ASCD.

Murphy, J. & Hawley, W. (2003). The AASA leadership for learning master's program. *Teaching in Educational Administration,* 10(2). Larchmont, NY:AASA.

NAESP. (2004). *What principals should know and be able to do: Overview of the six standards.* Video. Cerebellum Corporation and National Association of Elementary School Principals.

NASSP. (2004). *Breaking ranks II: Strategies for leading high school reform.* Reston, VA: National Association of Secondary Principals.

Peterson, K. D. (2002). *The professional development of principals: Innovations and opportunities.* Educational Administration Quarterly. *38*(2), 213–232.

Reeves, D. (2002). *Assessing educational leaders: Evaluating performance for improved individual and organizational results.* Thousand Oaks, California: Corwin Press.

Riley, R. (2002). Educational reform through standards and partnerships, 1993-2000. *Phi Delta Kappan, 83*(9), 700.

Sergiovanni, T. (1996). *The principalship: A reflective practice* perspective (2nd ed.). Boston, MA: Allyn & Bacon.

Southern Regional Educational Board (SREB). (2001, April). *Preparing a new breed of school principals: It's time for action.* Atlanta, GA: Author.

Southern Regional Educational Board (SREB). (2006). *Schools can't wait: Accelerating the redesign of university principal preparation programs.* Atlanta, GA: Author.

Stogdill, R. M., & Coons, A. E. (1957). *Leader behavior: Its description and measurement.* Columbus, OH: Columbus Bureau of Business Research, Ohio State University.

Stricherz, M. (2001). DC principal's training designed to boost instructional leadership. *Education Week.* Retrieved September 26, 2002, from Web site: http://www.edweek.com/ew/newstory.cfm?slug=02instruct.h21

Wilson, T. (2006). *The features and practices of three mid-south principal preparation programs.* (Unpublished Dissertation). Memphis, TN: University of Memphis.

PART TWO

Dimension 1
Understanding Self and Others

Values	Beliefs
Strengths	Other Personal Aspects

Chapter 2 Leading with an Understanding of Self
Chapter 3 Leading with an Understanding of Others

DIMENSIONAL CONCEPTS

In order to effectively lead a 21st century school, individuals must develop an understanding of self and others. With an understanding of self and others, they build a foundation for leadership. Once the foundation is built, individuals can strive to lead with confidence, embracing the skills and attributes of all stakeholders.

Dimension 1, Understanding Self and Others, combines Chapters 2 and 3 to present the purpose and processes that individuals might utilize to develop an understanding of self and the individuals with whom they work. Two basic theories underpin the dimension: Goleman's Emotional Intelligence Theory and Hertzberg's 2-Factor Motivational Hygiene Theory.

2

Leading with an Understanding of Self

(Standard 5)

"What lies behind us and what lies before us are tiny matters compared to what lies within us."

OLIVER WENDELL HOLMES

"Leaders cannot be thought of apart from the historic context in which they arise, the setting in which they function, and the system over which they preside. They are integral parts of the system, subject to the forces that affect the system. They perform (or cause to be performed) certain forces that affect the system. They perform (or cause to be performed) certain tasks or functions that are essential if the group is to accomplish its purpose."

JOHN W. GARDNER

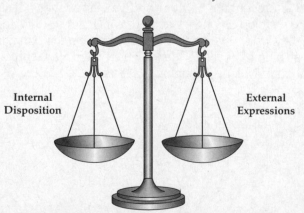

Internal
Disposition

External
Expressions

INTRODUCTION

As school leaders strive to facilitate the interaction of individuals and groups in schools, they are challenged by many different situations and personalities. To address those challenges, they need an in-depth understanding of themselves and the individuals they lead. Understanding one's strengths, beliefs, values, and other personal qualities enables one to establish a clear vision of purpose and acquire knowledge of how one's behavior influences the behavior of others (Bennis, 1994). With this knowledge and understanding, school leaders are able to suspend assumptions, refrain from making broad generalizations, and balance the inward forces of their personal values and beliefs with the outward display of their behavior. Consequently, they become secure and confident in their actions and are able to direct their energies toward organizational goal attainment, while considering the behavior of followers. In essence, they establish a foundation for leadership.

In this chapter, we explore the importance of school leaders understanding themselves, their values, beliefs, strengths, and other personal aspects that affect their behavior and influence the behavior of others. In addition, readers are afforded an opportunity to develop an appreciation for how school leaders' understanding of self, or lack of it, can affect their behavior and the behavior of others in a manner that fosters or inhibits goal attainment. We also illustrate how the behavior of followers affects the behavior of leaders. Having completed this chapter, readers should have a clear understanding of the purpose, process, and outcome of acquiring an understanding of self and other individuals affiliated with the school organization. In Chapter 3, we complete this dimension with a discussion of the importance of school leaders developing an understanding of the individuals with whom they work and serve.

Exploring Self

A number of researchers and writers have presented theories on the personal aspects of leaders and what it means for leaders to acquire an understanding of themselves. Goleman, Boyatzis, and McKee (2002), referring to it as self-awareness, define the concept as the ability of leaders to recognize and understand their motives, emotions and drives, and the effects they have on others. Senge (1990) speaks of the concept in terms of mental models—the ability of leaders to see pictures of the world in which they function and to achieve personal mastery—coming to a realization of what matters most and deepening their ability to see things objectively. In addition, leaders who understand themselves are able to formulate perceptions about how things are and why people behave in certain ways (McGregor, 1960; Murray, 1998). Bennis (1994), referring to the concept as management of self, offers that leaders should know themselves, their skills, and their strengths. Once this knowledge is acquired, these skills and strengths can be nurtured and utilized to assist leaders in becoming all they are capable of becoming. Some key theories, theorists, and the implications they hold for leadership appear in Table 2.1.

For the purpose of this work, we define understanding self as the knowledge an individual posseses relative to his/her personal beliefs and thought processes and how he/she might behave in a given situation or react to a particular issue. Specifically, it is what individuals believe about the environment in which they live and function, the people with whom they interact, the strengths they have acquired, and the values that influence their behavior.

TABLE 2.1   Theories, Theorists, and Their Implications for Leadership

Theories	Theorists	Implications for Leadership
Theory X / Theory Y	(Douglass McGregor, 1960)	Based on their belief about people, school leaders might take one of two approaches in motivating the people with whom they work. If they believe people naturally like work, they will give them autonomy, empower them, and allow them to assume organizational responsibilities. If they believe people dislike work, they will lead using an authoritarian style and closely supervise their work.
Goleman Emotional Intelligence	(Daniel Goleman, 2001)	There is power in the emotions; when that power is cultivated, school leaders can use it to acquire information, make connections, and influence behavior.
Mental Models	(Peter Senge, 1990)	Leaders should be knowledgeable of the manner in which they view situations, events, and possibilities.
Managing Self	(Warren Bennis, 1994)	Leaders should have knowledge of their values, beliefs, and strengths and effectively develop them for use in appropriate situations.
Social System Theory	(R. L. Green, 2005)	School leaders should view the organization as a whole, taking into consideration the interrelationship of the parts that makeup the whole and their interaction within the internal and external environments of the organization. They should also reflect on feedback received from all sources.

Source: Contents of the table were developed from the writings of the authors listed.

EXHIBIT 2.1   Elements Fostering an Understanding of Self and Others

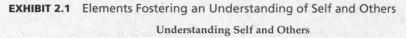

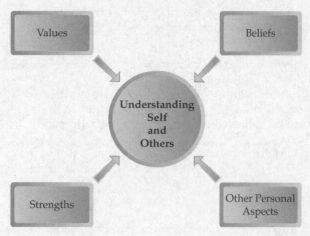

In addition, it refers to an acquisition of knowledge of how their behavior influences the behavior of others. Exhibit 2.1 contains a graphic overview of factors contributing to the makeup of the individual self. In the next section, we illustrate how each of these factors contributes to the makeup of the individual self.

THE VALUE OF UNDERSTANDING SELF

Self-understanding is a life-long process essential to effective human relations (Goleman, 1997). The strengths of school leaders and what they value, think about themselves, believe about people in the community, believe about children, and believe to be the purpose of schools, comprise their disposition, and it is the disposition of leaders that influences their behavior (Green, 2005). Without a clear understanding of one's self—values, beliefs, and strengths— it is difficult to successfully lead any group or organization. Emerson, in his essay *Art* (cf. Schlesinger, 1950), said, "No man can quite emancipate himself from his own age and country, or produce a model in which the education, the religion, the politics, usages, and arts of his time shall have no share."

As one progresses in a school leadership role, various events can bring significant shifts in the leader's values, beliefs, strengths, and behaviors. However, with an understanding of self, leaders can develop strategies for use in managing interpersonal struggles; then, the challenge of effectively managing outward expression becomes easier (DuBrin, 1996). School leaders cannot control the actions of others. However, they can control how they respond to the actions of others.

Standard 5

An education leader promotes the success of every student by acting with integrity, fairness, and in an ethical manner.

Functions
   a. Ensure a system of accountability for every student's academic and social success
   b. Model principles of self-awareness, reflective practice, transparency, and ethical behavior
   c. Safeguard the values of democracy, equity, and diversity

Source: Educational Leadership Policy Standards: ISLLC 2008.

The Influence of Values

As previously mentioned, school leaders must be keenly aware of their values, keeping in mind that their values influence their behavior, and their behavior influences the actions of followers. Values are goals, principles, qualities, or standards that a person perceives as having intrinsic worth. Individuals have a personal hierarchy of values that they use to categorize their behavior and the behavior of others, giving meaning to issues and decisions (Yero, 2002). Depending on the benefits derived from this behavior, values are perceived as favorable and desirable or detrimental and undesirable (Rebore, 2001).

The dichotomies used to illustrate the importance of this point are faux values and authentic values. Leaders must recognize the difference between the two. For example, some school leaders may profess that their practice is to treat people fairly, equitably, and with dignity and respect (an expressed value). Yet, their true values become evident when they exhibit behavior regarding a faculty member who has earned the right to lead a school event, and the privilege of leading that event is awarded to another (an operational value). The true essence of what the leader values is likely to be called into question. What the leader expressed in actuality is a faux value.

The values of leaders cannot always be judged by what they state about an issue; rather, in some instances, their values are judged by how they behave in regard to that issue. Thus, school leaders reveal, through their behavior, the authentic nature of their values. For example, if school leaders believe that all children can learn, that is a value that should influence their instructional behavior—the decisions they make and the energy they exert relative to the teaching and learning of all children.

Through their behavior, leaders can demonstrate that they value the ideas of others and will act with integrity, fairness, and in an ethical manner. To do otherwise, they run the risk of losing the respect of the faculty and other stakeholders. Therefore, the perception of followers regarding the connection between the values of leaders and the behavior they exhibit in leading the school is an important phenomenon that leaders must recognize and clearly understand.

The Influence of Beliefs

After the influence of values resonates, school leaders should develop a deep understanding of how their belief system influences their behavior and the behavior of others. Beliefs are generalizations that school leaders have about people, events, or issues—the mental acceptance of what they consider to be real and true and about which they hold a firm conviction. Beliefs form a frame of reference for how school leaders perceive situations or circumstances, giving them specific meaning (Dilts, 1999).

Beliefs are formed as a result of experiences or impressions and shape how school leaders view the world, building confidence relative to how they will achieve the desired results (Stone & Dahir, 2006; Yero, 2002). Therefore, largely, the belief system influences how leaders behave in the school environment. For example, a principal may believe that faculty members dislike working on the school improvement plan and are trying to avoid that assignment. In order to secure their participation, the principal is likely to closely supervise them and direct their behavior—directive behavior. Conversely, if the principal believes that faculty members are self-directed, cooperative, and enjoy such tasks as school improvement planning, the principal's attitude and behavior toward the faculty members are likely to be quite different. Rather than directing, the principal is likely to create an environment conducive to self-direction—facilitative behavior (McGregor, 1960).

Beliefs can also influence the vision school leaders have for the structure of the school, thus affecting the instructional program and student achievement. For instance, beliefs about students' ability to learn and teachers' ability to teach can affect a principal's leadership behavior and the decisions they make regarding the structure of the instructional program. This can be seen in the behavior of Alisha Kiner, Principal of B. T. Washington High School in Memphis, Tennessee. Principal Kiner has a strong belief about gender classes at the ninth-grade level. She believes that single-gender classes at the ninth-grade level are academically enhancing for both male and female students. Thus, one of her instructional program initiatives was the establishment of single-gender classes. Her espoused beliefs can be observed in her leadership behavior. However, espoused beliefs are not always observed in an individual's behavior, as will be explained in the next section.

ESPOUSED BELIEFS VS. OBSERVABLE BEHAVIOR Espoused beliefs of individuals are not always observable in their behavior. What individuals believe about students and what they communicate about them may be different.

School leaders must realize that faculty members might talk endlessly about their objectivity and willingness to work cooperatively to meet the needs of all students but behave in an entirely different manner. Thus, a contradiction exists between espoused beliefs and observable behavior.

Simply hearing individuals state that they believe in something is not sufficient. When espoused beliefs are not transformed into observable behavior, individuals can negatively affect the teaching and learning process. Deep seated resentment can surface, causing individuals to struggle in identifying objective strategies that can be used in developing the type of school culture and climate that is conducive to meeting the needs of all students. For example, a faculty member might state that he/she believes that all students can learn but not develop program plans that demonstrate that all students have the capability to function effectively in school—achieving high standards. In such a case, it is not likely that the faculty member will seek to implement instructional programs sufficient to leave no child behind; unless an individual truly believes in something, he/she will not pursue it with conviction.

Another example of espoused values not being observed in the actual behavior of individuals can be seen in the behavior of the school leader. If school leaders do not believe that a faculty should be racially diverse, then, it will be difficult to get them to pursue achieving a multicultural faculty that is consistent with the makeup of the student body. Thus, some students may be deprived of receiving instruction from individuals thoroughly knowledgeable of their heritage and rituals which define them as unique individuals.

Upon entering the schoolhouse, school leaders must pay close attention to their beliefs, realizing that their beliefs, as well as their values, influence their behavior. They must be willing to acknowledge, at least to themselves, what they believe about schools, the purpose of schools, and the processes and procedures that they have selected to use in leading schools (Green, 2005). It is easier to acquire the commitment of followers when they observe the leader pursuing a goal with true commitment (Maxwell, 1998).

The Influence of Strengths

The collective strengths of a leader is another significant element that influences leader behavior. It is the degree of intellect regarding a particular subject, issue, or task, that increases the leader's potential of being successful. The awareness of their strengths will enable leaders to make a determination of the areas in which they are capable of performing most effectively. In addition, through strength identification, they gain insight into where their passion lies and what motivates them to remain in pursuit of organizational goal attainment (Collins, 2001).

ALIGNING INDIVIDUAL STRENGTHS WITH ORGANIZATIONAL TASKS   A key to organizational effectiveness is aligning the strengths of individuals with organizational tasks to be accomplished (Collins, 2001; Sergiovanni, 1986). No one individual has developed sufficient strengths to solely administer a 21st century school. It takes a combination of individuals with diverse skills and attributes assigned to special areas. Therefore, leaders must identify their strengths and the strengths of other individuals working in the organization. Through this process, they identify areas where assistance is needed and make a determination if a void exists that needs to be filled. To be conscious that a void exists in an area is the first step in acquiring information, knowledge, and expertise to fill that void (Maxwell, 1998).

The Influence of Personal Aspects

In addition to values, beliefs, and strengths, other personal factors contribute to the behavior of leaders. Some of the most noted ones are disposition, style of communication, and approaches used in making decisions that affect individuals who work in the organization. These three factors create an environment that can either enhance or inhibit organizational effectiveness. They affect the motivational level of individuals, influencing the extent to which they are willing to commit to contributing to organizational goal attainment. Special attention will be devoted to each of these areas throughout the text, illustrating the impact that they have on leader effectiveness.

OBSERVING THE EFFECTS OF LEADER BEHAVIOR

In the preceding section of this chapter, we discussed the influence of values, beliefs, strengths, and other personal aspects of leader behavior. Much of the earlier discussion focused on the importance of leaders recognizing that their behavior influences the behavior of other individuals affiliated with the school and vice versa. To further illustrate that point, we turn to the scenario, "The Leadership Behavior of Principal Carter." While reading this scenario, readers are challenged to observe the behavior of both leader and followers with the intent of developing an understanding of how they influence the behavior of each other. After the scenario, a discussion is held on various behaviors with the goal of offering the reader an opportunity to develop a deeper awareness of factors that influence the behavior of leaders and followers, leader confidence, and the value of guarding against self-judgment.

Scenario: The Leadership Behavior of Principal Carter

Values, Beliefs, and Behavior

Because of her success in enhancing the academic achievement of students at Blue Lakes Middle School and her reputation for enhancing student/teacher and teacher/teacher relationships, Mrs. Carter was recruited to Northwood Middle School, located in the heart of a neighboring city. She accepted the position because she felt that she could contribute greatly to students who were struggling academically. The student population at Northwood Middle School was quite different from that of Blue Lake Middle as it consisted of 68 percent African-American, 30 percent Caucasian, and 2 percent Hispanic.

As Mrs. Carter reviewed the racial makeup of the Northwood faculty, she noticed that of the faculty totaling forty-three (43) teachers, there were only three African-Americans and one Hispanic teacher. However, because of escalating discipline problems, ten (10) faculty members had requested and received transfers. After interviewing teachers to fill the 10 open positions, Principal Carter was pleased that she was able to identify applicants who would enhance the diversity of the faculty. After reviewing the applicants a second time, she hired six (6) African-Americans and three (3) Hispanic teachers. She was particularly pleased with the employment of Ms. Jackson, an African-American teacher, who had expressed in her interview the desire to improve the human condition of all students, especially African-American students.

With a full staff in place, the school year got off to an excellent start. However, after just three weeks, one of the Caucasian teachers, Mr. Gray, approached Mrs. Carter with a dilemma. He noted that 27-year-old Carmen Jackson, one of the newly hired African-American teachers, often spoke negatively about her students. He stated that the negative reference occurred constantly in the teachers' lounge. When Principal Carter asked him for specifics, he stated that she often referred to the boys as "thugs" and the girls as "trash." He also advised Principal Carter that Ms. Jackson had informed other teachers on several occasions that she was from a middle class family; thus, she knew nothing about the street life of the students of Northwood. She also stated that the university from which she graduated did not prepare her for teaching inner-city students. He also reported hearing Ms. Jackson state that the only reason she took the job at Northwood was to have her student loans deferred by teaching in the inner-city for at least five (5) years. Most disturbing of all, he advised, due to her negative attitude toward her students, students were becoming more and more disrespectful in the classroom. Mr. Gray voiced a concern that his instructional time was constantly being interrupted by the arguments and confrontations that occurred in Ms. Jackson's class.

Principal Carter was not surprised at these comments as she had received several phone calls from parents stating that Ms. Jackson was very strict, required extensive assignments, and refused to allow students to make up work or to assist them when they did not understand an assignment. Principal Carter was stunned by the series of complaints; after all, she had hired Ms. Jackson, believing that she was her best choice. Ms. Jackson, an African-American teacher, was working with a predominantly African-American class.

In an attempt to correct the problem, Principal Carter began to frequent Ms. Jackson's classroom. However, even though Principal Carter made frequent visits to Ms. Jackson's classroom, and over time, offered a variety of suggestions and strategies, the complaints continued; in fact, they escalated. Because of the frequent visits, Ms. Jackson began to miss days from school and complained that she was being harassed. Perplexed by this turn of events, Principal Carter stopped visiting Ms. Jackson's classroom, avoided her, and began to discuss termination possibilities with central administrators.

REFLECTIVE QUESTIONS

Developing a Deeper Understanding of Behavior

1. What are the underlying principles influencing the behaviors of Principal Carter, Ms. Jackson, and Mr. Gray?
2. What are the values that may be influencing these behaviors?
3. In terms of strengths, what do you perceive are the void(s) that Principal Carter needs to fill? Justify your response using passages from the scenario.
4. Reflect on the values, beliefs, and strengths that would direct your behavior at Northwood Middle School. Respond both as a faculty member and as the school leader.

The Effects of Leader Behavior

In leading school organizations, leaders might display behavior that is task-oriented, relationship-oriented, or a combination of both. If they choose to structure organizational tasks, exhibiting power and control over individuals and the situation, it is likely because they do not believe that followers have developed the maturity level sufficient to complete the assigned tasks without guidance and assistance (Hersey, Blanchard, & Johnson 1996). This type of behavior might also exist because the leader values control and wants to ensure that a specific outcome is reached. Another reason may be that the leader has lost confidence in an individual or group and believes that structure, directions, and close supervision are necessary for task completion (Green, 2005; Sergiovanni, 1996).

In other instances, leaders might choose to exhibit relationship behavior because they believe that an individual has the capability of completing a task and meeting a predetermined standard with little guidance or assistance. Also, this type of behavior might be exhibited because a leader values the ideas and opinions of others and wants to include them in the decision-making process. A third reason could be that a leader values positive interpersonal relationships with followers and wants to enhance those relationships.

Regardless of the reason for the behavior or its effect, it is important to remember that people develop a perception of an individual's capability of performing a specific task based on their prior experience with that individual or the manner in which the individual is currently performing tasks (Allan & Harrison, 2004). This was the case with the recruitment of Principal Carter to Northwood Middle School. She came into a new situation, bringing a positive perception of her past behavior, which gave her instant credibility. In some instances, the converse is true; an individual's past behavior could convey a negative perception, robbing him/her of credibility. If school leaders are aware of how their past behavior is being perceived, they can strive to exhibit behavior that alters the perception.

The underlying principle relative to Principal Carter, in this case, is that school leaders must constantly seek to achieve a balance between the inside forces of values and beliefs and the outside forces that affect the culture and climate of the school. In responding to the question, "What are the values that may be influencing Principal Carter's behavior?," we quickly answer diversity and self-understanding. She was employed at Northwood partly because of her behavior in a previous assignment. When she presented that same behavior at Northwood, it was not a good fit for the Northwood culture. Equally important, she was not aware of how that behavior would be perceived. In addition, her belief about diversity and the need for students to interact with individuals of the same race or culture greatly influenced her decision regarding teacher selection. A rationale for her behavior, as well as the behavior of faculty members Jackson and Gray, can be acquired from Luft's (1970) and Janas' (2001) description of Johari Window.

The Johari Window: An Analysis of Principal Carter

Individuals leading 21st century schools should have as a primary objective, improving self-awareness, and the Johari Window model (Boje, 2001; Janas, 2001; Luft, 1970) is a useful instrument for that purpose. The model provides a graphic way for leaders to view the effects of what individuals know and do not know about their behavior. With an enhanced understanding of self, school leaders can improve the climate in the schoolhouse, influencing individuals to exhibit behaviors of empathy, collaboration, two-way communication, and unity of purpose. These behaviors lead to the development of relationships that exist in a professional learning community. It is critical for leaders to understand their behavior and the manner in which that behavior might be affecting others. Equally important is the leader's knowledge of how they are being perceived by others and the effect their behavior has on the motivation level of others. The concept is presented in four quadrants. A graphic analysis of the four quadrants can be seen in Table 2.2.

The four quadrants enable leaders to become aware of how public or private they are when they work with individuals and groups and the expectations individuals and groups hold for them. The following is an explanation of each quadrant:

1. *Quadrant I: The Public Self*—Frequently school leaders are aware of the behaviors they are exhibiting, and other individuals are also aware of those behaviors. Therefore, in order to reach the highest level of effectiveness, school leaders should strive to exhibit behaviors informed by the 13 core competencies outlined in Chapter 1. When these behaviors are exhibited, school leaders are at their best and are likely to be most effective.

2. *Quadrant II: The Blind Self*—There are instances when school leaders function in blind areas; others can see things of which the school leader is unaware. Therefore, school leaders should seek to reduce the negative aspects of the blind self. They can accomplish this desired outcome by being receptive to receiving feedback from faculty members and other stake-

TABLE 2.2   The Four Quadrants of Johari Window

	Known to Leader	Not Known to Leader
Known to Others	**1. Public Self:** The area of free activity, or public area, refers to behavior and motivation, is known to an individual and to others.	**2. Blind Self:** The blind areas are where others can see things of which the individual is unaware.
Not Known to Others	**3. Private Self:** The avoided or hidden areas represent things the individual knows but does not reveal to others, (e.g., a hidden agenda, or matters about which individuals have sensitive feelings).	**4. Unknown Self:** The areas of unknown activity are those where neither the individual nor others are aware of certain behaviors or motives.

Source: This diagram is developed based on the Janas and Luft Johari Window Model (Janas, M. 2001; Luft, J. 1970).

holders. Not only should they be receptive to receiving feedback, but they should be proactive and seek feedback regarding their behavior, as well as the programs and activities they are advocating. For example, there are instances when school leaders perceive their style of leadership to be positive when actually it has a negative effect on the faculty. In such instances, the leader is functioning in the blind quadrant and is overrating himself/herself. With an effective system of feedback in place, leaders are able to make an assessment regarding their blind self, develop an understanding of how they are perceived by others, and determine if their behavior is enhancing or inhibiting organizational goal attainment.

3. *Quadrant III: The Private Self*—In some instances, school leaders are aware of information about themselves that is not known to individuals in the schoolhouse or the community. School leaders have a right to privacy and to withhold from stakeholders information that has no relationship to the effectiveness of school programs or the operation of the school in general. How much information of a personal nature the school leader wishes to share is a matter of personal choice. Conversely, if the hidden information has a relationship to the effective operation of the school, it should become a part of the public arena. When school leaders share their true position with others, they minimize conflict, open the lines of communication, and enhance the potential of building the type of trust-based culture that exists in a professional learning community.

4. *Quadrant IV: The Unknown Self*—There are instances when school leaders have feelings and attitudes that are unknown to

them and others. This unknown information can influence the school leader's personality and/or his/her behavior. For example, a school leader may be highly capable of providing the leadership for a program that would enhance the academic achievement of underachieving students. However, if the leader in question has not had a previous opportunity to implement such a program, he/she might lack the confidence to make an attempt at its implementation. Another example would be lack of exposure. If a leader has functioned at a particular academic level for an extended period of time and experienced success, he/she may feel that the same level of success at a different academic level can be attained. However, when given an assignment at another level, he/she may discover that the challenges posed are beyond his/her level of preparation. To move from this unknown area, school leaders might enhance their working relationship with other school leaders, attend local, state, and national conferences, or participate in a variety of workshops. (Janas, 2001; Luft, 1970)

Of the four quadrants, quadrant four—the unknown self—is most critical in terms of school leadership. Leaders are often unaware of the behavior they are exhibiting. The challenge posed by the unknown self is that actions are not known to the leader or others; they become private, blind, or public only by circumstances that create a new awareness (Glickman, Gordon, & Gordon, 2004). Contingent on the circumstances under which the unknown self becomes public, the behavior could very well cause leaders to become ineffective in their duties or create an undesirable situation.

In the aforementioned scenario, Principal Carter's beliefs and values emerged unknowingly through her behavior. Based on her rationale for hiring Ms. Jackson, her values and beliefs influenced her behavior. When Mr. Gray shared his concerns regarding Ms. Jackson's behavior, it became evident that Ms. Jackson's behavior conflicted with Principal Carter's values and beliefs, as well as the culture of Northwood. In an attempt to rectify the situation, Principal Carter began to frequent Ms. Jackson's classroom and offer various suggestions and strategies which were met with great resistance from Ms. Jackson. Consequently, the behaviors of Principal Carter influenced the behavior of Ms. Jackson, causing conflict. In this situation, Principal Carter's blind self became public, influencing negative consequences.

Individuals are challenged to lead schools; if they are blind to their behavior and the effect that their behavior has on others, they are only able to correct the behavior of which they are aware (Glickman, Gordon, & Gordon, 2004). The values of Principal Carter, Ms. Jackson, and Mr. Gray influenced their behaviors toward each other (see Table 2.3).

It is not uncommon for individuals to host beliefs and exhibit judgmental behaviors that have been taught, practiced, and accepted through the years.

TABLE 2.3 Influencing Values		
Principal Carter	**Ms. Jackson**	**Mr. Gray**
Diversity	Egocentrism	Structure
Equality	Self-preservation	Outcomes
Progress	Stereotypes	Justice
	Independence	Interdependence

Such is possibly the case with Ms. Jackson and her expressed beliefs about some of the students attending Northwood. If individuals do not bring their beliefs to the surface and acknowledge and act on them, their beliefs may conflict with the behavior that they display. In most instances, an individual's behavior reveals what that individual truly believes (Green, 2005).

Ms. Jackson was not aware that other faculty members, mainly Mr. Gray, had observed her display of prejudiced behavior toward her students. She was "blind" to this prejudiced behavior. According to Janas (2001), when individuals have a "blind self," they exhibit behaviors that are known by others but are not known by them. Once the behavior of Ms. Jackson became public, she defended her actions by stating that she was from a middle-class family and that she knew nothing about the street life of the students at Northwood. The underlying principle relative to this particular situation is that an individual is not likely to exhibit behavior that is significantly different from what they believe and value.

Janas (2001) recommended that one's aim should be to reduce this area (the blind self), and increase the open area (the public self). By providing sensitive, yet constructive feedback, and encouraging acknowledgement of these behaviors, both Mr. Gray and Principal Carter could have possibly reduced the defensive attitude of Ms. Jackson. This would foster a non-judgmental climate that minimizes fear, anger, and hostility. In addition, it is imperative that school leaders realize that some individuals are more resistant than others when provided feedback, whether the feedback is constructive or destructive. Therefore, when school leaders confront faculty members regarding significant and/or sensitive issues, the emotional needs of the individual should be given consideration (Boyatsis & Skelley, 1995).

Safeguarding Against Self-Judgment

Having made the aforementioned observations, a caution regarding self-judgment is warranted. According to Branden (1997), "of all the judgments we pass in life, none is more important than the judgments we pass on ourselves. That judgment impacts every moment and every aspect of our existence. Our self-evaluation is the basic context in which we act and react, choose our values, set our goals, and meet the challenges that confront us. Our responses to events are shaped in part by whom and what we think we are."

Accordingly, leaders can be their best or worst critic. Therefore, it is vital that leaders develop an understanding of self.

In viewing the belief system of others, leaders must search inwardly. Through an inward search, they can seek an understanding of their outward behavior. However, this investigation must not simply be an observation that occurs on the surface; rather, leaders must probe deeply into their own personal beliefs and thought processes to acquire personal understanding. Once they understand their personal belief system, they can challenge their own interpersonal struggles, which will open the door to a change in their outward expression toward colleagues and others. We now turn to a discussion of benefits leaders derive from having an understanding of self.

BENEFITS FROM ACQUIRING AN UNDERSTANDING OF SELF

A number of theories can inform the benefits of developing an understanding of self. However, for the purpose of this discussion, the focus is on (1) Open Social Systems Theory; (2) Jacob Getzels and Egon Guba Two-Dimensional Organizational Theory; (3) Situational Leadership Theory, and (4) Goleman's Emotional Intelligence Theory.

Open Social System Theory

Schools are often viewed as open social systems, not operating as separate entities, but functioning as part of a larger system. They consist of a set of interrelated parts that interact within its environment. The system receives input from the external environment and transforms that input into a product (output) that goes into the external environment and eventually returns as input. To obtain school goals, school leaders must understand the parts, the whole, and how their behavior influences the interaction between and among the parts.

Jacob Getzels's and Egon Guba's Two-Dimensional Organizational Theory

An organization is explained by Jacob Getzels and Egon Guba (1957) as having two dimensions, an institutional dimension and an individual dimension. The institutional dimension addresses roles and expectations designed to fulfill the goals of the organization, and the individual dimension addresses the individuals who inhabit the organization with certain personalities and need dispositions. When school leaders develop an understanding of self, they enhance the potential of exhibiting behavior that brings the two dimensions together (Lunenburg & Ornstein, 1996). This congruence fosters school organizational goal attainment. A more detailed explanation of this organizational theory will be provided in Chapter 3.

Situational Leadership Theory

Understanding self also enables leaders to identify their strengths and align those strengths with tasks to be performed in the schoolhouse. When school leaders are aware of their strengths, they can compensate for any voids that might exist by utilizing the skills of others. In addition, they are positioned to become a facilitator, building capacity in others sufficient for them to lead in a trust-based culture.

Goleman's Emotional Intelligence Theory

True leadership is power derived from relationships and service (Kouzes & Posner, 2002). Therefore, to be effective, school leaders must develop effective relationships. A critical factor in building and managing those relationships is emotional intelligence, knowing oneself. Therefore, leaders must first understand and lead themselves before they can effectively understand and lead others (Goleman, 1998). More will be said about emotional intelligence later in the chapter. First, we discuss processes an individual might use to develop self-understanding.

Assessment Tools for Use in Developing Self-Understanding

Various scholars have produced a number of assessment tools that have contributed significantly to a leader's understanding of self. In addition, school leaders can acquire an understanding of self by consistently engaging in reflective practice and utilizing the results to improve their performance. The following section consists of tools used by school leaders to acquire a deep understanding of self. The results produced by these tools can be used by school leaders to develop an individual profile. Then, the profile can be used to inform the development of an individualized professional enhancement plan.

THE MYERS-BRIGGS INVENTORY®   Isabel Myers and Katharine Briggs (1998) published a self-assessment type indicator designed to help show leaders how they prefer to analyze and address situations and tasks. The inventory, based on C. G. Jung's theory of psychological types, primarily focuses on four psychological dichotomies that consist of eight preferences: extroversion/introversion; sensing/intuition; thinking/feeling, and judging/perceiving, which can be determined by the following directives:

1. Where individuals prefer to focus their attention and get energy (Extroversion or Introversion)
2. The way individuals take in information (Sensing or Intuition)
3. The way individuals prefer to make decisions (Thinking or Feeling)
4. Whether individuals favor a lifestyle that is more decisive and planned or a lifestyle that is more flexible and spontaneous (Judging or Perceiving)

A summary of the dichotomies appear in Table 2.4.

TABLE 2.4 The Four Psychological Dichotomies

Extrovert or Introvert	Sensing or Intuition
Thinking or Feeling	Judging or Perceiving

Since each of the eight preferences is represented by a letter (E, I, S, N, T, F, J, or P), a four-letter code can be used as an acronym for indicating the determined type. Therefore, an individual's type is the combination of one's preference selected from each of the four dichotomies suggesting that everyone has a natural preference for one of the two opposites on each of the four dichotomies. For example, ENTJ would offer that an individual's preference is to draw his/her energy from others (Extroversion); take in information by focusing on the relationships and connections between facts (Intuition); look at the logical consequences of choices or actions (Thinking), and plan activities in an orderly way (Judging). When the four dichotomies are combined in all possible ways, 16 types result (Myers et al., 1998). A summary of the 16 types appear in Exhibits 2.2 and 2.3.

EXHIBIT 2.2   The Personality Type Matrix

		Personality Type Matrix - 16 types			
		Sensing Types (S)		Intuitive Types (N)	
		Thinking (T)	Feeling (F)	Feeling (F)	Thinking (T)
Introverts (I)	Judging (J)	**ISTJ** Serious, quiet, earn success by concentration and thoroughness, practical, orderly, matter-of-fact, logical, realistic, and dependable; take responsibility	**ISFJ** Quiet, friendly, responsible and conscientious, work devotedly to meet their obligations, thorough, painstaking, accurate, loyal, considerate	**INFJ** Succeed by perseverance, originality, and desire to do whatever is needed or wanted, quietly forceful, conscientious, concerned for others, respected for their firm principles	**INTJ** Usually have original minds and great drive for their own ideas and purposes, skeptical, critical, independent, determined, often stubborn
	Perceiving (P)	**ISTP** Cool onlookers—quiet, reserved, and analytical, usually interested in impersonal principles, how and why mechanical things work, flashes of original humor	**ISFP** Retiring, quietly friendly, sensitive, kind, modest about their abilities, shun disagreements, loyal followers, often relaxed about getting things done	**INFP** Care about learning, ideas, language, and independent projects of their own, tend to undertake too much, then somehow get it done, friendly, but often too absorbed	**INTP** Quiet, reserved, impersonal, enjoy theoretical or scientific subjects, usually interested mainly in ideas, little liking for parties or small talk, sharply defined interests
Extroverts (E)	Perceiving (P)	**ESTP** Matter-of-fact, do not worry or hurry, enjoy whatever comes along, may be a bit blunt or insensitive, best with real things that can be taken apart or put together	**ESFP** Outgoing, easygoing, accepting, friendly, make things fun for others for their enjoyment, like sports and making things, find remembering facts easier than mastering theories	**ENFP** Warmly enthusiastic, high-spirited, ingenious, imaginative, able to do almost anything that interests them, quick with a solution and to help with a problem	**ENTP** Quick, ingenious, good at many things, may argue either side of a question for fun, resourceful in solving challenging problems, but may neglect routine assignments
	Judging (J)	**ESTJ** Practical, realistic, matter-of-fact, with a natural head for business or mechanics, not interested in subjects they see no use for, like to organize and run activities	**ESFJ** Warm-hearted, talkative, popular, conscientious, born cooperators, need harmony, work best with encouragement, little interest in abstract thinking or technical subjects	**ENFJ** Responsive and responsible, generally feel real concern for what others think or want, sociable, popular, sensitive to praise and criticism	**ENTJ** Hearty, frank, decisive leaders, usually good at anything that requires reasoning and intelligent talk, may sometimes be more positive than their experience in an area warrants

EXHIBIT 2.3   The Myers-Briggs Preferences

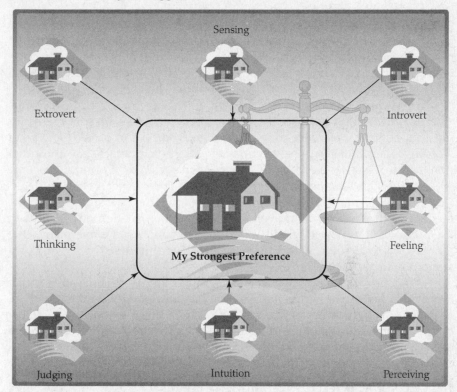

Source: The above Exhibit was designed by Dr. S. Cypress based on the contents of the 1998 MBTI manual, page 64.

Usually, the preference type that is determined for individuals is the one in which they feel most competent, natural, and energetic (Myers et al., 1998). Therefore, one can view the 16 preference types as a house with sixteen rooms. One room may be identified as an individual's favorite as determined by a combination of the four specific preferences. However, this does not mean that the individual never enters other rooms in the house.

Individuals must keep in mind that their preference types may be influenced by their values, beliefs, religion, and/or the situation or task to be addressed. It is not uncommon for leaders to change the way they prefer to become energized, take in information, make decisions, or orient themselves to the external world. An individual's preference may change based on a specific situation.

Specific situations or circumstances may warrant the individual entering other rooms which would represent a different combination of preferences. Simply put, the second set of preferences is not the favorite, rather a selection of choice (see Exhibit 2.2). Whereas, it is "ok" to step into a room that requires a change in behavior to address a certain issue or task, leaders must understand that they may not accomplish the task with equal confidence as they would if they had remained within their preferred type. It is also critical that leaders understand that other individuals who work within the organization may address similar situations and tasks by utilizing a different preference type—one that may be totally opposite of the leader's preferred type. Such behavior should not be perceived as good or bad, just different.

In the case of Principal Carter, her preference for making decisions changed due to the situation she encountered with Ms. Jackson. Her prior decision-making preference may have included the act of considering what was important to her and to others involved, placing herself into the situation, and making decisions based on her values relative to honoring people (Feeling). In this situation, her preference is to think logically and to determine the consequences of the choices or actions that she takes. Thus, she mentally and physically removed herself from the situation and examined the pros and cons objectively (Thinking). Accordingly, her preference is the identification of a solution to address the challenge, more so than giving consideration to Ms. Jackson's feelings.

The value of the use of the Myers-Briggs Inventory by school leaders is that it provides descriptions of preferences that help them understand themselves, as well as the individuals with whom they work. When school leaders know their own preferences and the preferences of others, they have a deeper understanding of how people with different preferences can relate to one another and contribute to the organization (Kummerow & Hirsh, 1998; Myers et al., 1998).

THE EMOTIONAL INTELLIGENCE QUOTIENT   Another assessment tool school leaders can use to develop an understanding of self is the "Emotional Intelligence Quotient" (EIQ). This assessment is comprised of a group of questions related to different aspects of one's emotional intelligence called emotional competencies. It is the particular combination of these competencies possessed by individuals that contributes to their uniqueness (Salovey and Mayer, 1990).

The test measures aspects of an individual's emotional intelligence by asking him/her questions specifically about understanding his/her emotions and feelings, as well as their attitudes and reactions in various situations. The results of the assessments offer information on the ability of an individual to (1) perceive emotions (reading people); (2) access and generate emotions so as to assist thought (using emotions); (3) understand emotions, and (4) reflectively regulate emotions so as to promote emotional and intellectual growth (managing emotions).

Goleman (1995, 1998) contends that leaders can develop their emotional intelligence and learn a great deal about themselves by focusing on the following five competencies:

1. *Self-Awareness:* This is the ability to accurately perform self-assessments, to have confidence in oneself, to recognize and to understand one's

feelings and moods as they occur. It is important for school leaders to recognize their emotions, feelings, and drives and, in particular, the impact that they have on others and the work environment.

2. *Self-Regulation and Motivation:* This is the ability of an individual to remain focused under pressure, effectively managing his/her potentially disruptive emotions and impulses. When the emotions of individuals are self-regulated, they remain composed and think clearly during challenging situations.
3. *Social Skills:* This is defined by proficiency in managing relationships and building networks. It includes the ability to influence and persuade others without coercion, to listen openly, to manage conflict effectively, to inspire and guide individuals, as well as groups and be able to serve as a change catalyst.
4. *Empathy:* This requires the ability to understand the needs of faculty members and provide them with constructive feedback.
5. *Self-Management:* This includes the ability to accept current conditions, concentrate on one's strengths and nurture them, seeing the possibilities in all situations.

School leaders need high EIQ because they represent the school, interact with a large number of people within the internal and external environment of the school, and set the tone for a positive school culture that fosters high employee morale. Therefore, they must be able to recognize and label their feelings and needs and to reconcile those needs with both their long-term goals and the needs of the faculty and the people they serve. In essence, they must be able to manage themselves, as management of self is critical to effective school leadership. If school leaders fail to manage themselves, they can do more harm than good. By taking the EIQ, they can determine the extent to which they are able to fulfill these tasks which is another step in understanding who they are and what they are capable of becoming.

THE 360° LEADERSHIP ASSESSMENT A third assessment is the 360° Leadership Assessment. This assessment provides school leaders with feedback on the perception of their behavior from multiple sources, such as supervisors, faculty members, students, parents, and peers. It places an emphasis, not only on leaders' behavior and what they accomplish for the organization, but also how they accomplish it. A leader's awareness of the perceptions of followers has important consequences because followers make decisions as to whether to follow a leader based on their perceptions of the leader (Ashford, 1989; Moshavi, Brown, & Dodd, 2003). Therefore, school leaders can use data from this assessment tool to alter their behavior in a manner that promotes a school climate that fosters faculty collaboration and enhanced academic achievement for all students.

OUTCOME FROM ACQUIRING AN UNDERSTANDING OF SELF

Whether school leaders attempt to develop a comprehensive understanding of self through the use of theories, assessments, or relationships, the result is an increased capacity to lead with the ability to monitor and adjust their leadership behavior as warranted by various situations. Self-understanding is tantamount to leader effectiveness, as it fosters a belief in oneself and one's ability to achieve the goals of the organization. When leaders truly understand themselves, they enhance their self-confidence and are willing to accept total responsibility for their circumstances—avoid blaming others. The following descriptors enumerate additional benefits to be derived by school leaders who acquire an understanding of self.

1. *Receptivity* An individual's willingness to accept honest feedback and utilize it to enhance himself/herself personally and professionally
2. *Inquiry* An individual's willingness to explore his/her inner strengths and the outside forces that impact him/her for the sole purpose of identifying processes and procedures to use in becoming all one is capable of becoming
3. *Direction* An individual's commitment to a vision and plan of action for goal attainment, accepting the fact that he/she may not be able to control the forces in the environment but can control how he/she responds to them
4. *Insight* The ability of an individual to acquire a deep understanding into what sets him/her apart from others—unique ingrained talents

■ ■ ■

Implications for Leadership

- Understanding self can be described as the ability of leaders to recognize their motives, emotions, and drives, the effect these factors have on their behavior, and the effects their behavior has on the behavior of others. Self-understanding provides leaders with an in-depth knowledge of their perception of the world (Goleman, Boyatsis, & McKee, 2002; Green, 2005).
- The process of understanding self occurs through a multifaceted approach which includes the leader's ability to (a) recognize the value of understanding self; (b) acknowledge values; (c) understand the influence of one's beliefs on his/her behavior; (d) identify and differentiate between espoused beliefs and observable behavior, and (e) acknowledge the effects of leader behavior on followers.
- Although many valuable benefits can be derived from the leader's understanding of self, one must understand that the process can be rather complex.

• With a true understanding of self, leaders are able to demonstrate absolute clarity about who they are, the purpose of their goals, and their potential for inspiring others to do the same.

By clarifying their values, internalizing and assessing their beliefs, and reflecting on their behavior, leaders can establish the foundation needed to lead today's schools.

Reflective Practice

1. What approach do you use to develop an understanding of self?
2. What approach do you use to determine how your behavior is influencing others?
3. As a leader, how important is it for you to feel accepted as a part of the group?
4. When are you most effective as a leader? What leadership style are you employing when you feel effective?
5. What tools do you use to conduct a self-assessment?

Chapter Essentials

Interstate School Leaders Licensure Consortium: Standard 1

An education leader promotes the success of all students by facilitating the development, articulation, implementation, and stewardship of a vision of learning that is shared and supported by all stakeholders.

Interstate School Leaders Licensure Consortium: Standard 5

An education leader promotes the success of every student by acting with integrity, fairness, and in an ethical manner.

Principle

An individual is not likely to exhibit behavior that is significantly different from what he/she believes and values.

Dichotomy
Internal Dispositions or External Expressions

School leaders must constantly seek to achieve a balance between the inside forces of their values and beliefs and the outside forces that affect the culture and climate of the school.

References

Allan, M., & Harrison, E. (2004). *Enabling and empowering authentic transformational leaders, or . . . "How to achieve all that you ever meant to in your life!* Retrieved June 11, 2004, from Web site: http://www.authenticbusiness.co.uk/archive/atleadership/

Ashford, S. (1989). Self-assessments in organizations: A literature review and integrative model. In L. L. Cummings & B. M. Staw (Eds.), *Research in organizational behavior* (Vol. 11, pp. 133–174). Greenwich, CT: JAI Press.

Bennis, W. (1994). *On becoming a leader*. Cambridge, MA: Perseus Books.

Boje, D. (2001). *Johari window and the psychodynamics of leadership and influence in intergroup life*. Retrieved September 3, 2006, from Web site: http://cbae.nmsu.edu/-dboje/503/johari_window.htm

Boyatzis, R. E., & Skelley, F. R. (1995). The impact of changing values on organizational life: The latest update. In D. A. Kolb, J. S. Osland, & I. M. Rubin (Eds.) *The Organizational Behavior Reader* (pp. 1–17). Upper Saddle River, NJ: Prentice Hall.

Branden, N. (1997). *What self esteem is and is not*. (adapted from the article, *"The Art of Living Consciously."* Simon & Schuster, 1997). Retrieved September 3, 2006, from Web site: http://www.nathanielbranden.com/catalog/articles_essays/what_self_esteem.html

Collins, J. (2001). *Good to great: Why some companies make the leap . . . and others don't*. New York: Harper Collins Publishers, Inc.

Dilts, R. B. (1999). *Sleight of mouth: The magic of conversational belief change*. Capitola, CA: Meta Publication.

DuBrin, A. J. (1996). *Human relations for career and personal success*. (4th ed.) Upper Saddle River, NJ: Prentice Hall.

Educational Leadership Policy Standards: ISLLC 2008. National Policy Board for Educational Administration. Washington, D.C.: Council of Chief State School Officials. Getzel, J. W., & Guba, E. G. (1957). Social behavior and the administrative process. *School Review, 65*, 423–441.

Glickman, C. Gordon, S., & Gordon, J. (2004). *SuperVision and instructional leadership: A developmental approach*. Upper Saddle River, NJ: Prentice Hall.

Goleman, D. (1995). *Emotional intelligence: What it is and why it can matter more than IQ*. New York: Bantam Dell Publishing Company.

Goleman, D. (1998). *Working with emotional intelligence*. New York: Bantam Dell Publishing Company.

Goleman, D., Boyatzis, R., & McKee, A. (2002). *Primal leadership: Realizing the power of emotional intelligence*. Boston, MA: Harvard Business School Press.

Green, R. L. (2005). *Practicing the art of leadership: A problem-based approach to implementing the ISSLC standards*. (2nd. Ed.) New Jersey: Merrill Prentice Hall.

Hersey, P., Blanchard, K. H., & Johnson, D. E. (1996). *Management of organizational behavior: Utilizing human resources*. Upper Saddle River, N.J.: Prentice-Hall.

Interstate School Leaders Licensure Consortium of the Council of Chief State School Officers. (1996). *Candidate information bulletin for school leaders assessment*. Princeton, NJ: Educational Testing Service.

Janas, M. (2001). Getting a clear view. *Journal of Staff Development, 22*(2), 32–34.

Kouzes, J., & Posner, B. (2002). *The leadership challenge*. San Francisco: Jossey-Bass.

Kummerow, P., & Hirsh, S. K. (1998). *Introduction to type in organizations*, (3rd ed). Palo Alto, CA: Consulting Psychologists Press, Inc.

Luft, J. (1970). *Group processes: An introduction to group dynamics*: New York: National Press Books.

Lunenburg, F. C., & Ornstein, A. C. (1996). *Educational administration: Concepts and practices* (2nd ed.). Belmont, CA: Wadsworth.

Maxwell, J. (1998). *The 21 irrefutable laws of leadership.* Nashville, TN: Thomas Nelson Inc.

McGregor, D. (1960). *The human side of enterprise.* New York: McGraw-Hill.

Moshavi, D., Brown, F. W., & Dodd, N. G., (2003). Leader self-awareness and its relationship to subordinate attitude and performance. *Leadership and Organization Development Journal, 24,* 407–418.

Murray, B. (1998). Does "emotional intelligence" matter in the workplace? *The APA Monitor Online, 29*(7). The American Psychological Association.

Myers, I. B., & Briggs, K. (1998). *Introduction to type* (6th ed.). Palo Alto, CA: Consulting Psychologists Press.

Rebore, R. W. (2001). *The ethics of educational leadership.* Upper Saddle River, NJ: Merrill Prentice-Hall.

Salovey, P., & Mayer, J. D. (1990). *Emotional intelligence.* Imagination, Cognition, and Personality, *9*(3), 185–211.

Schlesinger, A. M. (1950). *The American as reformer.* Cambridge, MA: Harvard University Press.

Senge, P. (1990). *The fifth discipline: The art of practice of the learning organization.* New York: Doubleday.

Sergiovanni, T. J. (1996). *Leadership for the schoolhouse.* San Francisco: Jossey-Bass.

Sergiovanni, T. J., & Corbally, J. E. (Eds.). (1986). *Leadership and organizational culture: New perspectives on administrative theory and practice.* Urbana, IL: University of Illinois Press.

Stone, C. B., & Dahir, C. A. (2006). *The transformed school counselor.* Boston, MA: Lahaska Press.

Yero, J. L. (2002). *Values.* Hamilton, MT: MindFlight Publishing. Retrieved on June 16, 2004, from Web site: http://www.teachermind.com/values/htm

Yero, J. L. (2002). *Beliefs.* Hamilton, MT: MindFlight Publishing. Retrieved on June 16, 2004, from Web site: http://www.teachermind.com/beliefs/htm

3

Leading with an Understanding of Others

(Standards 2 and 5)

"Knowing the skills and attributes of each faculty member enhances the capacity of the school leader to lead."

"Before an individual can become a leader, that person must first believe that he can lead; that others will accept and support him, and that the position as leader will involve accomplishments which lead to a reward. Many individuals fail in their attempt to lead because they fear rejection by others."

HEMPHILL

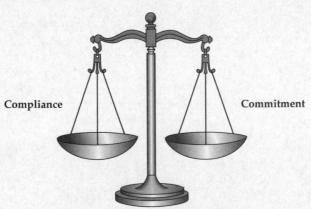

Compliance   Commitment

INTRODUCTION

The process of understanding self and others establishes the foundation for leadership in schools. In Chapter 2, our focus was on the importance of leaders having an understanding of self. In this chapter, as previously stated, we complete the equation of understanding self and others by directing the reader's attention to the importance of school leaders acquiring an in-depth understanding of individuals with whom they work, building a capacity to lead, and maintaining that capacity by balancing their behavior with the skills and attributes of followers.

The fundamental premise of the chapter is that effective school leaders acquire an understanding of followers and lead, seeking to achieve the delicate balance between compliance and commitment. Once that balance is achieved, school leaders must maintain it by continuously aligning the needs of the school organization with the needs of the individuals in both the internal and external environments of the schoolhouse.

DEVELOPING AN UNDERSTANDING OF OTHERS

Leaders of today's schools build leadership capacity by developing a deep understanding of individuals with whom they work and serve. On any level, it is beneficial for school leaders to know the strengths and interests of the individuals with whom they work. They also have to know group processes and processes and procedures of change. This knowledge will allow them to utilize the strengths and interests of individuals to effectively and efficiently move the organization toward its vision. Although the behavior of leaders is critical to school operations, the behavior of faculty members, individually and collectively, can be equally important because the behavior of followers influences the behavior of leaders. Therefore, in order to effectively lead a school, it is imperative that school leaders build a capacity to lead. Building that capacity requires them to have an understanding of individuals affiliated with the school.

As was introduced in Chapter 2, schools are open social systems consisting of individuals who work in organizations and have values, desires, and goals that they are attempting to achieve. Consequently, the effectiveness of an organization, in this instance the school, is dependent on the compatibility that exists between the school as an organization and the individuals who work in that organization. The greater the compatibility of the two forces, the more effective the organization is likely to function (see Exhibit 3.1). The challenge for school leaders is balancing the needs of the school with the goals and desires of followers. If school leaders want commitment, rather than compliance, they have to assume responsibility for orchestrating a community of learners in a manner that connects individuals and the organization, realizing that it is just as important for followers to achieve their personal goals as it is for the organization to reach its goals.

EXHIBIT 3.1   Organizational Dimensions

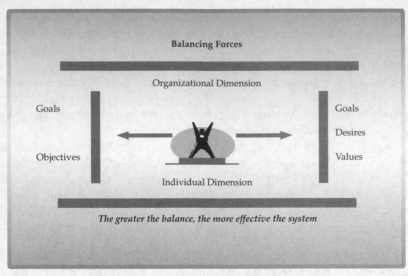

To fulfill this responsibility, school leaders must know and understand what followers and other stakeholders expect and desire from the school. In addition, they must gain insight into leadership practices that center not only on the behavior of followers, but the reason they behave in a specific manner. When leaders have knowledge and understanding of the behavior and expectations of individuals and groups with whom they work, they can maximize the interconnectedness between them and the school. They can also address the needs and goals of faculty and staff members and assist them in reaching their full potential. As a result, the efficiency and effectiveness of the school are increased.

The Process of Understanding the People with Whom We Work

It is not uncommon for emerging school leaders, or even practicing school leaders, to espouse theoretical concepts that offer a purpose for developing a deep understanding of individuals with whom they work. However, in some instances, when they are asked to share processes and procedures that can be used to operationalize these concepts in a school situation, a void in their preparation surfaces. This void can be problematic. If school leaders want to effectively utilize the skills and attributes of followers, they must have a process in place to identify them. They must also be able to determine the strengths and expectations of those individuals, gain insight into their values, beliefs, interests, levels of motivation, and understand how they view the school and the behavior of the leader. For example, when Georgia Edwards served as principal of Lexington Elementary School in District 89 of

Standard 2

An education leader promotes the success of every student by advocating, nurturing, and sustaining a school culture and instructional program conducive to student learning and staff professional growth.

Functions
  a. Nurture and sustain a culture of collaboration, trust, learning, and high expectations
  b. Create a comprehensive, rigorous, coherent curricula program
  c. Create a personalized and motivating learning environment for students
  d. Supervise instruction
  e. Develop assessment and accountability systems to monitor student progress
  f. Develop the instructional and leadership capacity of staff
  g. Maximize the time spent on quality instruction
  h. Promote the use of the most effective and appropriate technologies to support teaching and learning

Maywood, Illinois, she assessed the teaching strengths of teachers across all grade levels. The results of this assessment revealed that the instructional strengths of teachers in Reading, English, and Language Arts were highly concentrated in Grade 5. In fact, every teacher at that grade level was proficient in the areas of Reading, English, and Language Arts. In addition, they were achieving results at or above the established standard. The data also revealed a void in Grade 4, as none of the teachers assigned to that grade level were proficient in the areas of Reading, English, and Language Arts, and no one was meeting the established standard. It was quite apparent that a change was necessary. Reviewing information from teachers about their interests and desires and having an understanding of their dispositions, Principal Edwards knew which teacher to talk with in Grade 5 to suggest a move to Grade 4. She was also able to identify the skills and attributes the selected teacher could bring to the fourth grade in terms of serving in a teacher-leader role and providing professional development activities to the grade level in a manner that would be acceptable to the fourth-grade team.

Gaining Follower Commitment: Applying Theory to Practice

A number of theories inform practices that leaders can use as they strive to acquire the commitment of their followers. Some of the most noted ones that are related to school leadership are Path-Goal Theory, Expectancy Theory, Situational Leadership Theory, Social System Theory, and Emotional Intelligence Theory. A graphic delineation of the aforementioned theories and the implication they hold for understanding individuals who work in schools is presented in Table 3.1.

Approaches Used for Understanding Others

In addition to using the aforementioned theories, school leaders may find "The Inquiring Leadership Model;" "The Total Faculty Interview," and leadership practices that respect diversity beneficial in assisting them in acquiring an understanding of the people with whom they work.

THE INQUIRING LEADERSHIP MODEL   *The Inquiring Leadership Model* advocates a questioning technique that can be used to gain insight into the strengths and interests of followers. Questions are asked to gather accurate and timely information about individuals and their perceptions of the school and its operations. Some examples of questions that might be asked individual faculty members are:

1. What is your greatest challenge as a teacher at this school?
2. What is your idea of an effective working relationship between a principal and teacher?
3. From your perspective, how might we enhance teaching and learning?
4. How would you like to contribute to vision attainment?

The inquiring leader has to be a skillful questioner, as the results obtained from the inquiry process depend on the questions asked, and the questions posed reveal the internal questions (thinking) of leaders, their experience, mindset, values, knowledge, and skills (Golderg, 1998; Goldberg, 1998; Zintz, 1999).

THE TOTAL FACULTY INTERVIEW   *The Total Faculty Interview* is another approach school leaders may find beneficial in their attempt to understand the individuals with whom they work. Principal Shirley Johnson of Washington Elementary School in Maywood, Illinois and a number of principals in the Memphis City Schools in Memphis, Tennessee reported this practice to be very effective. Within the first two weeks of their assignment, school leaders might interview every faculty member, asking such questions as:

1. What position do you currently hold?
2. To what position do you aspire?
3. What are some of your greatest strengths?
4. What are your career goals?
5. What are ways that I might assist you in achieving those goals?

This interview process conveyed to faculty members that Principal Johnson valued them as individuals and was interested in involving them in the leadership of Washington Elementary School. It also provided Principal Johnson with valuable information that she could use in structuring the school for effective teaching and learning, making use of the skills and attributes of her faculty.

TABLE 3.1   Theories, Theorists, and Their Implications

Theories	Theorists	Implications for Leadership
Hierarchy of Needs Theory	(Abraham Maslow, 1970)	Factors in the workplace influence employee satisfaction and dissatisfaction. Individuals who work in schools have desires and goals that they want to achieve. Their level of motivation is enhanced if they work in an environment that is conducive to meeting their needs and acquiring their personal desires and goals.
Path-Goal Theory	(Robert House, 1971)	An understanding of goals and motivational levels of followers is required for effective leadership. With this knowledge, school leaders can assign tasks, clarify expectations, remove roadblocks to goal attainment, and facilitate meaningful rewards for followers.
Situational Leadership Theory	(Paul Hersey and Richard Blanchard, 1982)	There is no one best way to lead a school. Therefore, the leader's style should be determined by the situation, the environment, and the maturity level of followers. When this occurs, school leaders can assign tasks to faculty members whose readiness level is commensurate with the tasks to be completed.
Social Systems Theory	(R. L. Green, 2005)	There is social interaction between and among individuals who work in the schoolhouse—an interdependency. When school leaders have an understanding of individuals and groups who work in the schoolhouse, they can foster effective interpersonal relationships and structure the school for effective teaching and learning.
Emotional Intelligence Theory	(Daniel Goleman, 2001)	The intrapersonal and interpersonal constructs, such as self-awareness, self-confidence, and self-control, comprise the emotional intelligence of individuals. Understanding others is the foundation of developing a nurturing environment, and it is important for school leaders to sense others' developmental needs and bolster their self-efficacy.
Expectancy Theory	(Victor Vroom, 1969)	Followers are likely to be highly motivated to complete tasks if they believe they are capable of performing the task in an acceptable manner and if they value the reward to be received for completing the assigned task.

In Chapter 2, we discussed a number of tools that leaders can use to develop an understanding of self. Among them were the Myers-Briggs Inventory®, Emotional Intelligence Test®, and the 360° Leadership Assessment®. These same assessment tools can be used by school leaders to explore and develop a deeper understanding of the strengths, interests, and levels of motivation of individuals with whom they work.

RESPECTING DIVERSITY   A third approach to developing an understanding of others is modeling a genuine respect for diversity, which must be done in a manner that demonstrates respect for the values, beliefs, and strengths of all individuals. Some leaders tend to ignore or simply tolerate diversity that exists inside and outside of the schoolhouse, as it is difficult for them to admit their preferences and biases. In such instances, the school suffers, as the behavior exhibited by school leaders can have a tremendous negative influence on the faculty, staff, and community stakeholders. Anyone or all of the affiliated groups may perceive the leader as an individual who exhibits preferences and biases that prevent fair and respectful treatment of all individuals. When leaders exhibit such behavior, followers are not likely to reveal their true feelings, robbing the leader of follower commitment to school goal attainment. Therefore, school leaders have to affirm their beliefs and the beliefs of others; after all, it is difficult for school leaders to respond to the challenges of a diverse school and community if they are not aware of their biases and the biases of others (Washington Protection & Advocacy System, 2006).

Leaders can further demonstrate their respect for others by developing a clear understanding of the era or generation in which individuals belong. Quite clearly, the personal generational aspects of individuals, such as their experiences, ideas, and values, have significant influence on their job performance (Thielfoldt, & Scheef, 2004). These personal aspects that are shaped and shared by people of different generations make for a melting pot of work approaches and priorities. If school leaders are aware of generational factors (i.e., ethics, values, beliefs, and behaviors) that affect follower behavior, they will enhance their ability to identify the leadership style that best fosters collaborative working relationships between and among followers. Consequently, biases and preconceived notions can be eliminated, and everyone within the organization can be afforded the opportunity to appreciate and make constructive use of each other's differences and similarities, thus enhancing a respect for diversity.

Employing a series of assessment tools and processes can provide school leaders with knowledge of individuals inside and outside of the schoolhouse, as these tools and processes reveal many significant factors. As school leaders move to the facilitative style recommended for leaders of today's schools, they will find that placing leadership in every facet of the school, sensing the feelings and perspectives of followers, understanding their strengths, and taking an active interest in their concerns will prove to be valuable leadership behavior.

Standard 5

An education leader promotes the success of every student by acting with integrity, fairness, and in an ethical manner.

Functions
   a. Ensure a system of accountability for every student's academic and social success
   b. Model principles of self-awareness, reflective practice, transparency, and ethical behavior
   c. Safeguard the values of democracy, equity, and diversity
   d. Consider and evaluate the potential moral and legal consequences of decision making
   e. Promote social justice and ensure that individual student needs inform all aspects of schooling

Having acquired this understanding, leaders can convey to followers the belief that it truly takes people with different skills and attributes working together to accomplish school goals. Equally important, to facilitate goal attainment, school leaders will be equipped with knowledge of how to align their skills and attributes with those of followers, maximizing the connection between the organizational and individual dimensions of the school.

THE BENEFIT OF UNDERSTANDING OTHERS

From my years of working in schools, researching leader behavior, and observing principals exhibit leader behavior in schools across the United States, I have noted several benefits that come as a result of leaders acquiring an understanding of individuals with whom they work and serve. For the purpose of this text, three are significant: (1) an opportunity for school leaders to fulfill the psychological contract of followers; (2) an opportunity for school leaders to utilize follower creativity, and (3) an opportunity for school leaders to acquire follower commitment to goal attainment. A discussion of each of these significant benefits follows.

Attending to the Psychological Contract

The basis for the behavior that occurs in organizations is the psychological contract—an individual's beliefs regarding the agreement that exists between him/her and the organization (Rousseau, 1995). It is a mental model or an unwritten agreement that individuals use to characterize events and frame concepts, such as promises, acceptance, and reliance as they relate to the expectations and obligations of their work experience (Rousseau, 1995).

THE INFLUENCE OF THE PSYCHOLOGICAL CONTRACT   The beliefs, values, and behavior of individuals in the schoolhouse are greatly influenced by the psychological contract. When there is agreement between individuals and the organization concerning the contract, working relationships are satisfactory. When the contract is perceived to have been broken, unsatisfactory working conditions exist, which can prove to be quite damaging to the effectiveness of the school, as a broken contract can foster feelings of mistrust, injustice, deception, anger, and/or betrayal among the individuals involved. Consequently, for effective leadership to exist, it is critical that the leader has an understanding of the expectations of individual faculty members.

CONTRACT VIOLATIONS   Psychological contracts are built on trust and commitment. Individuals who work in the schoolhouse characterize events and develop expectations for the school in return for services that they plan to render. These expectations are based on their past experiences and their perception of reality (Rousseau, 1995). When the behavior of the leader and/or other individuals does not fit with these expectations, individuals perceive that their contract has been violated, and a violation may lessen an individual's commitment to the organization and his/her participatory behavior. Violations are most likely to occur:

- when there is a history of conflict and low trust in relationships;
- when there are social differences between the faculty and the school leadership;
- when actions are not taken to ensure that the perspectives of different individuals are understood;
- when faculty members feel they have no alternatives;
- when a faculty member feels the principal places little value on their relationship (Rousseau, 1995).

Some examples of actions that a faculty member might view as a contract violation include the following:

1. "I was promised that I would teach Advanced Placement English, and here I am teaching four sections of remedial English and only one Advanced Placement class."
2. "The school leader promised that I would not have to serve on lunch duty. In return, I agreed to take the drama club. Now he is saying that everyone will have to serve on lunch duty."
3. "The individual who received 'Teacher of the Year' award did not really complete all the projects that were listed by her name. I completed more projects than she did."

When individuals feel that their contracts have been violated, they may take one or more of several actions. They may (1) voice feelings, which helps to reduce losses and restore trust (active-constructive); (2) keep silent—a form of non-response, which reflects a willingness to endure or accept unfavorable circumstances, hoping that they may improve (passive-constructive); (3) engage in destruction/neglect, which can involve more active examples of counterproductive behaviors (passive negligence or active destruction), or (4) they may simply exit the school, which is voluntary termination of the violated relationship (Robinson & Rousseau, 1994).

The psychological contract is a major component in establishing and maintaining effective relationships between and among school leaders and the individuals they serve. Because psychological contracts are continually being created and sustained, it is vital that school leaders develop a deep awareness of their followers. They need to understand the expectations of faculty members, how they feel they are being treated, what inspires them, and how they react in various situations. With an understanding of each faculty member and other individuals affiliated with the school, school leaders can take into consideration their copious implications. Most specifically, they can be clear on the expectations individuals hold for the leadership of the school and the obligations of the school to them. When leading the school and making organizational decisions, a major responsibility of school leaders is to ensure that contracts are understood and honored or at least considered.

Utilizing the Creativity of Followers

Schools are complex multifaceted organizations, so much so that no one individual can lead them. It takes a combination of individuals with different skills and strengths who are committed to collaborating to achieve a shared vision. In Chapter 2, the focus was on the leader developing an understanding of self, which consisted of an identification of the values, beliefs, and strengths that influence the behavior of the leader. Here, we discuss the need for leaders to assess the skills, strengths, and attributes of followers. With that understanding, they can make a determination of how to distribute leadership responsibilities, utilizing the creativity of followers in a manner that maximizies the potential for school goal attainment.

Quite clearly, the school leader is ultimately responsible for the total school program. However, school leadership is becoming more facilitative and distributive in nature, necessitating the sharing of power and responsibility. With the acceptance of this advocated direction, the idea of shared responsibility becomes the key to effective leadership in schools (Gardner, 1990). Faculty members are engaged in such a way that, depending on the condition or event, they become leaders. Then, school leaders become followers, each raising each other to higher levels of motivation and morality (Burns, 1978; Gardner, 1990). In essence, the school leader becomes the lead learner—facilitating, advocating, nurturing, collaborating, influencing, and responding to diverse needs in the schoolhouse (ISLLC Standards, 1996).

In today's schools, leaders and followers may have different roles and functions; however, professionally, their purpose is the same—enhancing the academic achievement of students. To that end, school leaders and followers develop a relationship with one another, and support is reciprocated; they lead each other and "raise each other up." In that sense, the terms "leader" and "follower" become interchangeable based on depth of knowledge or ability to motivate and influence (Burns, 1978; Gardner, 1990).

An example of the exchange of roles and functions described in the preceding paragraph can be seen in the implementation of the instructional program for which the school leader is ultimately responsible. In some instances, the school leader will delegate tasks to an assistant or a group of high-performing teacher-leaders and simply monitor the process, offering suggestions and guidance. In such an instance, teachers and other members of the faculty make decisions regarding the developmental process. When this occurs, leaders become followers, and followers become leaders.

It is likely that school leaders will always have position power and authority. However, the real challenge seems to lie within the area of influence and acceptance of the realization that in today's schools, followers have about as much influence on their leaders as their leaders have on them (Gardner, 1990; Hook, 1955). Knowing that followers have a tremendous influence on leaders, an in-depth understanding of followers is imperative. With this understanding, leaders can seek follower commitment and align their skills and talents with tasks that lead to goal attainment.

Acquiring Follower Commitment for Goal Attainment

Realizing that even the most effective school leader cannot lead a school alone, school leaders must facilitate the development of a shared vision and acquire follower commitment for its attainment. The first step in the process is for school leaders to acknowledge their strengths and identify areas where they need assistance. Then, they can proceed to assess the background knowledge, skills, attributes, and experiences of followers for the purpose of filling any voids that might exist. If school leaders want to acquire the commitment of followers, rather than have them to simply comply, they have to utilize their skills and attributes in a meaningful way.

In addition, they have to be willing to collaborate and respond to diverse needs of followers, and their behavior has to exhibit interest in them to the extent that they can mobilize the support of, not only followers in the schoolhouse, but members of the larger external community (ISLLC Standards 1–6, 1996). In essence, to acquire commitment, rather than obtain compliance, school leaders have to become partners with the faculty and community in examining school needs, identifying best practices, and implementing those practices in a fair and equitable manner (Lieberman, 1995). In essence, their leadership behavior is transparent.

Effective 21st-century school leaders enhance their relationship with followers by being transparent. When school leaders choose to be transparent, they close the gap between themselves and their followers and gain follower commitment. Many leaders are criticized for not being open and honest about school-related issues or for having a hidden agenda. When school leaders choose to be transparent, they foster integrity, and their decisions can withstand scrutiny.

It is often difficult for school leaders to please everyone, as different individuals and groups hold different expectations for their leader. However, when the behavior of leaders is transparent and they use fair processes, acting with integrity, followers may not like the decisions that are made, but if the process was fair and equitable, they are likely to accept the decisions and commit to their implementation.

LEADER/FOLLOWER RELATIONSHIPS   To achieve the mission and goals of the school, there has to be leadership in every facet of the school organization, and that type of leadership requires interaction between the leader and followers (Maxwell, 2005). In addition, elements in the environment must be taken into account. Consequently, the effectiveness of the school and especially the leader, depends, to a large extent, on the quality of the relationship that exists between the leader, followers, and elements in the environment (Green, 2005).

In some instances, the style of the leader might necessarily be relationship-oriented and, in other instances, it might be necessary for leaders to exhibit task-oriented behavior. Each style has the potential of positively or negatively affecting the relationship between leaders and followers. Thus, the challenge becomes selecting the style most appropriate for a given situation. This determination is best made when consideration is given to the readiness level of individuals (Hersey, Blanchard, & Johnson, 1996).

IDENTIFYING THE READINESS LEVEL OF FOLLOWERS   The effective leader affirms the readiness level of followers, first by determining which followers can contribute most to the school, and then by influencing them to strive to reach their full potential. As a result, when school leaders assign tasks to followers, they can assign them in accordance with the follower's skills, abilities, and level of readiness. In some instances, it will be necessary for leaders to initiate structure, set work standards, carefully organize tasks, and identify methods followers can use in completing the assigned tasks. At other times, because of the readiness level of followers, it will be unnecessary for leaders to structure tasks, providing detailed directions (Green, 2005). In still other instances, it may be necessary for the behavior of leaders to be supportive, directive, participative, or possibly achievement-oriented. Given that school situations and/or tasks dictate leader behavior, school leaders have to keep in mind that different situations will require different approaches, and they will have to align their behavior with the behavior of followers. The behavior utilized should be informed by the follower's level of maturity, requiring school leaders to have knowledge of their capability (Hersey & Blanchard, 1982).

In addition to making a determination of the readiness level of followers to gain their commitment, leaders have to set clear expectations and standards of performance. Expectations and standards help to determine and clarify reality. If the readiness level of followers is ignored and/or not addressed, group performance can be affected. This may negatively affect school goal attainment. Consequently, when leaders set expectations and establish standards for followers, they have to be aware of the ability and confidence level of followers—their self efficacy. Followers' level of motivation and commitment to task completion are often determined by their mental expectation regarding their ability to complete the assigned task, their ability to achieve the desired level of performance, and their belief as to whether the reward will be meaningful (House, 1971). Therefore, the leader must clarify the tasks, make the expectations clear, remove roadblocks that inhibit goal attainment, and assure followers that they will be meaningfully rewarded for task completion.

With an understanding of followers, school leaders can exhibit the appropriate behavior, lead with insight and passion, clearly articulate the vision, mission, and goals of the school to the extent that followers and the larger community share the vision and make a commitment to its attainment. It is not only the responsibility of leaders to articulate the vision, mission, and goals, but they must also remove roadblocks or pitfalls that inhibit their attainment. The benefit to be derived is that individuals will feel respected, valued, and appreciated for the contribution that they make to the school. Essentially, they will see themselves in their leaders (Holmes, 2006).

■   ■   ■

Implications for Leadership

- Twenty-first century schools are complex, multifaceted organizations, so much so that no one individual can lead them.
- Today's school leaders have the awesome task of seeking and finding ways to transform schools into learning organizations that are adaptive to the demands of society.
- When school leaders understand others, they establish a foundation for leadership effectiveness.
- When school leaders establish a climate of trust in the schoolhouse, followers are provided an environment wherein they feel respected, nurtured, motivated, and empowered.

- Effective school leaders acknowledge the psychological contract of faculty and staff members. In doing so, they create and honor expectations and standards.
- Expectations and standards determine reality.
- Acquiring follower commitment for goal attainment enables the leader to distribute leadership to every facet of the organization, creating a professional learning community wherein the skills, talents, and attributes of all individuals are valued, respected, and utilized.
- Before leaders can understand the people with whom they work, they must first understand themselves.
- School leaders have to assemble a set of assessment tools and utilize them to develop a deep understanding of their faculty and staff.
- School leaders must put a process in place to utilize in developing a deep understanding of the people the school serves.
- Theories inform processes that can be utilized to understand others.
- A plan has to be put into place to identify resources in the community that are available for use by the school.
- School leaders have to keep in mind that their behavior influences the behavior of followers.
- Organizational tasks to be completed have to be aligned with the skills and attributes of followers.
- When leaders seek to achieve the goals and objectives of the organization, they have to keep in mind that the faculty and staff have goals and objectives that they are desirous of achieving.
- Organizational decisions have to be made in a manner that will facilitate the attainment of goals and objectives by both the school and the individuals who work in the school.
- The standard of excellence that is used to measure the project outcome should be embedded in the vision that is shared by stakeholders.

Reflective Practice

1. How do you determine if you have the right people assigned to the right tasks?
2. How do you determine the capability of faculty members?
3. How do you give people feedback concerning their performance?
4. What process do you use to ensure compatibility between the goals and objectives of the school and the desires and goals of individuals who work in the school?
5. How can you honor the psychological contract of individuals without minimizing the primary objectives of the school program?

Chapter Essentials

Interstate School Leaders Licensure Consortium: Standards 2 and 5

An education leader promotes the success of every student by advocating, nurturing, and sustaining a school culture and instructional program conducive to student learning and staff professional growth.

An education leader promotes the success of every student by acting with integrity, fairness, and in an ethical manner.

Principle

To lead with an understanding of others, the leader must first establish a trust-based foundation; then, he can develop and maintain the capacity to lead with an understanding of others.

Dichotomies

Compliance or Commitment

Leadership for today's schools requires collaboration. Therefore, compliance is not an option; rather school leaders will necessarily have to build the type of relationships that will influence followers to become committed to vision, mission, and goal attainment.

References

Burns, J. M. (1978). *Leadership*. New York: Harper & Row.

Gardner, J. W. (1990). *On leadership*. New York: Simon & Schuster.

Goldberg, M. C. (1998). The spirit and discipline of organizational inquiry: Ask questions for organizational breakthrough and transformation (as cited in *Organizations & People*, the Quarterly Journal of AMED). Association for Management Education and Development.

Goldberg, M. C. (1998). *The art of the question*. New York: John Wiley & Sons.

Goleman, D. (2001). What makes a leader? In J. Osland, D. Kolb, & I. Rubin (Eds.). *The Organizational Reader*. Upper Saddle River, NJ: Prentice Hall.

Green, R. L. (2005). *Practicing the art of leadership: A problem-based approach to implementing the ISSLC standards*. New Jersey: Merrill Prentice Hall.

Hersey, P., & Blanchard, K. H. (1982). *Management of organizational behavior: Utilizing human resources* (3rd ed.). Upper Saddle River, NJ: Prentice Hall.

Hersey, P., Blanchard, K. H., & Johnson, D. E. (1996). *Management of organizational behavior: Utilizing human resources*. Upper Saddle River, NJ: Prentice Hall.

Hemphill, J. K. (1961). Why people attempt to lead. In L. Petrullo and B. M. Bass (Eds.) *Leadership and interpersonal behavior* (pp. 201–205). New York: Holt, Rinehart, and Winston.

Holmes, M. (2006). Composing and conducting: How our top leaders make beautiful music. *Business Day*. Retrieved September 3, 2006, from Web site: http://www.realbusiness.co.za/Article.aspx?articleID=3758&typeID=4

Hook, S. (1995). *The hero in history*. Boston, MA: Beacon Press.

House, R. J. (1971). A path-goal theory of leader effectiveness. *Administrative Science Quarterly, 16*, 331–333.

Interstate School Leader Licensure Consortium (ISLLC). (1996). *Standards for school leaders*. Washington, DC: Council of Chief School Officers.

Levine, S. R., & Crom, M. A. (1993). *The leader in you: How to win friends, influence people, and succeed in a changing world*. New York: Simon & Schuster.

Lieberman, A. (1995). Restructuring schools: The dynamics of changes, practice, structure, and culture. In A. Lieberman (Ed.) *The work of restructuring schools: Building from the ground up*. New York: Teacher College Press.

Maxwell, J. C. (2005). *The 360° leader: Developing your influence from anywhere in the organization*. Nashville, TN: Thomas Nelson.

Maslow, A. (1970). *Motivation and personality* (Rev.ed.) New York: Harper & Row.

Robinson, S. L., & Rousseau, D.M. (1994). Violating the psychological contract: Not the exception but the norm. *Journal of Organizational Behavior, 15*, 245–259.

Rousseau, D. M. (1995). *Psychological contracts in organizations: Understanding written and unwritten agreements*. London: Sage.

Thielfoldt, D., & Scheef, D. (2004). *Generation X and the millennials: What you need to know about mentoring the new generations*. Retrieved August 15, 2006, from Web site: http://www.abanet.org/lpm/lpt/articles/nosearch/mgt08044_print.html

Washington Protection & Advocacy System (2006). *Identifying your biases*. Seattle, WA. Retrieved September 3, 2006, from Web site: http://www.wpasrights.org/What%20is%20Advocacy/identifying_your_biases.htm

Vroom, V. H. (1969). Industrial social psychology. In G. Lindzey & E. Aronson (Eds.), *Handbook of social psychology* (2nd. Ed., 5, pp.196–268) Reading, MA: Addison-Wesley.

Zintz, A. (1999). *Leadership, inquiry, and innovation*. Princeton, NJ: The Institute for Inquiring Leadership.

PART THREE

Dimension 2

Understanding the Complexity of Organizational Life

Structure	Culture
Climate	The Interaction of People

Chapter 4 The Social Interaction in Schools
Chapter 5 Perspectives on School Structure: Chaos or Efficiency
Chapter 6 The Principal's Role in Establishing and Retaining a Quality Teaching Faculty

DIMENSIONAL CONCEPTS

Schools are multifaceted and complex organizations. Contributing to that complexity is the structure of the school, its culture, climate, and the interaction of people. In this dimension, Chapters 4 and 5 combine to foster the position that schools and situations differ. As a result, the behavior of individuals and groups working in schools is understandably different.

To lead effectively, transforming the vision of a school into reality, school leaders must understand the complexities of organizational life, assess current conditions, establish a standard of excellence, and implement solid plans for goal attainment, while focusing on (1) respect for diversity; (2) principles of fair process; (3) ethical behavior, and (4) removal of fear and intimidation from the schoolhouse.

CHAPTER

4

The Social Interaction in Schools

(Standards 2, 3, and 4)

"The internal organizational culture is a quality inherent within a school environment that creates an atmosphere setting it apart from other schools that are similar in nature."

REBORE

"Learning organizations are places where people continually expand their capacity to create the results they truly desire, where new and expansive patterns of thinking are nurtured, where collective aspiration is set free, and where people are continually learning how to learn together."

SENGE

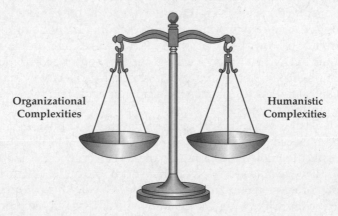

Organizational Complexities   Humanistic Complexities

INTRODUCTION

There is nothing simple about schools; schools are multifaceted and complex open social systems. Their structures are varied, and their challenges are influenced by a number of different components and situations. These contributing factors differ from school to school and, as a result, the behavior of individuals leading them necessarily has to be varied and different. To achieve effectiveness, school leaders must develop a deep understanding of these complexities and identify strategies that can be used to address them.

While we recognize that many factors contribute to the complexity of organizational life in schools, in this chapter, the focus is on four: (1) culture; (2) climate; (3) structure, and (4) the interaction of people. The underlying tenet is that schools are social systems with interacting component parts. There is interdependency between the parts, and the leader's understanding of their working relationship is tantamount to school goal attainment. With this understanding, school leaders can facilitate the development of a structure that fosters collaborative relationships between and among the parts.

To begin the chapter, organizations are defined. Next, a scenario that provides readers an opportunity to analyze the complexities of school organizations in a practical situation is presented. We then proceed to discuss the complex nature of school organizations functioning as open social systems by reviewing the aforementioned four components as they appear in the scenario. The chapter concludes with a discussion of processes that school leaders can use to develop an understanding of the complexities of school organizational life.

ORGANIZATIONS DEFINED

Organizations are a collection of individuals with varying interests embedded in broader environments and functioning on a relatively continuous basis to achieve a goal or set of common goals (Robbins, 1998; Scott, 2003). They are durable in that they are designed to persist over time and reliable in that the same functions are performed repeatedly in the same way. In addition, they foster accountability in that the behavior of individuals takes place within a framework of rules that provides guidelines and justifications for decisions and activities. When a school faculty, comprised of individuals with various skills, attributes, values, and beliefs, collectively implements programs and activities to enhance the academic achievement of students, a school organization is operationalized.

There is a real social and professional connection and interdependence between organizational members. To lead effectively, school leaders must have a deep understanding of the interconnectedness of all individuals in the organization. They have to take an action-oriented approach and facilitate the establishment of a professional learning community—a cohesive constituent team that focuses on the achievement of a common goal. Through the process, team members fashion a shared vision, empower and motivate each other, gain commitment, and facilitate goal attainment (Levine & Lezotte, 1990).

To assist the reader in understanding this interconnectedness and exploring the complex nature of a school organization in practice, the scenario "Harpo Allen Middle School" is presented. In reading the chapter, the reader is encouraged to reflect on the events in the scenario, describe the action that he/she would take to address the various occurrences, and identify any additional information he/she would need to fully understand the culture, climate, structure, and the interactions of people in the schoolhouse. The reflective questions following the scenario are designed to assist the reader in transforming the theoretical concepts of the chapter into practical application. After reading Chapter 5, the reader will have an opportunity to design a school structure to address the challenges posed in the scenario.

Scenario: Harpo Allen Middle School

Harpo Allen Middle School has a composition of Grades 6, 7, and 8, serving a student population of 1600. The breakdown of the student population is:

Grade 6	597 students
Grade 7	532 students
Grade 8	471 students

The school is staffed with eighty (80) faculty and staff members, a leadership team comprised of one principal, four assistant principals, and three professional school counselors. The school is located in a major urban city bordered by two states.

The makeup of the faculty and staff covers four distinct eras: (1) one third (1/3) of the faculty and staff members were born between 1940 and 1960; (2) one third (1/3) of the faculty and staff members were born between 1960 and 1970; (3) ten (10) members of the faculty and staff were born between 1970 and 1980, and (4) the remainder of faculty and staff members were born after 1980.

Most of the faculty and staff live outside of the school community. Some live in neighboring states or in suburban areas that are far away from the school; they do not have to drive through the entire community in order to get to Harpo Allen Middle School. Each year, as many as sixteen (16) teachers are new to the faculty.

Because of the annexation of suburban areas into the city, the school and the community have been in transition for the past six years. While not documented, the high teacher turnover rate is attributed to the annexation, posing a challenge to keep highly qualified teachers with the appropriate certification.

Due to urban blight, the city is overhauling its housing projects. Many of the residents are moving into the Harpo Allen district, causing the demographics of the area to change. The city's new trend in housing is the development of single units, allegedly to give low-income families the opportunity to become first time homeowners. However, these families are unable to purchase the newly constructed homes. To the contrary, middle class whites are purchasing the new homes, and the low-income residents are being relocated to the Harpo Allen area. They are becoming more destitute, as they do not have access to public transportation and cannot afford many of the conveniences enjoyed by others in the Harpo Allen area. In addition, over the past five years, the area has had an influx of Hispanic and Asian families.

Student achievement and discipline are less than desirable. The school has been on the corrective action list for the last three years. When speaking with the faculty, there is a lot of finger pointing, very little ownership, and little commitment to resolving the situation. Most of the faculty make comments such as, "The kids are not interested. The parents do not support or value education. I really cannot make a difference. I am not a social worker; I am a teacher." One can easily see the divisiveness that exists among the faculty and the community.

Parents do not participate in the school program, as they feel that the school is not warm and open. They do not feel that there is a role for parents in the educational process. They will often make comments such as "They don't care about my child. They are just earning a paycheck. They are always picking on my child." For whatever reason, the school leadership has not been able to involve parents. The faculty and staff attribute low student achievement and high incidents of discipline to lack of parental involvement.

William Jefferson has just completed a leadership preparation program and was invited to assume the Principalship at the Harpo Allen Middle School. He is very energetic and enthusiastic. He has scheduled his first faculty meeting at 3:30 P.M. He is so excited and can hardly wait to implement some of the ideas that he learned in his leadership preparation program. Mr. Jefferson has prepared an agenda for the meeting, focusing on student achievement, school climate, and the rules and procedures for Harpo Allen Middle School. It is now 3:25 P.M., time for the meeting to begin.

Mr. Jefferson entered the meeting with a heartfelt welcome. He proceeded with the agenda. The meeting was progressing successfully until Mr. Jefferson presented his action plan designed to address the aforementioned problems. Soon after, hands of faculty members began to fly in the air, requesting an opportunity to speak. Feelings of contentment and agreement were quickly replaced with feelings of frustration and disgruntlement.

REFLECTIVE QUESTIONS

1. Describe some approaches that could be used to establish a culture of high expectations for students and staff performance at Harpo Allen Middle School?

2. How would you use the demographic data pertaining to students and their families to develop a school mission and goals for Harpo Allen

Middle School? What additional information might prove to be helpful in the process?

3. What core beliefs would have to be built into the vision of Harpo Allen Middle School in order for all stakeholders to be included?
4. What are some program activities that could be implemented by Principal Jefferson to influence parents in the community to participate in developing new and innovative programs?
5. What strategies would you use to assess the school climate with the intent of identifying and removing barriers to student learning?
6. How would Harpo Allen Middle School have to be structured in order for all stakeholders to be involved in decisions affecting the school?
7. What group process and consensus skills will Principal Jefferson need?
8. What type of instructional program would you recommend for Harpo Allen Middle School? Describe the change strategies that you would employ to ensure its effective implementation.
9. Identify the elements in the internal and external environments of the school that are likely contributing to the complexity of organizational life in Harpo Allen Middle School.

ELEMENTS CONTRIBUTING TO THE COMPLEXITY OF ORGANIZATIONAL LIFE

People often refer to schools as if they are all the same, but, quite the contrary, they are all unique and different. The first step to understanding the complex nature of schools is to recognize that they are open social systems and, as such, they do not function in isolation as separate entities. Rather, they are dependent on the flow of information and resources from their external environment, and their activities are subject to laws, policies, and procedures that are often enacted by agencies that exist in their external environment (Green, 2005).

In Chapters 2 and 3, we introduced the concept of schools functioning as open social systems. Here, we build on that concept by identifying elements that contribute to the complexity of the system. These elements are culture, climate, structure, and the interaction of people functioning in the schoolhouse. For a graphic view of these elements, see Exhibit 4.1. In the following section, we provide the reader with an explanation of how each of these elements contributes to the complexity of organizational life in schools.

The Organizational Culture of Schools

One of the most essential elements contributing to the complexity of organizational life in schools is its internal and external culture. Culture shapes the organization as it consists of the deep patterns of shared values, beliefs, and traditions formed in the organization over a period of years (Schein, 1992). As people function in the organization, culture drives their behavior

EXHIBIT 4.1   Elements Contributing to the Complexity of Organizational Life in Schools

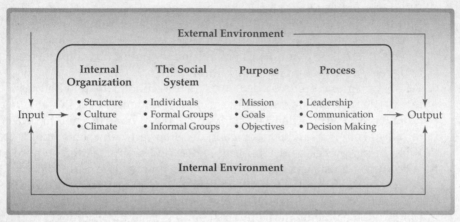

describing how they react to things, where they commit their energy, and what captures their enthusiasm (Schein, 1992).

School leaders encounter a myriad of people and situations daily, and as society changes, they are expected to lead, addressing those changes. This is not an unrealistic expectation as it is quite reasonable to expect leaders to lead with an understanding of the organization for which they are responsible. Yet, if they fail to acquire answers to pertinent questions about the culture of the school and how it affects organizational life, they lead blindly and without knowledge of the social dynamics of the organization; this was the situation at Harpo Allen Middle School.

When entering a new position or observing someone else entering a new position, perhaps you have heard the phrase, "Do not go in making a lot of changes; wait a while before you start making changes." In essence, the individual is being advised to develop an understanding of and an appreciation for the culture of the school, prior to attempting to lead organizational change.

The culture of an organization contributes to relationship building, commitment of followers, establishment of policies and procedures, program development, and the level of trust that exists among organizational members (Sashkin, Rosenbach, & Taylor, 1993). Given these factors, one can easily see how culture is a major contributor to the complexity of organizational life and why it is advisable that individuals leading today's schools become aware of the existing culture of the school, as well as factors influencing that culture. To acquire this understanding, a new or experienced school leader might seek answers to the following questions:

1. How is business transacted by school personnel?
2. What are the norms and standards of behavior?
3. What are the patterns of basic assumptions?

Standard 2

An education leader promotes the success of every student by advocating, nurturing, and sustaining a school culture and instructional program conducive to student learning and staff professional growth.

Functions
- **a.** Nurture and sustain a culture of collaboration, trust, learning, and high expectations
- **b.** Create a comprehensive, rigorous, and coherent curricular program
- **c.** Create a personalized and motivating learning environment for students
- **d.** Promote the use of the most effective and appropriate technologies to support teaching and learning

4. How does information flow?
5. What are the lines of communication?
6. What process is used to socialize new members?
7. Who does what and when is it done?
8. How are decisions made?
9. What are the established operational procedures?
10. What are the formal lines of authority?
11. What are the informal lines of authority?
12. Who are the power brokers in the schoolhouse and the community?

As one seeks answers to these questions, it should be kept in mind that both the internal and external cultures of each school organization are unique and consist of many variables. Therefore, in the following section, we discuss variables that exist in the internal and external cultures of schools.

THE INTERNAL CULTURE OF SCHOOLS   The teaching and learning process that takes place in the schoolhouse is influenced both by the internal and external culture of the school. New school leaders, or school leaders transferring from one school to another, are likely to find that each school has its own unique identity, even though it functions at the same structural level, elementary, middle, or secondary, and has the same mission—enhancing the academic achievement of students. Largely, the difference rests in the internal culture of the school—the behavior of people, their values, their beliefs, the content of their conversation, their dress, and their interaction with each other.

A major function of the internal culture is to socialize individuals to the values and goals of the school and to exercise coordination and control of the teaching and learning process. Through the socialization process, a faculty and staff might personally identify with the purposes and values of the school and become motivated to align their personal goals and needs with those of the school (Rebore, 2001). It is also through the socialization process that individuals new to the school acquire the skills needed to participate effectively (Dunn, Rouse, & Seff, 1994). Thus, the internal culture of the school organization epitomizes, not only what the school stands for, but also the work style and aspirations of individual participants.

Critical to understanding how the internal culture of schools contributes to their complexity is understanding the makeup of schools, their ethos, rituals, patterns of behavior, traditions, values, beliefs, and what individuals hold true and dear. Of particular importance, in many instances, are the traditions that make up school culture. They are the elements that are passed down from class to class and often from generation to generation. As leaders enter schools and contemplate change, these elements should be given considerable consideration as teachers, students, parents, alumni, and members of the community value and identify with them and often have a vested interest in their existence. To say the least, they bring a sense of pride to the school and community. For example, school colors, school mascots, instructional program schedules, extracurricular program activities, class arrangement, instructional assignments, band programs, sports activities, and patterns of behavior are just a few of the elements of school culture that must be understood and factored into the plans of the leader.

These elements are the glue that holds the school together, making it a family or a community with a shared sense of purpose. To alter any of these elements without careful thought and planning could prove to be very disruptive. Adding to the importance of understanding this phenomenon is the fact that individuals and groups have a vested interest in different elements of the culture, making it necessary for the leader to not only have knowledge of the various elements, but also individuals and groups that lay claim to those elements.

SUBCULTURES IN THE SCHOOLHOUSE Another internal cultural factor adding to the complexity of organizational life is the different subcultural groups that comprise the faculty and staff. Any given school may not only have various racial, ethnic, and religious cultural groups, but each of the identified groups might divide themselves into one or more subcultures. Additionally, the groups might divide themselves by socioeconomic status, language, and friendships. Whereas each of these cultural groups and/or subcultural groups contributes to the internal culture of the school organization, they also function as a separate and autonomous subculture group. They warrant a depth of understanding and appreciation on behalf of the school leader. For example, a faculty may consist of Christians, Jews, Muslims, African-Americans, Hispanics, Asians, Caucasians, and other nationalities. Each of these religious and ethnic groups possesses beliefs, values, folkways, and norms that can have a decisive impact on the culture of the school organization.

As the different cultural groups strive to be acculturated into the culture of the school organization, they also seek to maintain their individual identities. To avoid conflict, it is imperative that school leaders gain insight into both the culture of the school organization and the culture of the various groups that make up the school organization. If school leaders focus solely on the culture of the school organization, failing to give consideration to cultural groups that make up the organization, conflict is likely to surface, provoking a disconnect that minimizes the desired level of commitment from individual faculty members (Yukl, 2002).

School leaders are further challenged by competing value systems, preconceived notions, and stereotypical behavior that exist between sub-cultures. These differences create a mosaic of organizational realities, rather than a uniform corporate culture (Morgan, 1997). To acquire faculty cohesiveness that fosters goal attainment, school leaders are challenged to first understand the various subgroups, then, develop strategies to connect them.

THE EXTERNAL SCHOOL CULTURE   The culture of the school community consists of "an evolved form of social practice that has been influenced by many complex interactions between people, situations, actions, and general circumstances" (Morgan, 1997, p. 151). This composition is different for each school and adds to the complexity of understanding organizational life in the schoolhouse. It defines the community and the people the school serves (Scott, 2003). To effectively lead a school, school leaders need to deeply probe the school community and gain insight into its diverse cultural makeup— values, expectations, traditions, rituals, and folkways. Community stakeholders hold these features true and dear to their hearts and have expectations for what the school should stand for and what it means to the alumni and the community-at-large.

Examining community elements is critical to the success of the school. In fact, it is the beginning point of linking the school and community in a meaningful way, and, to a large extent, it can be more critical to leadership effectiveness than connecting the elements in the internal environment of the schoolhouse (Scott, 2003). For example, at Harpo Allen Middle School, the external culture of the school is greatly influencing the teaching and learning process. Therefore, Mr. Jefferson needs to examine that culture and obtain critical information that will inform any attempt for effective change. Having

Standard 4

An education leader promotes the success of every student by collaborating with faculty and community members, responding to diverse community interests and needs, and mobilizing community resources.

Functions
a. Collect and analyze data and information pertinent to the educational environment
b. Promote understanding, appreciation, and use of the community's diverse cultural, social, and intellectual resources
c. Build and sustain positive relationships with families and caregivers
d. Build and sustain productive relationships with community partners

gained insight into the culture of the school community, the leadership (administrators and faculty) can make a determination of current reality, establish shared goals and objectives, and give meaning to actions that lead to enhanced academic achievement and improvement of the human condition.

School leaders have to know and understand community stakeholders and convey to them that their desires, ideas, and opinions are valued, and that programs and activities are being implemented for the good of the total community. Parents, students, and community stakeholders feel something special about their school; they have expectations and want to feel that they can collaborate with the leadership in making decisions and providing directions for the school.

Equally important, with an understanding of the external culture, a positive environment for lasting change can be established, and a communication network that facilitates the constant monitoring of public thinking regarding school operations can be operationalized. In addition, the needs of the community and the goals of the school can be reconciled; competing values and beliefs can be minimized, and a broad-based constituency can be built, avoiding the occurrence of crises. To further enhance this subject, in Chapter 5, we discuss how school leaders might structure schools to engage community stakeholders in the educational process.

The Organizational Climate of Schools

Another factor that contributes to the complexity of organizational life in the schoolhouse is the internal climate of the school. School climate is a characterization of the atmosphere, the tone, the personality, or the ethos of the school. In essence, it is a description of how people feel about the quality of their life inside of the schoolhouse and the extent to which they are engaged or disengaged in ongoing activities (Halpin & Croft, 1963; Owens, 2004). The single most important purpose for schools is the enhancement of academic achievement for all students, and this purpose is best achieved in a climate that is conducive to effective teaching and learning.

The literature on school climate offers evidence that when characteristics of a professional learning organization are in place, the type of climate that enhances teaching and learning will exist (Owens, 2004; Rebore, 2001). In our work at the University of Memphis, we have found success in this area by implementing a three-step process. First, we accepted the proposition that in a professional learning community, teaching and learning can be enhanced. Having accepted this proposition, we assist emergent school leaders in becoming knowledgeable of the characteristics of a professional learning community and processes that can be utilized to effectively implement them in a school. Next, using several survey instruments, they assess the existing climate of schools with a focus on: (1) people expanding their learning capacity; (2) the atmosphere of the building; (3) the manner in which individuals address each other; (4) the extent to which individuals collaborate with each other; (5) the manner in which people enter the building; (6) the statements they make about the school and the activities ongoing in the school, and (7) whether or not the general perception is that effective teaching and learning are taking place. The survey process necessarily has to be extensive, collecting data from principals, teachers, students, parents, and citizens in the community. Through analyses of the data, hindering and enabling forces in the existing school climate can be identified.

The third step is the selection of a process that can be utilized effectively to remove the hindering forces or to transform them into enabling forces. In addition, the enabling forces can be enhanced, aligning them with characteristics of a professional learning community.

The outcome of this three-step process is a positive school climate wherein school leaders, teachers, and staff are able to collaborate and participate in identifying what is needed to enhance academic achievement of students. To illustrate the concept, the following scenario is offered. When Sharon Williams-Griffin was appointed principal of Airways Middle School in Memphis, Tennessee, upon entering the schoolhouse for the first time, she observed a building in major disrepair. Realizing that academic achievement and school climate were directly related, her first action was to enhance the climate of the school. In doing so, she made direct contact with the superintendent and invited her to tour the building. After the tour, Principal Griffin made several requests that were necessary if meaningful and sustained change were to occur. The building was painted inside and outside; all lockers were cleaned, and gang signs were removed. A security system was installed that consisted of safety-video cameras, walkie-talkies, and an intercom. Additionally, a system was established to remove any marks or drawings on walls daily. With these changes, the school began to take on a school-like environment. The climate was further enhanced with the establishment of a progressive discipline system, which required one voice; all faculty and staff assumed responsibility for obtaining positive student behavior. Finally, Principal Griffin secured adopters from the community to assist in maintaining and growing what was to become "The New Airways Middle School." As a result of these and other changes, the academic achievement of students was significantly enhanced (see Exhibit 4.2)

It is important for school leaders to understand that the climate inside and outside of the schoolhouse can influence the behavior of the faculty and

EXHIBIT 4.2   Enhanced Academic Achievement at Airways Middle School

School Year	Mathematics	Reading/Language Arts	Attendance
2006	77%	71%	93%
2007	84%	85%	95%
2008	93%	92%	94%

Source: Developed from Airways Middle School Progress Report.

staff in various ways. Also, the motives and behavior of a faculty and staff can positively or negatively affect the school climate, ultimately determining if the school organization works effectively as a social system fostering goal attainment (Rebore, 2001). Just as the sum total of the characteristics of an individual equates to an individual's personality, the sum total of the characteristics of a school equates to the personality of that school. Ultimately, it is the personality of the school that people accept or reject.

To change the personality of a school, the characteristics have to change, and this change begins with school leaders, as they must model the characteristics that are desired. Because of the makeup of a social system, this might appear to be a simple and reasonable request. Quite the contrary, because of the differences in attitudes, values, beliefs, and dispositions of people, changing a school climate can be very challenging, adding to the complexity of school organizational life. You cannot factor out people because schools are about people. They are all about people; the purpose is about people; people implement the process, and the outcome is in the form of a product, which is people.

Creating an effective teaching and learning environment relates to ownership and assuming responsibility for the challenges that exist. For example, in a school environment that is perceived to be hostile and unproductive, individuals might be characterized as highly disengaged, uncooperative, apathetic, aloof, inconsiderate, and projecting low levels of trust. When this type of climate exists, the school as a whole might be viewed as being stagnant and not meeting its goals or the academic, social, and emotional needs of students. In this type of climate, more often than not, the behavior of the leader discourages faculty involvement in the leadership process, as task completion is the major focus. The faculty and staff feel disconnected from the school and often express a concern that their social and emotional needs are not being met.

Conversely, in a school environment that is perceived to be a positive wholesome school climate, faculty and staff express a high degree of satisfaction with working conditions; they care about each other, take pride in their work, trust the administration, function in a lively manner, and energetically strive to achieve the goals and objectives of the school. Equally important, they identify the school as one which they would like for their children to attend. In this type of climate, more often than not, the behavior of the leader influences faculty involvement in the leadership process, and there is a balance between work tasks and the social and emotional needs of the faculty and staff.

The climate in the schoolhouse can also influence external relationships that positively or negatively impact the teaching and learning process and the flow of material resources from the external environment. Given that the climate is the personality of the school organization, it conveys a perception to parents and external stakeholders regarding the extent to which they are welcome in the schoolhouse and a part of their children's education. Climate can also influence the manner in which parents and other community stakeholders perceive that their ideas are accepted and their concerns are being addressed.

Finally, school climate truly adds another dimension to an already complex social organization. Therefore, school leaders must be able to analyze it and make judgments about the extent that it influences stakeholder satisfaction and dissatisfaction. They should also make judgments about what is needed to increase the motivation level of individuals and enhance organizational efficiency. Indeed, climate is a contributing factor to the complexity of organizational life in schools.

The Organizational Structure of Schools

A third contributing factor to the complexity of life in the schoolhouse is the structure of the organization. Organizational structure refers to coordination and control—how tasks are assigned in a formal manner, how individuals are grouped to complete work assignments, how lines of communication are established, and the enactment of rules and regulations that govern the behavior of individuals (Robbins, 2000).

For a number of years, the structure of schools was hierarchical in nature with the leadership focusing on efficiency and exhibiting behavior governed by principles of bureaucratic, scientific, and administrative management. Today, because of the challenges of leading schools, there is the call for school leaders to abandon the classical concept of one-person leadership and move to a more facilitative style of leadership, focusing on the creativity and competence of followers (Allen, 1990; Chirichello, 2001; Liontos, 1994; Palestini, 2003). To facilitate this change, the structure of the school must shift from a classical hierarchical structural to one that is more humanistic and inclusive, involving all stakeholders in a leadership role.

Initially, transitioning from a bureaucratic hierarchical structure of leadership to a participative structure may appear simplistic, but it really is not. Making the transition adds many challenges to organizational leadership. Some school organizations may need to be highly structured, focusing on task and goal attainment, while others may need a flexible structure that focuses on relationships as a means of completing organizational tasks. Developing an effective balance between these two general concepts to foster organizational effectiveness adds to the complexity of life in school organizations. Given that organizational structure is a dominant influence in school organizational life, Chapter 5 is entirely devoted to a discussion of the organizational structure of schools.

Interactive Behavior of People

A fourth factor that contributes to the complexity of organizational life in schools is the interactive behavior of people as they strive to achieve the goals of the organization, as well as their personal goals. The process becomes complex as differences in the values of individuals and groups foster competition for human and material resources, as well as time. Three critical elements contributing to that complexity are: (1) the diverse needs of students and their effect on teaching and learning; (2) the motivation level of faculty and staff, and (3) the style of leadership exhibited by school leaders.

THE DIVERSE NEEDS OF STUDENTS   In today's schools, students differ in terms of ethnicity/culture, social class, personal development, academic ability/ disability, and gender. In many schools, the student body is likely to consist of Native Americans, African-Americans, Asians, Caucasians, and any number of non-English speaking students. Each of these groups brings differences into the schoolhouse. These differences may influence the climate of the classroom, the beliefs of school leaders and teachers relative to student ability levels, and the structure and design of the curriculum (DuFour & Eaker, 1998; Levin, 1988; Slavin, Karweit, & Madden, 1989).

To accentuate the complexity that the diverse needs of students bring to the teaching and learning process, we refer the reader to the section of this chapter where we discussed the internal culture of the school. In that section, values and core beliefs were noted and explored as contributors to the culture of a school, and the culture of the school shapes the foundation for teaching and learning. It has also been associated with high levels of academic achievement (Parkay & Stanford, 2004). What the faculty believes about students' ability to achieve and learn, whether good teaching will make a difference in student learning, who should maintain power and control over the instructional process, and who is to be accountable for the lack of student achievement impacts the instructional program (DuFour & Eaker, 1998; Shellard, 2003). The competing values of individuals regarding how these questions should be addressed add to the complexity of life in schools.

In effective schools, all students are held to high standards of learning, and the teaching and learning process involves school leaders and teachers and should accommodate all students, regardless of their developmental, cognitive, and social levels (Slavin, 2003). Students who are experiencing crisis during specific developmental stages should be provided assistance in addressing their cognitive, emotional, social and/or physical needs. Rather than relying on generalizations about students, teachers have to disaggregate data and identify the specific needs of each student. It may also be necessary to visit the home, the community, and investigate the interpersonal interests of students. In that way, teachers can make sure the curriculum is free of race and gender bias and provide the opportunity for all students to learn whether they are thriving academically or having learning difficulties. To achieve these outcomes, school leaders must exhibit mastery of the core competencies of unity of purpose, curriculum and instruction, and collaboration.

THE MOTIVATIONAL LEVEL OF FACULTY AND STAFF   Another factor relative to the interaction of individuals in the schoolhouse is the motivational level of faculty and staff. The interdependency of the teaching and learning process requires members of the faculty and staff to interact with one another for instructional goal attainment. However, individuals have competing values causing members of the faculty and staff to disagree regarding appropriate operational procedures to use in addressing select issues.

Standard 3

An education leader promotes the success of every student by ensuring management of the organization, operation, and resources for a safe, efficient, and effective learning environment.

Functions
  a. Monitor and evaluate the management and operational systems
  b. Obtain, allocate, align, and efficiently utilize human, fiscal, and technological resources
  c. Promote and protect the welfare and safety of students and staff
  d. Develop the capacity for distributed leadership
  e. Ensure teacher and organizational time is focused to support quality instruction and student learning

For positive interaction to occur, the motivation level of faculty and staff members has to be commensurate with their assigned responsibilities. First, they have to feel that they have the skills necessary to complete assigned tasks; then, they have to believe that they can complete the tasks in line with the established standards, in the allocated timeframe. Additionally, they have to value the reward afforded them for completion of the assigned tasks (House, 1971).

Teachers enter the schoolhouse with various levels of preparation and expertise. Some are experienced with fully developed skills and attributes, and others are novices with little or no experience to couple with the training they acquired during their teacher preparation program. Then, there are other teachers, who fall along the continuum between the two. Therefore, to enhance teacher motivation and increase interaction between and among faculty members, school leaders have to assess the capability of each faculty member and align his/her skills and attributes with tasks to be performed and goals and objectives to be achieved.

In some instances, it is necessary for school leaders to collaborate with faculty in the planning and implementation of professional development activities that address voids in the faculty's preparation. Determining appropriate professional support begins with both the leader and teacher identifying challenges that the teacher may be experiencing in his/her work, along with the sources of the challenges. Once the challenges and their sources have been determined, school leaders can identify various solutions, choose the best option, and establish priorities for their implementation (Seyfarth, 1999). Through such a process, the needs of individual faculty members can be identified and addressed before they become debilitating. An instructional supervisory model that school leaders may find helpful is discussed in Chapter 6.

Leaders should be mindful that addressing the individual needs of faculty members relative to their instructional assignments is just one way to provide professional support. The unique needs of the school program must also be considered. This is of practical importance when change is occurring in the form of modifications, program additions, or a complete restructuring of the instructional program.

School leaders also motivate their faculty through non-academic related activities. They host dinners for faculty members and their spouses; they provide suggestion boxes to secure faculty input, and afford faculty members release time to address personal needs.

To address the complexity that is created in schools because of the level of motivation of faculty and staff, it is imperative that school leaders give consideration to both the faculty's professional and personal needs. When this occurs, their motivation level is likely to increase, and they will have a greater sense of commitment to school goal attainment.

THE LEADERSHIP STYLE OF SCHOOL LEADERS   A third factor contributing to the complexity of school organizational life, because of the interactive behavior of people, is the leadership style of school leaders. This factor cannot be overemphasized, as school leaders are constantly interacting with all stakeholders. However, their leadership style can shift from an authoritarian top-down style to an inclusive facilitative style, allowing teachers, parents, and other community stakeholders to interact and play a lesser or greater role in making decisions that affect schools.

Between the years of 2003 and 2008, we observed the leadership style of school leaders and the influence those styles have on the interaction of the faculty in eighteen (18) schools. Our observations suggest that a significant determinant of the quality of the interaction among faculty members is the style of leadership exhibited by the school leader.

In one instance, a school faced challenges relative to the leadership style of the principal and the negative interaction between the principal and members of the faculty and community. Conflict also existed among members of the faculty; thus, we observed the school appearing in the electronic and print media daily. With a change in principal, a change in leadership styles occurred, and thus, a positive change occurred in all of these groups. In short order, the media coverage was nonexistent.

In a second instance, we observed a principal using an autocratic style of leadership for a period of two years. The style negatively impacted the faculty, causing them to split into three different factions. Visits from outside staff development facilitators had little or no effect on changing the negative interactions that were occurring between the school leadership and the faculty, or among faculty members. The principal was reassigned, took the same leader behavior to the reassigned school and achieved the same results with the faculty; serious negative interaction occurred between the principal and the faculty.

In a third instance, three or four faculty members were negatively impacted by the leadership style of the principal, so they reported. Our observations suggested something different. We observed a group of teachers who had a difference of opinion with the leadership of the school. Our opinion was supported by reports from a large number of faculty members.

Nevertheless, the interaction among the faculty as a whole was negatively impacted, as was student achievement. In this instance, as was the case in the second instance, the principal was reassigned and carried the same leadership style to the new assignment. In the new assignment, the transferred principal was well received; faculty interaction was positive, and student achievement is currently at or above the established standard of excellence.

From a quality standpoint, the style of leaderships exhibited by school leaders frequently affects the interaction among faculty members. Thus, the quality of leadership that exists in the schoolhouse may dictate, to a great extent, the quality of the relationship that exists between and among faculty members and subsequently their interaction with one another. In the final analysis, individuals in schools are dependent on each other, and the leadership style of school leaders must foster the type of interpersonal relationships among faculty members that enhance organizational goal attainment.

Obviously, there are multiple approaches to leading a school. Our suggestion is for school leaders to enhance their capacity to lead by developing a deep understanding of the complexities of school organizational life. To that end, it is important for school leaders to understand the culture and climate of the school, its structure, the strengths and weaknesses of stakeholders, and the relationships that influence the interaction between and among them.

Every school is unique and different. When school leaders understand the complexities of school organizational life, they can determine the adjustments they need to make in order to succeed. Consequently, the challenge for school leaders is to become knowledgeable of the school they lead and identify processes that can be used to move the school to the next level of excellence. Success in one school does not equate to success in another school. For these and other reasons, understanding the complexities of school organizational life becomes a meaningful element in school leadership.

■ ■ ■

Implications for Leadership

- Schools are multifaceted organizations. For school leaders to be effective, they must not only understand the complexities of schools, but they must be able to identify and implement processes to generate the desired results.
- Factors inside and outside of the schoolhouse contribute to the complexity of school organizational life, and school leaders must be able to identify and understand these factors.
- School culture, climate, structure, and the teaching and learning process are key factors of school organizational life. When these factors are understood and adequately addressed, the result is an organization built on trust—one with open communication and void of coercive behavior that alienates faculty, staff, and community stakeholders.

• Organizations have a mission and goals to achieve, and organizational participants have needs and desires that must be satisfied. When the leadership strikes a balance between the two, organizational effectiveness is likely to be the end-result.

Reflective Practice

1. What are some approaches that you would use to adequately assess life in a school organization?
2. What are some approaches that you would use to assess the external community of a school?
3. Describe the type of professional program that really focuses the attention of a faculty on student learning.
4. What strategies would you use to assess the climate of a school for the purpose of identifying and removing barriers to student learning?
5. What are some strategies that school leaders can implement to influence parents in a community to participate in developing new and innovative programs for their school?

Chapter Essentials

Interstate School Leader Licensure Consortium Standards 2, 3, and 4

An education leader promotes the success of every student by advocating, nurturing, and sustaining a school culture and instructional program conducive to student learning and staff professional growth.

An education leader promotes the success of every student by ensuring management of the organization, operation, and resources for a safe, efficient, and effective learning environment.

An education leader promotes the success of every student by collaborating with faculty and community members, responding to diverse community interests and needs, and mobilizing community resources.

Principle

Schools leaders do not have to have the answer, but it is imperative that they know the question.

Dichotomy

Organizational Complexities or Humanistic Complexities

School leaders must constantly seek a balance between complexities that are influenced by the culture and climate of the school organization and those influenced by individuals affiliated with the school organization.

References

Allen, J. (1990). *Mechanistic organization.* Retrieved October 21, 2004, from Web site: http://ollie.dcccd.edu/mgmt1374/p135

Chirichello, M. (2001). Collective leadership: Sharing the principalship. *Principal, 80*(1) 46, 48, 50–51.

DuFour, R., & Eaker, R. (1998). *Professional learning communities at work: Best practices for enhancing student achievement.* Bloomington, IN: National Educational Service.

Dunn, D., Rouse, L., & Self, M. (1994). New faculty socialization in the academic work place. *Higher Education: Handbook of Theory and Research, 10,* 374–413.

Gardner, J. W. (1990). *On leadership.* New York: Free Press.

Green, R. L. (2005). *Practicing the art of leadership: A problem-based approach to implementing the ISLLC Standards.* Upper Saddle River, NJ: Pearson Merrill Prentice Hall.

Halpin, A. W., & Croft, D. B. (1963). *The organizational climate of schools.* Chicago, IL: The University of Chicago Midwest Administration Center.

House, R. J. (1971). A path-goal theory of leader effectiveness. *Administrative Science Quarterly, 16,* 331–333.

Interstate School Leader Licensure Consortium (ISLLC). (1996). *Standards for school leaders.* Washington, D.C.: Council of Chief School Officers.

Levin, H. (1988). Accelerated schools for disadvantaged students. *Educational Leadership, 44*(6), 19–21.

Levine, D., & Lezotte, L. (1990). *Unusually effective schools.* Madison, WI: National Center for Effective Schools.

Liontos, L. B. (1994). *Shared decision making.* Eugene, OR: ERIC Clearinghouse on Educational Management.

Morgan, G. (1997). *Images of organization.* (2nd ed.) Thousand Oaks, CA: Sage Publications.

Owens, R. G. (2004). *Organizational Behavior in Education.* (8th ed.) Boston: Pearson Education, Inc.

Palestini, R. H. (2003). *The human touch in educational leadership: A postpositivist approach to understanding educational leadership.* Lanham, MD: Scarecrow Education.

Parkay, F. W., & Stanford, B. H. (2004). *Becoming a teacher.* Boston, MA: Pearson. Education, Inc.

Rebore, R. W. (2001). *The ethics of educational leadership.* Upper Saddle River, NJ: Merrill Prentice Hall.

Robbins, S. P. (1998). *Organizational behavior: Concepts, controversies, applications.* (8th ed.) Upper Saddle River, NJ: Prentice Hall.

Robbins, S. (2000). *Managing today.* (2nd ed.). Upper Saddle River, NJ: Pearson Prentice Hall.

Sashkin, M., Rosenbach, W. E., & Taylor, R. Eds. (1993). *A new leadership paradigm future: Contemporary issues in leadership.* Boulder, CO: Westview Press.

Schein, E. H. (1992). *Organizational culture and leadership.* (3rd ed.) San Francisco, CA: Jossey-Bass.

Scott, R. W. (2003). *Organizations: Rational, natural, and open systems.* Upper Saddle River, NJ: Prentice Hall.

Seyfarth, J. T. (1999). *The principal: New leadership for new challenges.* Upper Saddle River, NJ: Prentice Hall.

Shellard, E. (2003). Using assessment to promote reading instruction. *Principal, 83*(2), N/D, Retrieved August 7, 2006, from Web site: http://www.naesp.org

Slavin, R., Karweit, N., & Madden, N. (1989). *Effective programs for students at risk.* Boston, MA: Allyn & Bacon.

Slavin, R. E. (2003). *Educational psychology.* (7th ed.) Boston, MA: Allyn & Bacon.

Yukl, G. (2002). *Leadership in organizations* (5th ed.) Upper Saddle River, NJ: Prentice Hall.

CHAPTER

5

Perspectives on School Structure: Chaos or Efficiency

(Standards 1, 3, 5, and 6)

"If organizational activities and/or events are important, have value, and are expected to exist, then, they should be facilitated by the structure of the organization."

"In order to be effective and productive, leaders need to know and understand the organizational structure within which they maneuver. The people who work within the organization, the structure of the organization, and the leader's personal beliefs all influence the leader's style. Leaders need to be adaptable and flexible in their structure."

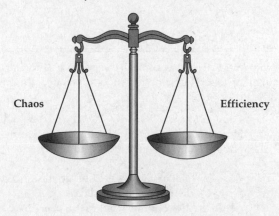

Chaos   Efficiency

INTRODUCTION

In Chapter 4, we discussed a set of elements that allowed readers to understand that schools are multifaceted, complex organizations. Here, we demonstrate how school leaders can minimize that complexity through school organizational structure.

Schools are complex in that they are both technical and social in nature. The technical aspect is embedded in the traditional mechanistic, bureaucratic structure of schools, whereas the social aspect stems from the need for school personnel to engage in human interaction. Effective 21st-century school leaders must be skilled in achieving a balance between these areas. They must embrace the traditional mechanistic, bureaucratic structure while facilitating human interaction in a positive manner. The challenge of achieving the needed balance can be visualized by examining the following fundamental questions: (1) What is organizational structure? (2) Why is structure necessary? (3) What are the elements of structure? (4) What are the different types of structure? and (5) How can school leaders develop the type of structure that is advocated for 21st-century schools?

The major thesis of the chapter is that when a school leader integrates the critical elements of a humanistic, organic structure into elements of a mechanistic, bureaucratic structure and finds a balance between the conflicting forces, chaos is minimized, and efficiency is maximized. In such a structure, individuals can fully utilize their expertise to satisfy organizational, as well as personal goals.

ORGANIZATIONAL STRUCTURE DEFINED

People in school organizations cannot be allowed to function at will; consequently, there must be a predetermined means of directing behavior, making decisions, communicating, and coordinating roles and functions. Organizational structure performs those functions.

Standard 3

An education leader promotes the success of every student by ensuring management of the organization, operation, and resources for a safe, efficient, and effective learning environment.

Functions
  a. Monitor and evaluate the management and operational systems
  b. Obtain, allocate, align, and efficiently utilize human, fiscal, and technological resources
  c. Promote and protect the welfare and safety of students and staff
  d. Develop the capacity for distributed leadership
  e. Ensure teacher and organizational time is focused to support quality instruction and student learning

Through structure, the purpose of the organization is identified, and formal rules and regulations are put in place to govern the behavior of individuals and to foster the achievement of stated and sometimes unstated goals (Morgan, 1997; Robbins, 1998; Scott, 2003). It is the foundation of all organizational activities in that it provides direction and coordinates behavior in a manner that eliminates chaos and enhances efficiency (Scott, 2003). Structure consists of several elements of which the most noted ones are formalization, specialization, coordination, chain of command, power and authority, and centralization (Morgan, 1997; Robbins, 1998; Scott, 2003). To some extent, these elements are found in most organizations. Graphic delineation of some theories, theorists, and the implications they hold for organizational structure appears in Table 5.1.

TABLE 5.1 Theories, Theorists, Definitions, and Implications for Leadership

Theories	Theorist(s)	Definitions	Implications for Leadership
Contingency Theory	Fred Fiedler	Effectiveness of task completion is contingent on three factors: the relationship that exists between the leader and follower; a clear definition of the task to be completed, and the influence of the leader over followers.	Effective school leaders develop a deep understanding of the situation, build positive relationships with the faculty, and exhibit behavior based on those two factors.
Two Factor Motivational-Hygiene Theory	Frederick Herzberg	There are two-types of factors in the work place: hygiene and motivation. Hygiene factors can cause or prevent worker satisfaction, and motivational factors can foster worker satisfaction.	School leaders must develop an understanding of the faculty and structure the school in a manner that enhances faculty satisfaction.
Open Social Systems Theory	Katz and Kahn	The organization consists of individuals who perform a set of activities by interacting with one another in the internal environment of the organization, using resources from the external environment.	Effective school leaders are concerned with the interaction that occurs between and among members of the faculty. They structure the school in a manner that fosters the type of relationships between faculty members

(continued)

TABLE 5.1 Theories, Theorists, Definitions, and Implications for Leadership (*continued*)

Theories	Theorist(s)	Definitions	Implications for Leadership
		Through the social interaction between and among individuals in the internal environment, a product is produced and returned to the external environment.	that motivates them to work cooperatively to address the needs of students. Additionally, the school is structured in a manner that enables the faculty and staff to respond to a variety of external environmental factors.
Transformational Leadership	Bernard Bass	Leaders influence followers to become aware of the importance of task completion. As a result, followers place task completion above self-interest and are highly motivated and committed to the completion of the task. During the course of events, leaders assist followers in reaching a level of self-actualization.	Leaders must begin with a clearly articulated vision. Then, they motivate the faculty to place the attainment of the vision above personal interests. Through this process, faculty members are led to understand that their personal goals and objectives will be met.
Classical Organizational Theory	Frederick W. Taylor, Henri Fayol, Luther Gulic, and Max Weber	The focus of work in the organization is based on principles of scientific management and administrative management. In regard to scientific management, the focus is on the worker and the one-best way of performing a task. In regard to administrative management, the focus is the organization, rules, policies, procedures, and an organizational structure to use in governing task completion.	Effective school leaders identify programs that meet the needs of students, hire faculty to implement them, and structure the organization in a manner that fosters student achievement.

(*continued*)

Theories	Theorist(s)	Definitions	Implications for Leadership
Path-Goal Theory	R.J. House	The behavior of the leader has an effect on the performance and satisfaction levels of followers. The motivational function of the leader is to clarify the routes followers must travel to reach goal-attainment and remove any roadblocks or pitfalls that may exist. The type of behavior the leader exhibits should depend on the situation. A leader's function is to clear the path toward the group's goal by meeting the needs of subordinates.	School leaders must clarify goals to be achieved by the faculty and staff and remove roadblocks and pitfalls to goal attainment.

Source: The content of the table was developed from information on theories in *Practicing the Art of Leadership: A Problem-Based Approach to Implementing the ISLLC Standards* (3rd ed.).

THE DIFFERENT TYPES OF STRUCTURE

In structuring today's schools, two general perspectives warrant consideration, the mechanistic, bureaucratic model and an open social system perspective that informs an organic, humanistic model. In the bureaucratic model, operational procedures are based on principles of scientific management, and efficiency and effectiveness are achieved utilizing formalized rules and regulations in a centralized hierarchy. Conversely, in an open social system, where the organic, humanistic model is in existence, operational procedures are based on democratic principles; efficiency and effectiveness are achieved largely through relationships developed between and among individuals who are functioning in the organization. To effectively lead 21st-century schools, school leaders must balance the essential elements of the two models.

Elements of the two models have the potential of clustering at extreme ends of the structural continuum, hindering or enabling organizational effectiveness (see Exhibit 5.1). To emphasize this point, we first discuss

EXHIBIT 5.1 The Structural Continuum

Mechanistic, Bureaucratic Model ◀━━━━━━━▶ Organic, Humanistic Model

characteristics of the mechanistic, bureaucratic model, and then proceed to a discussion of the elements of the organic, humanistic model.

The Mechanistic, Bureaucratic Model

Clustering at one end of the continuum are elements of the bureaucratic model. The bureaucratic model is grounded in classical theory and principles of scientific management—the one best way of completing a task. It is the creation of Max Weber, a German sociologist who was famous for his study of organizations (Weber, 1947). The model is highly formalized, consisting of rules and regulations that group work assignments according to functions.

Weber (1947) advanced the concept, offering that an organization could be effective and efficient by dividing work into subunits and employing people with the expertise necessary to function in those subunits. The structure of the bureaucratic model consists of several elements of which the most noted ones are formalization, specialization, coordination, chain of command, power and authority, and centralization (Morgan, 1997; Robbins, 1998; Scott, 2003). See Exhibit 5.2. This structure, though somewhat modified, is used today by most school leaders.

It is not uncommon to find school leaders who identify an instructional process, present that process to their faculty, require them to implement it, and establish controls to ensure that directions are followed. For those reasons, a description of each of the aforementioned elements is provided in the following section.

FORMALIZATION   Formalization refers to rules, regulations, and procedures that govern the behavior of individuals functioning in organizations. School officials at the top echelon of the hierarchy of the organization usually enact and enforce these rules, regulations, and procedures in an attempt to achieve standardization. The types and effects of formalization vary from punitive to representative or from high to low. Scott (2003) offers that through a punitive, formalized structure, rules that govern behavior are formulated and stated in a precise and explicit manner, independent of individuals serving in organizational positions. When this occurs, formalization is high; individuals in authority are very directive and unilaterally establish rules and regulations to control and punish individuals who fail to follow them. For example, a

EXHIBIT 5.2   Elements of the Mechanistic, Bureaucratic Model

Formalization
Specialization of Assignments
Departmentalization
Chain of Command
Centralization

school leader who establishes a set of rules and regulations from the confines of his office and distributes them in a faculty meeting, expecting that they will be followed unquestioned, is using a highly formalized structure. In such instances, the end results can be a hostile school climate—one that plagues the organization with chaos, negatively affecting the work performance of the faculty (Rousseau, 1978).

Conversely, formalization can be representative; individuals in authority and individuals serving in organizational positions jointly make formal rules and regulations (Gouldner, 1954; Robbins, 1998). For example, a problem exists in the area of school dismissal. The principal discusses the problem situation with the faculty, and collaboratively they establish rules and regulations to resolve the problem. Then, the faculty implements the rules and regulations using professional judgment. In this instance, formalization is considered low, as faculty members participated in the development of the rules and regulations and exercised flexibility in their implementation. Usually, when low formalization exists, rules and regulations serve the purpose of guiding work behavior and preventing challenging situations, resulting in improved problem solving and enhanced professionalism.

SPECIALIZATION OF ASSIGNMENTS　Another element of structure relative to schools is organizing individual faculty members into work groups by areas of specialization. This is a critical element and, in most instances, state law mandates it. Through their university preparation programs, individuals obtain certification in specialized areas, which qualifies them to teach select subjects or to work in specific areas. Rather than acquiring training to teach all subjects, they specialize and become highly qualified to teach a specific subject or subjects. It is a widely held belief that individuals who have been trained in specialized instructional areas teach in those areas with greater effectiveness (Sergiovanni, 2001). They are expected to get the same results from students, notwithstanding their readiness level to teach or the background knowledge of students. For example, an individual might have a license to teach English, History, or Mathematics. If a school vacancy occurs in one of those specific areas, it is expected that the school leader will enhance instruction by seeking to employ an individual certified in that area. If the appropriate individual is not employed, the instructional program can be negatively impacted.

DEPARTMENTALIZATION AND COORDINATION　To coordinate and enhance the delivery of instruction, many schools are structured into departments. Departmentalization is an element of school structure that groups teachers by subjects—organizing the faculty members into departments in a manner that will enable them to deliver a particular subject area of the curriculum to students. For this arrangement to work effectively, extensive planning and coordination are required by the school leadership, and a cooperative working relationship must exist between and among the faculty, staff, and other stakeholders. When positive working relationships do not exist, the coordination of work assignments for task completion can be inhibited. For example, several high school teachers are grouped for the purpose of teaching English. One of the teachers may be assigned as Department Chair with the responsibility of facilitating instructional decisions using student data. The effectiveness of task completion will depend, to a large extent, on the leadership style of the Department Chair, the delineation of work assignments, and the establishment of a standard of excellence. Without effective coordination between the Department Chair and members of the department, creativity can be stifled; fragmentation will probably occur, and individuals are likely to work at cross-purposes.

When positive relationships exist among departmental members, departmentalization can be an effective process to use in maximizing opportunities for successful student learning. Members of the department work collaboratively to design, manage, and monitor instruction on a regular basis, using effective problem framing and problem solving skills to make instructional modifications as needed.

CHAIN OF COMMAND, POWER, AND AUTHORITY A fourth element of the bureaucratic school structure is the existence of a chain of command and the power and authority of individuals within that chain. As was discussed in the section on formalization, school organizations can be structured in a hierarchical manner with authority extending from individuals who serve in the highest positions of the organization to individuals who serve at the lowest echelon (see Exhibit 5.3). Through the chain of command, there is clarification of who is responsible and accountable for work assignments.

EXHIBIT 5.3 School Organizational Chart

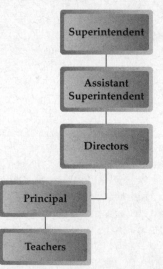

Individuals at one level in the organization have the authority to make decisions and work assignments for individuals at the next descending level in the organization. For example, directions and work assignments are given to assistant superintendents by superintendents; assistant superintendents give directions and work assignments to directors who in turn give directions and work assignments to principals who supervise teachers.

School leaders, at each of these levels, have power and authority inherent in their position, and it is expected that one would comply with a directive issued by individuals at the next highest level (Green, 2005).

There are advantages and disadvantages to following a strict chain of command and investing power and authority in a limited number of people at the top of the organization. However, in today's schools, where a professional learning community is advocated, little emphasis should be placed on the chain of command (Senge, 1990; Sergiovanni, 1994; Sparks, 1999). Whereas a degree of supervision and direction is needed to ensure accountability and goal attainment, there are instances when individuals in the chain of command will use their position to direct and control the behavior of others. Such actions are viewed by many as authoritarian, stifling creativity, hindering participatory decision making and reducing professionalism (Barth, 1990; Fullan, 1999; Lashway, 1999; Senge, 1990). This point will be explored in greater detail in a later section of this chapter.

CENTRALIZATION   A fifth element of the bureaucratic school structure is centralization. Centralization refers to the extent to which faculty members participate in decisions at the building level and the extent to which principals and teachers participate in decisions made at the central office level of the school district. In a highly centralized organization, decision making is concentrated at the top of the organization; communication flows downward, and power and authority are perceived to be concentrated at the top of the organization. Centralization is an elitist process as individuals who hold top-level positions issue directives, and many other individuals who have knowledge and expertise that could contribute to decision quality are left out of the process. It does not foster professionalism, as some top-level school leaders use their positions to control and discipline individuals at lower levels in the organization.

THE EFFECTS OF THE BUREAUCRATIC STRUCTURE ON SCHOOL LIFE   As well intended as the bureaucratic structure may be, it has some features that negatively impact the operation of today's schools. When schools are operated using the strict bureaucratic model, the height of the organization is extended, consisting of many levels of management. People are driven by directives and a controlled approach; thus, they have a tendency to become complacent and focus on simply following rules and regulations. Authority and control replace professionalism and, as a result, the job becomes less challenging, and individuals become relatively content to be confined to their area of specialization (Allen, 1990). Another difficulty with this model is that individuals become predisposed to achieving predetermined goals and are not challenged nor motivated to foster innovations (Allen, 1990).

The bureaucratic structure also challenges lines of communication. Whereas the model advocates two-way communication, achieving effective responses to inquiries is sometimes inhibited by fear of reprisal from top-level supervisors and/or the high degree of specialization in different functional areas. Consequently, school leaders or colleagues do not always benefit from the thinking of individuals who work closest to challenging situations. In addition, communication and coordination between departments become problematic, and people develop a myopic view of what is occurring because they are not provided a comprehensive picture of the challenges facing the organization (Morgan, 1997).

Although some school leaders are effective in obtaining school goals using a bureaucratic structure, there is little flexibility in the implementation of rules and regulations; the involvement of followers is minimized, and creativity is stifled, as leaders assume total responsibility for moving the organization forward. Therefore, many educators and scholars have become advocates for replacing this type of structure with one that offers fewer controls and less rigidity (Abbott & Caracheo, 1988; Barth, 1990; Liontos, 1992; Senge, 1990; Seyfarth, 1999). In the following section, we address a model that falls at the other end of the continuum, one that is closely aligned with the structure advocated for today's schools.

The Organic, Humanistic Model

Clustering at the other end of the continuum are elements of the organic, humanistic model. This model is grounded in Human Relations Theory and principles of Social System Theory. With the onset of the Human Relations movement, a change occurred in the scientific and administrative management elements of Classical Theory. The traditional one best way of doing things in a highly structured, formalized manner gave way to suggestions that productivity was based more on group dynamics and efficient leadership than rigid demands and controls of management (Mayo, 1939). Due to the findings from the "Hawthorne Studies," the leadership focus shifted from production to producer, as the study established the importance of leaders developing an understanding of human behavior in the work place. Specifically, the focus shifted to the activities of individuals and groups and the interdependent nature of their working relationships.

In school settings where the organic, humanistic structure is in place, a comprehensive information network has replaced formalization. This network fosters open communication, participatory decision making and effective relationships between and among members who function in cross-hierarchical and cross-functional teams. Of primary importance is the fact that effective school leaders ensure that consideration is given to the human element at all times.

EXHIBIT 5.4   Elements of the Organic, Humanistic Model

> Open Communication
> Participatory Decision Making
> Collaborative Teaming
> Interpersonal Relationships
> Consideration for the Human Element

Elements of the organic, humanistic model are listed in Exhibit 5.4. These elements have a profound effect on leadership for 21st-century schools and, for that reason, they are defined under the inclusive structure and discussed throughout the text.

THE EFFECTS OF THE ORGANIC, HUMANISTIC MODEL ON SCHOOL LIFE   The organic, humanistic model is based on principles of social system theory and when a structure is based on principles of social system theory, the leader assesses the skills and interests of followers; they are afforded opportunities to define their work assignments while interacting with other individuals with whom they work. Leadership roles are constantly changing as the leadership for task completion is defined and redefined with the occurrence of changes in organizational challenges and circumstances. Supervisory controls and positions of authority are replaced by employee commitment to the completion of organizational tasks.

Because of the dedication and commitment of individuals to the organization, technological advances soar, and suggestions for improvements in the teaching and learning processes are limitless. Changes in the organization occur as a result of individuals conducting inquiries into new instructional programs and innovative ways of addressing student needs (King, 2002; Huffman, 2003).

Having reviewed two models and the effects of their elements on the structure of schools, we now turn to a discussion of an appropriate structure for 21st-century schools, seeking a balance between enabling elements of each of the models.

STRUCTURAL CONFIGURATIONS FOR THE 21ST-CENTURY SCHOOLHOUSE

The challenges faced by 21st-century school leaders call for a structure that is significantly different from the bureaucratic structure previously described. Schools are unique; thus, the "cookie cutter" design presupposed by the bureaucratic model is not appropriate. School leaders of today are challenged to design the type of structure that will align with the needs of that school; then, they must operationalize that structure in a manner that fosters effective communication among all stakeholders, allowing them to be involved in making decisions that affect the school.

Standard 3

An education leader promotes the success of every student by ensuring management of the organization, operation, and resources for a safe, efficient, and effective learning environment.

Functions
a. Monitor and evaluate the management and operational systems
b. Obtain, allocate, align, and efficiently utilize human, fiscal, and technological resources
c. Promote and protect the welfare and safety of students and staff
d. Develop the capacity for distributed leadership
e. Ensure teacher and organizational time is focused to support quality instruction and student learning

In today's schools, structure, in and of itself, is not the problem; rather, it is the type of structure and the manner in which the structure is operationalized that create chaos and reduce efficiency in schools. To be effective in 21st-century schools, the structure has to facilitate an interactive planning process where school leaders and members of the faculty collaboratively confront and resolve problems in a timely manner, creating a circularity of responsibility and accountability measures that ensures enhanced student achievement (Hoy & Sweetland, 2001; Huffman, 2003; ISLLC Standard 3, 1996). They have to implement a structure wherein they can facilitate the development, implementation, and stewardship of a shared vision and nurture and sustain a school culture and instructional program conducive to student learning and staff professional growth (ISLLC Standards, 2008).

Standard 1

An education leader promotes the success of every student by facilitating the development, articulation, implementation, and stewardship of a vision of learning that is shared and supported by all stakeholders.

Functions
a. Collaboratively develop and implement a shared vision and mission
b. Collect and use data to identify goals, assess organizational effectiveness, and promote organizational learning
c. Create and implement plans to achieve goals
d. Promote continuous and sustainable improvement
e. Monitor and evaluate progress and revise plans

School leaders are also being asked to manage the organization, ensuring a safe and effective learning environment, while collaborating with and responding to the diverse needs of all stakeholders (ISLLC Standards, 2008).

In doing so, they are expected to exhibit behavior that is fair and ethical and develop an understanding of the influences that affect the teaching and learning process in the internal and external environments of the schoolhouse (ISLLC Standards, 2008).

Standard 5

An education leader promotes the success of every student by acting with integrity, fairness, and in an ethical manner.

Functions
  a. Ensure a system of accountability for every student's academic and social success
  b. Model principles of self-awareness, reflective practice, transparency, and ethical behavior
  c. Safeguard the values of democracy, equity, and diversity
  d. Consider and evaluate the potential moral and legal consequences of decision making
  e. Promote social justice and ensure that individual student needs inform all aspects of schools

Basically, today's school leaders are being asked to create a new structure that will enable them to lead an open social system structured in a traditional bureaucratic manner. Both the aforementioned models can contribute elements to that structure. See Table 5.2.

To develop and implement such a structure, school leaders must acquire an in-depth understanding of the two models previously presented with the intent of combining the critical elements of each. The elements identified must be able to coexist in a manner that fosters organizational effectiveness.

TABLE 5.2   A Comparative View of Elements of the Bureaucratic and Humanistic Model

Elements of the Mechanistic, Bureaucratic Model Autocratic Leadership	Elements of the Organic, Humanistic Model-Democratic Leadership
Formalization	Open Communications, Collaborative Teaming
Specialization of Assignments	Participatory Decision Making
Departmentalization	Interpersonal Relationships
Centralization	Consideration for the Human Element
Chain of Command	

In addition, school leaders must be able to combine their instructional skills with their managerial skills and become excellent managers and outstanding instructional leaders. Moreover, to provide this dual leadership function, school leaders will necessarily have to trust people and their judgment, collaborate, and involve stakeholders in management processes; they must also communicate effectively, share decision making, and respect diversity (ISLLC Standards, 2008).

There is sufficient evidence from research studies and reports to support a theoretical framework for a structure that will address this complex challenge (Calhoun, 1996; Cushman, 1999; Joyce & DuFour, 1999; Lashway, 1995; Sinden, Hoy, & Sweetland, 2004). Using the findings from these studies and reports, at the University of Memphis, we have characterized a structure that encompasses the elements of both models and offer it for use by leaders of today's schools.

The Inclusive School Structure

The inclusive school structure is circular, and participatory leadership exists in every facet of the school organization. The elements of the structure are a combination of enabling elements of both the mechanistic, bureaucratic model and the organic, humanistic model and can be viewed from two perspectives: the inclusive behavior of individuals and benefits derived by the organization.

The inclusive behavior of individuals is governed by a standard of excellence, and they are afforded the opportunity to exercise flexibility in the implementation of rules and regulations. They participate in the establishment of goals and priorities and collaborate in teams to achieve them while effectively utilizing the resources of the school and community. There is a connection between the school leader, faculty, staff, students, and community, and a professional development plan is in place to assist all individuals in reaching their full potential.

The benefit derived by the organization is a teaching faculty who exhibits a greater commitment to the organization, and functions with unity of purpose, conducts inquiry into instructional processes to use in their classes, and works in collaborative teams for enhanced goal attainment. In essence, the model suggests that the structure of the school should foster the existence of any educationally sound activities and/or events that have value and are expected to enhance teaching and learning. Mrs. Angela, Brown, Principal of Douglass Elementary School in Memphis, Tennessee, used this model to transform Douglass into a professional learning community that is addressing the needs of all students the school serves. After assuming the role as lead learner (the fifth principal in seven years), she quickly developed an understanding of the complexity of organizational life at Douglas. She then involved individuals in the internal and external environment of the school in developing a vision that all stakeholders shared and built bridges to the attainment of that vision through relationships. Visiting Douglass, one would observe teachers utilizing best practices, parent and community involvement, and students meeting established local, state, and national academic standards.

In the remaining section of the chapter, we will provide other examples that illustrate how an inclusive school organizational structure can be beneficial to leaders of 21st-century schools, reducing chaos and enhancing efficiency. However, before proceeding to that section, we invite readers to read the scenario entitled "Superintendent Chooses First Year Principal to Lead Fresh Start School." Then, as the remainder of the chapter is read, we invite the readers to place themselves in the role of Principal Collins and reflect on how they would utilize elements of an inclusive structure to lead New Meadows Middle School.

Scenario: Superintendent Chooses First Year Principal to Lead Fresh Start School

State Department Announcement

The State Department of Education (SDE) announced today that New Meadows City School System (NMCS) dramatically increased the number of schools that met all state standards for student achievement under the No Child Left Behind (NCLB) federal law. Seventy-seven schools, of the one hundred forty-eight (148) schools identified last year as not meeting NCLB standards, have been cleared off the list.

Speaking to the success of the schools, NMCS Superintendent Walter Jones said, "We are certainly pleased that many of our schools have achieved or exceeded state standards. First, we must recognize the dedicated principals, teachers, and staff who achieved these positive results. Over the next several days, we will analyze these results and identify specific strategies that have proven successful so that we can share them across the system. Already, we have increased our focus on literacy and offered more professional development in mathematics and science. All of our schools are emphasizing ninety-five (95) percent attendance, and many have employed family specialists to better connect with parents."

Dr. Jones added, "We will not be satisfied until all of our schools and students are achieving high standards. To that end, we are Fresh Starting five schools; the first is New Meadows Middle School, and Mr. Stephen Collins has been named principal. We will continue to implement our action steps and also review the progress and data for each site so we know where to focus interventions. As you are aware, we must work with the State Department of Education to determine which additional steps might be required."

New Meadows Middle School

New Meadows Middle School has an enrollment of twelve-hundred (1200) students of whom sixty (60) percent are African American, twenty-five (25) percent Hispanic, ten (10) percent Caucasian, and five (5) percent Asian. The family unit, comprising the school's attendance zone, consists of mostly single-parent homes with low-socioeconomic backgrounds. Student suspensions were high; attendance rates were low, and many parents spoke of changing their children to a different school. Whereas, the school had a number of challenges and did not meet the NCLB standards, some strategies put in place by the previous administration and faculty appear to be working. Therefore, the news of becoming a Fresh Start School was received with mixed emotions in the community, as many students and parents liked some of the changes that were occurring and often described the actions of the assistant principal as being educationally sound and effective.

The Appointment of Steven Collins

On June 6, Steven Collins completed an intense non-traditional principal preparation program that exposed him to every aspect of the principalship, specifically for urban school settings. Steven felt very confident that if he received a principalship for the upcoming school year, he would be ready. On the 8th of July, he received a phone call from the superintendent's office to come in for an interview. The interview went really well, and he was confident about being offered a principalship. However, he was very much surprised on the 20th of July when he received a call to invite him to become principal of New Meadows Middle School, one of the district's five Fresh Start Schools. After some deliberation, he accepted the appointment.

Challenges Facing Principal Collins

On July 25th, Principal Collins attended a special meeting to orient the five principals assigned to Fresh Start Schools. He welcomed the meeting, as he did not have many details about the Fresh Start Program. He had participated in discussions regarding the program; however, he had no indication that a first year principal would be assigned to one of the schools.

During the meeting, the principals of Fresh Start Schools were told that everyone in the schools had been relieved of their positions, and it was their responsibility to staff the schools. As a part of the re-staffing process, they were given the flexibility to select any of the previous faculty and staff. This became a real dilemma for Mr. Collins as the previous assistant principal (James Rivers) had participated in the exciting, innovative preparation program with him. The group of twenty-one (21) participants had bonded, established collaborative working relationships, and informally agreed to support the upward mobility of each other. Mr. Collins was also faced with a program restriction. Due to the high suspension and low attendance rates at New Meadows, he was told he had to continue action steps provided by the Board of Education and the State Department of Education. Finally, he was advised that data should be reviewed, and the progress of the school should be frequently assessed, focusing on implementing interventions that would enhance the academic achievement of all students at New Meadows Middle School.

Community Reactions

As Principal Collins started to ponder the major challenges facing him, he received a flood of phone calls from parents who had heard of his outstanding leadership abilities and his energetic approaches to various challenges in his previously assigned schools. The parents asked for assurance that their children would have a place in the new program. Of course, Mr. Collins was flattered by the compliments; however, the excitement from the flattery did not last. He was feeling stressed due to the rigorous tasks of staffing the school, selecting an assistant principal, projecting the new student enrollment, attending community meetings to explain the new program concept, addressing individuals (often hostile) who resisted the change, and responding to the high expectations being placed on him by the superintendent, parents, students, and others.

As the days passed and challenges surfaced, decisions had to be made, and Principal Collins had to make them.

REFLECTIVE QUESTIONS

1. Would you use collaborative teaming at New Meadows Middle School? If so, how would you structure the teams? If not, what alternative structure would you employ to ensure collaboration among the faculty and staff?
2. What are some of the expectations that you would establish for the faculty and staff of New Meadows Middle School, and how would you communicate those expectations?
3. How would you address formalization at New Meadows Middle School?
4. Describe some structural elements that would foster an ongoing focused professional development program that meets the needs of all faculty and staff members.
5. What are some structural elements that would ensure that all stakeholders are treated with dignity and respect?
6. What structural procedures would you put in place to ensure that the principal, faculty, and staff at New Meadows Middle School know the students who attend the school?

Elements of the Inclusive Organizational Structure

Today's schools are serving a new and different population, and the current reform movement is calling for a structure that addresses principles of human relations theory. Therefore, the structure needed for 21st-century schools is one that contains enabling elements of the bureaucratic model implemented in a manner that addresses principles of human relations theory operating in an open social system. The essential elements of that structure are: (1) collaborative teaming that reduces the hierarchy of the bureaucratic model; (2) an inclusive organizational standard of excellence that informs efficiency and effectiveness; (3) flexibility in the implementation of policies, rules, and regulations that eliminates high formalization; (4) decentralization that provides a comprehensive information network, and (5) distributive leadership that fosters democratic principles throughout the organization. The structure is graphically depicted in Exhibit 5.5.

COLLABORATIVE TEAMING Given the interdependent nature of the teaching and learning process, the organizational structure of schools has to foster collaborative teaming. Power and control can no longer be vested in a few individuals at the top of the bureaucratic hierarchy. Rather, there has to be a renewed understanding of the role of school leaders, as the viewpoint that no one individual can control all aspects of the school is accepted. Instead, schools leaders must put a structure in place that facilitates the establishment of a collaborative

EXHIBIT 5.5 Elements of the Inclusive Organizational Structure

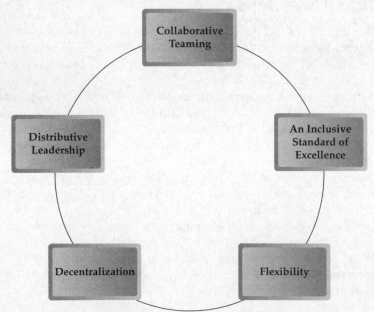

team, one in which power is shared among all stakeholders. In such a structure, there is the realization that all individuals have skills and attributes, and those skills and attributes can be critical to school goal attainment. Accordingly, all individuals assume responsibility for leading tasks. In addition, all individuals are empowered to do so, thereby creating a circularity of responsibility and accountability. For example, just as school leaders are the experts in school administration, teachers are experts in instruction and should contribute to decisions that fall in their area of expertise. Consequently, in an inclusive structure, teachers become members of a collaborative leadership team and participate in reaching decisions involving teaching and learning, as well as other school matters. The focus for school leaders has to be on giving people energy, and people are given energy by acts of inclusion and kindness; they feel a sense of belonging. The school leader, faculty, and staff have to be fully engaged to understand and facilitate the process that is necessary for school goal attainment.

In 21st-century schools where a collaborative culture is advocated, lines of authority, the bureaucratic chain of command, and the span of control are minimized (Robbins, 1998). Everyone shares a common goal which is promoting the academic achievement of students. In such a culture, an inclusive structure can eliminate the vertical communication lines of a hierarchical structure that creates barriers between departments.

When members of a school faculty work in separate traditional departments, there is disconnect, as the traditional hierarchical structure does not provide a means of connecting one department with another. Working separately, departmental faculty may effectively attain departmental goals; however, working in cross-functional teams, information can be exchanged, new ideas developed, and complex problems can be solved, facilitating the attainment of school-wide goals. It is not the independent work of departments that fosters the academic achievement of all students, but, rather, the collective efforts of the faculty working collaboratively to achieve a shared vision (Lashway, 1997). When individuals work in teams, flexibility, cooperation, and collaboration replace rigid, autocratic, and controlling behavior. Individuals work across recognized authority boundaries while maintaining their distinctive roles. Expertise is valued more than position; teachers feel confident, and they are able to exercise professional judgment.

Collaboration and cross-functional teaming are practices widely advocated in most educational leadership literature. However, it cannot be assumed that everyone is knowledgeable of how to collaborate. For collaboration to be practiced effectively, the process of collaborating has to be learned, and a particular type of structure is required. There must be time for team meetings; the right people have to be placed on the right teams and assigned to perform specific tasks.

Teachers selected to serve on committees should have the desire to serve, knowledge sufficient to contribute to the quality of the outcome sought, and ability necessary to effectively engage in collaborative dialogue. If they do not have this depth of knowledge, the leadership facilitates a process that allows them to conduct inquiry into the subject sufficient to acquire knowledge necessary to effectively participate in reaching the outcome sought.

According to John Maxwell (2006), author of *The 360° Leader*, ninety-nine (99) percent of all leadership occurs, not from the top, but from the middle of an organization. Such is the case with leadership in an inclusive structure. The voice of all faculty members is valued, a team concept established, and the expertise of all individuals is utilized. There is a school leader; however, the leadership that is exhibited using the strengths and talents of others enhances that leader's capabilities and strengths. There are no big I's or little You's. Rather, all individuals are respected and invited to participate in the decision-making process. The benefit to the organization is the establishment of a community of learners, consisting of a team of individuals who are empowered to use their expertise to create and implement programs and activities that move the organization toward goal attainment.

A STANDARD OF EXCELLENCE The bureaucratic model was put into place partly to ensure efficiency and effectiveness from individuals as they pursued organizational goal attainment. However, it is no longer an acceptable management framework. In 21st-century schools, efficiency and effectiveness can be achieved through the establishment of a standard of excellence—a predetermined goal set by stakeholders as a criterion of effectiveness. With the establishment of a standard of excellence, expectations are clarified for individuals working in the organization, as well as those receiving services from the organization.

The school leader's role is critical in establishing a standard of excellence. Through organizational structure, he/she facilitates the staff's understanding of the need to establish a clear sense of purpose, a shared vision, goals, and criterion against which the outcome of activities are measured. For example, working with the faculty, the school leader may determine that excellence in student attendance is reached when ninety-six (96) percent of all students attend school daily. When all faculty members understand and commit to this standard, focus can be given to the work of the organization in the area of student attendance. However, if faculty members are not aware of the standard of excellence, or do not understand that the standard is an established expectation, they could become frustrated when participating in activities designed to increase attendance.

As the standard of excellence is pursued, there is value to be derived from acknowledging progress made by individuals or the faculty en route to the standard. The measure of excellence should not be based solely on what has been accomplished once the standard is reached, but also on what has been accomplished en route to the established standard. An example of this would be if the standard of excellence for attendance is ninety-five (95) percent, and the effort of the faculty has increased attendance from seventy-nine (79) percent to eighty-nine (89) percent. Even though the standard of excellence has not been achieved, progress toward the standard could be motivational if recognized, acknowledged, and celebrated. Clearly, efficiency and effectiveness can be achieved with the establishment of a standard of excellence. Over time, strategies for goal attainment may change, but the standard by which organizational effectiveness is measured should only change after the previous standard has been met.

FLEXIBILITY IN THE IMPLEMENTATION OF POLICIES, RULES, AND REGULATIONS

Formal policies, rules, and regulations are necessary to govern the behavior of individuals functioning in the organization. Some rules and regulations are created internally, and many are formulated by the central administration of the school district, the state department of education, the federal government, and agencies that establish program requirements and set accreditation standards.

Regardless of where policies, rules, and regulations are formulated, they affect the teaching and learning process. Therefore, individuals charged with the responsibility of implementing them should be included in their development and afforded flexibility in their implementation. When members of a faculty are included in policy development and afforded flexibility in the implementation of those policies, they can exercise professional judgment and effectively utilize their expertise. Such involvement creates a feeling of empowerment, fosters open communication, and facilitates problem solving (Weick & Sutcliffe, 2001). Thus, a critical element in structuring schools is the provision of opportunities for stakeholders to cooperatively participate in formulating policies, rules and regulations, and to be afforded the appropriate amount of flexibility in their implementation.

A caution for note by school leaders is the need to balance high formalization of the Mechanistic, Bureaucratic Model with low formalization/flexibility of the Organic, Humanistic Model as policies, rules, and regulations can be restrictive, or they can be facilitative. If they are too restrictive, the leader is perceived as being coercive and exhibiting autocratic behavior. In such instances, the end result is a lack of trust, and the presence of fear which is likely to minimize the participation of faculty, parents, and community stakeholders in establishing goals. It could also deter them from making a commitment to the attainment of those goals (Adler & Borys, 1996; Gouldner, 1954). Conversely, if policies, rules, and regulations are understated or too much flexibility is allowed in their implementation, followers tend to perceive the leader as exhibiting laissez-faire behavior and failing to give directions. This type of perception fosters uncertainty among faculty members and creates a lack of continuity and consistency in their behavior (Adler & Borys, 1996; Gouldner, 1954). Therefore, the structure has to provide a balance between rules being too strict or too permissive.

Striking a balance between high formalization—strict adherence to rules and regulations, and low formalization—allowing individuals flexibility to utilize their skills and attributes in the implementation of rules and regulations is what a leader should seek in structuring the school (Sinden, Hoy, & Sweetland, 2004). When this balance is reached, a climate of professionalism is created wherein people exercise professional judgment; collaboration is enhanced, and individuals are motivated to conduct inquiry into best practices (Weick & Sutcliffe, 2001).

DECENTRALIZATION   A fourth element of the inclusive structure is decentralization. Schools are unique with unique challenges, and they should be structured so those challenges can be addressed in the most efficient and effective manner possible. People closest to the challenges are in the best position to understand them and should be actively engaged in finding solutions to them (Wohlsterter & Buffett, 1991). Given this assumption, the needs of students and the community should become essential factors informing the structure of 21st-century schools.

Before putting a structure in place, school leaders should acquire an understanding of the current conditions of the school, the needs of students, and knowledge of the school's external environment. From this understanding, they should acquire guidance as to how to structure the school so that multiple roles and functions can be performed. Challenges posed by the diverse instructional needs of students, as well as elements in the school's external environment, must be addressed. If schools are serving a particular group of stakeholders in a select community, those stakeholders not only have a right to participate in the educational process, but it is their responsibility to do so (Burke, 1992).

Diverse Instructional Needs of Students.   Students enter the schoolhouse with diverse educational needs. When a faculty has a working knowledge of all students, they have a greater opportunity to enhance the academic achievement of those students (Cushman, 1999). Therefore, developing the capacity of the faculty and staff to address those needs is a challenging process that must have, at its center, the creation of a structure that affords individual faculty members an opportunity to develop a working knowledge of all students.

With knowledge of all students, the faculty can establish a shared vision and an instructional program that meets the needs of all students. Decision making becomes critical to instructional effectiveness, as it may be necessary for the school leader to reduce class size, limit the number of daily student/teacher contacts, or implement any one of a variety of special programs. These could include single sex classes, schools within a school,

Standard 6

An education leader promotes the success of every student by understanding, responding to, and influencing the political, social, economic, legal, and cultural context.

Functions
   a. Advocate for children, families, and caregivers
   b. Act to influence local, district, state, and national decisions affecting student learning
   c. Assess, analyze, and anticipate emerging trends and initiatives in order to adapt leadership strategies

multi-age grouping, high schools that work, or any number of other research-based programs. Implementation of either of these instructional concepts requires a particular type of structure and knowledge of the diverse needs of students. Having the required knowledge will enable the faculty to participate in decisions that inform student achievement.

Community Involvement. There is indisputable evidence that links the scholastic achievement of students to the involvement of families in their education (NASSP, 2006). Therefore, school leaders must structure schools in a way that facilitates the involvement of the community in the educational process. They have to create initiatives that will connect the school and the community in an effective manner. It is not sufficient to make parents feel welcome when they enter the schoolhouse; rather, they have to feel a part of the school and feel comfortable engaging in the decision-making process. This necessarily requires the leadership, the faculty, and the staff to develop an in-depth understanding of the culture of the community. Evidence of this element can be obtained at Frayser Elementary School, in Memphis, Tennessee. Principal Elaine Stewart Price has implemented it with tremendous success. She has a special parking place for parents, a parent room, and a number of other amenities in place for parents and members of the community. Under her leadership, the school has become a treasured spot in the community, one which parents and community stakeholders visit frequently. They voice the sentiment that this is our school, and we play a major role in decisions that lead to its success.

Stakeholders, inside and outside of the schoolhouse, have information about the students being served. In many instances, the information they offer can produce effective instructional concepts. Regardless of the source of the concept, if it is educationally sound and meets the needs of the students in attendance, it should be administratively and structurally possible.

DISTRIBUTIVE LEADERSHIP In several earlier sections of this text, we have discussed the concept of distributive leadership. In each instance, the concept was addressed because it is of primary importance in 21st-century schools. Again, we make note of the importance of the concept. In this instance, it is mentioned as a factor influencing the structure of schools. Society is changing, and the changes occurring are affecting the way schools are led. These changes are adding to the complex nature of schools, requiring a different type of leadership, and that leadership necessarily has to be distributed throughout the school organization. Thus, the fifth element of the inclusive structure is distributive leadership. As school leaders commit to collaborating with faculty to facilitate the implementation of various processes that involve them in meeting organizational needs, they must be provided time to learn and plan—time to conduct inquiries into best practices of addressing specific student needs and engaging in professional dialogue with colleagues. The structure of the school must provide teachers with this opportunity (DuFour & Eaker, 1998; King et al., 2004).

Roadblocks, such as scheduling conflicts and voids in preparation, have to be removed in order to facilitate faculty participation in leadership matters. For example, Ms. Allen, a member of the principal's advisory committee who happens to have two children under the age of five, may feel that it is inconsiderate if the school leader schedules all advisory committee meetings before or after the school day. Furthermore, being a mother of two children should not prohibit her from serving as a contributing member of the committee. Some meetings could be scheduled at a time when it is not necessary for her to make special arrangements for her children. In addition, when she does remain after school or come prior to the opening of school, some special incentive, such as compensatory time, could be provided.

Another critical factor in fostering distributive leadership is professional development, which must become a life-long process. When appropriate professional development is in place, the school leader provides the faculty members with relevant assistance to ensure that they have the required preparation and support to obtain and master skills that enable them to better achieve the overall goals of the school. With adequate professional development, individual members of the faculty become equipped to engage in any number of leadership projects, including, but not limited to, providing workshops and seminars on instructional best practices for peers, serving as mentors, and effectively collaborating with colleagues on plans for school improvement (King et al., 2004).

Within the confines of the mechanistic, bureaucratic structure, school leaders cannot successfully address the challenges of 21st-century schools. At best, the structure is laden with regulations and mandates that subordinate individuals, robbing the organization of flexibility and creativity. More importantly, it serves the interest of a few top-level individuals who provide legal authority over specifically defined workplace tasks. The structure of 21st-century schools must free individuals from these restraints and constraints, fostering the ability of school leaders and their faculty to lead in a manner that responds to student and community needs.

■ ■ ■

Implications for Leadership

- Because schools are complex, multifaceted organizations, it is necessary for school leaders to structure the school for the effective and efficient coordination of activities and to direct the behavior of individuals.
- Prior to designing the school structure, it is necessary for the leader to acquire an in-depth understanding of the internal and external cultures of the school.
- With knowledge and understanding of the internal and external cultures of schools, school leaders can facilitate the design of programs and activities that meets the needs of students while respecting the values and beliefs of the community served.
- The design of the structure must take into account the critical need to establish interpersonal relationships between individuals in the workplace.
- Positive interpersonal relationships are necessary for individuals to effectively fulfill their roles and responsibilities.

- The structure must foster the participation of all stakeholders in decisions that affect the organization.
- The structure must address collaboration, as it is required in today's schools.
- As leadership for goal attainment is being distributed throughout the organization, the faculty must be treated in a professional manner, and their talents, strengths, and skills must be recognized and valued.
- The faculty must be afforded flexibility in the implementation of rules and regulations, as well as time to plan and engage in dialogue with colleagues.

Reflective Practice

1. What are some major challenges facing Principal Collins?
2. How will you structure your school?
3. What elements of the Mechanistic, Bureaucratic Model are most appealing to you?
4. What elements of the Mechanistic, Bureaucratic Model are least appealing to you?
5. What are some strategies that school leaders can use to implement a school structure that fosters stakeholder involvement in teaching and learning?

Chapter Essentials

Interstate School Leader Licensure Consortium Standards 1, 3, 5, and 6

An education leader promotes the success of every student by facilitating the development, articulation, implementation, and stewardship of a vision of learning that is shared and supported by all stakeholders.

An education leader promotes the success of every student by ensuring management of the organization, operation, and resources for a safe, efficient, and effective learning environment.

An education leader promotes the success of every student by acting with integrity, fairness, and in an ethical manner.

An education leader promotes the success of every student by understanding, responding to, and influencing the political, social, economic, legal, and cultural context.

Principle

Facilitation is different from directing. Both the leader and the follower must assume some responsibility.

Dichotomy

Chaos or Efficiency

The school leader must structure the school in a manner that eliminates chaos and fosters efficiency.

References

Abbott, M., & Caracheo, F. (1988). *Power, authority, and bureaucracy*. In N. Boyan (ed.), Handbook of Research on Educational Administration (pp. 239–257). New York: Longman.

Allen, J. (1990). *Mechanistic organization*. Retrieved October 21, 2004 from Web site: http://ollie.dcccd.edu/mgmt1374/ p.135

Adler, P., & Borys, B. (1996). Two types of bureaucracy: Enabling and coercive. *Administrative Science Quarterly, 41*, 61–89.

Barth, R. (1990). *Improving schools from within*. San Francisco, CA: Jossey-Bass.

Burke, C. (1992). Devolution of responsibility to Queensland schools: Clarifying the rhetoric critiquing the reality. *Journal of Educational Administration, 30*(4), 33–52.

Cushman, K. (1999). Essential school structure and design: Boldest moves get the best results. *Horace, 15*(5), 5–17.

DuFour, R., & Eaker, R. (1998) *Professional learning communities at work: Best practices for enhancing student achievement*. Bloomington, IN: National Education Service.

DuFour, R. (1999). Changing role: Playing the part of the principal stretches one's talent. *Journal of Staff Development, 20*(4),1–4.

Fullan, M. (1999) *Change forces: The sequel*. Philadelphia, PA: Falmer Press.

Green R. L. (2005). *Practicing the art of leadership: A problem-based approach to implementing the ISLLC Standards*. Upper Saddle River, NJ: Pearson Merrill Prentice Hall.

Gouldner, A. (1954). *Patterns of industrial bureaucracy*. New York: Free Press.

Hoy, W., & Sweetland, S. (2001). Designing better schools. The meaning and measure of enabling school structures. *Educational Administrative Quarterly, 37*, 296–321.

Huffman, J. (2003). The role of shared values and vision in creating professional learning communities. *NASSP Bulletin, 87*(637), 21–34.

Interstate School Leader Licensure Consortium of the Council of Chief State School Officers. (1996). *Candidate information bulletin for school leaders assessment*. Princeton, NJ: Educational Testing Service.

Interstate School Leader Licensure Consortium (ISLLC). (2008). Educational Leadership Policy Standards, Washington, D.C.: Council of Chief School Officers.

Joyce, B., & Calhoun, E. (1996). School renewal: An inquiry, not a prescription. In *Learning experiences in school renewal: An exploration of five successful programs*. Eugene, OR: (ERIC Clearing House on Educational Management No. ED 401 600).

King, D. (2002). Beyond instructional leadership: The changing shape of leadership. *Educational Leadership, 59*(8), 61–63.

King, D. et al. (2004). *Instructional coaching: Professional development strategies that improve instruction*. Providence, RI: Annenberg Institute for Education Reform.

Lashway, L. (1995). *Facilitative leadership*. Eugene, OR: ERIC Clearinghouse on Educational Management.

Lashway, L. (1997). *Leading with vision*. Eugene, OR: ERIC Clearinghouse on Educational Management.

Lashway, L. (1999). Measuring leadership potential. *ERIC Digest, 5*.

Liontos, L. B. (1992). *Transformational leadership*. Eugene, OR: ERIC Clearinghouse on Educational Management.

Mayo, E. (1939). *The human problems of an industrial civilization*. New York: Macmillan.

Maxwell, J. (2006). *The 360 degree leader: Developing your influence from anywhere within the organization*. Nashville, TN: Thomas Nelson.

Morgan, G. (1997). *Images of organization* (2nd ed.) Thousand Oaks, CA: Sage Publications.

National Association of Secondary School Principals. (2006). *Breaking ranks in the middle: Strategies for leading middle level reform.* Reston, VA.

Robbins, S. P. (1998). *Organizational behavior: Concepts, controversies, applications* (8th ed.). Upper Saddle River, NJ: Prentice Hall.

Rousseau, D. (1978). Characteristics of departments, positions and individuals: Contexts for attitudes and behavior. *Administrative Science Quarterly, 23*, 521–40.

Rousseau, D. (1997). Organizational behavior in the new organizational era. *Annual Review of Psychology, 48*, 515–46.

Scott, R. (2003). *Organizations: Rational, natural, and open systems* (5th ed.). Upper Saddle River, NJ: Prentice Hall.

Senge, P. M. (1990). *The fifth discipline: The art and practice of the learning organization.* New York: Doubleday.

Seyfarth, J. T. (1999). *The principal: New leadership for new challenges.* Upper Saddle River, NJ: Prentice Hall.

Sergiovanni, T. J. (1994*). Building community in schools.* San Francisco, CA: Josey-Bass, Publishers, Inc.

Sergiovanni, T. J. (2001). *The principalship: A reflective practice perspective.* Boston, MA: Allyn & Bacon.

Sinden, J. E., Hoy, W.K., & Sweetland, S. R. (2004). An analysis of enabling school structure: Theoretical, empirical, and research considerations. *Journal of Educational Administration, 42*, 462–478.

Sparks, D. (1999). Real-life view: Here's what a true learning community looks like. *Journal of Staff Development, 20*(4), 53–57.

Weber, M. (1947). *The theory of social and economic organizations. Trans.* T. Parsons. New York: Oxford University Press.

Weick, K., & Sutcliffe, K. (2001). *Managing the unexpected: Assuring high performance in an age of complexity.* San Francisco, CA: Josey-Bass Publishers, Inc.

Wohlstetter, P., & Buffet, T. (1991, April). *School-based management in big city districts: Are dollars decentralized too?* Paper presented at the annual meeting of American Educational Research Association, Chicago, IL.

CHAPTER

6

The Principal's Role in Establishing and Retaining a Quality Teaching Faculty

(Standards 2, 3, and 5)

"True Greatness Is Found in Serving"

JAMES MacDONALD

"Knowing what to do is the central problem of school improvement. Holding schools accountable for their performance depends on having people in schools with the knowledge, skills, and judgment to make the improvements that will increase student performance."

R. ELMORE

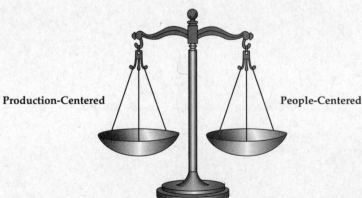

Production-Centered   People-Centered

INTRODUCTION

In order to effectively enhance the academic achievement of all students, principals must develop and maintain a quality faculty. Placing a teacher who does quality teaching in every classroom everyday, all day is the hallmark of an effective school. Having acquired an in-depth understanding of the culture, climate, and interaction of people from the previous two chapters, the reader is positioned to begin the process of understanding the importance of the principal's role. This specifically refers to selecting quality teaching personnel and structuring the school for effective teaching and learning.

This chapter focuses on the principal's role in developing a faculty of quality teachers. We begin with a perspective on teacher recruitment, selection, induction, and placement. Next we present a model designed for instructional enhancement. Then, we focus on the retention of teachers by presenting a mentoring program that provides teachers with support and enhances their career aspirations. The chapter concludes with a discussion that focuses on professional development and career advancement.

TEACHER RECRUITMENT, SELECTION, INDUCTION, AND PLACEMENT

One of the greatest resources in a school is a quality teaching faculty. In fact, the literature refers to it second only to the principal (Barth, 1990; Schlechty, 2002). Therefore, the recruitment, selection, induction, placement, and retention of teachers of quality have become major concerns of leaders of 21st-century schools (see Exhibit 6.1).

Teacher Recruitment

The major responsibility for the recruitment of quality teachers rests with central office administrators in the district's human resources department. However, principals play a crucial role in that process. At the school level, principals assess the instructional needs of the school to identify the type of program that will be implemented and the instructional services that are needed. Then, the skills and attributes of teachers needed to implement any new program or improve existing ones have to be determined. The process of making this determination requires the principal to assess the current teaching faculty's capacity to meet instructional program needs and communicate any identified personnel needs to the district's human resources administrator.

ASSESSING THE SCHOOL'S PERSONNEL NEEDS Instructional improvement is the primary purpose of the school program. Therefore, principals have to be able to determine the current conditions of the school program and identify any discrepancy that lies between the current conditions and the vision. The two kinds of assessments most often conducted are program and student assessments. Either of these assessments can surface a void in program effectiveness, student needs, teaching personnel, or all three. In either case, the

EXHIBIT 6.1 Teacher Recruitment, Selection, Induction, and Placement

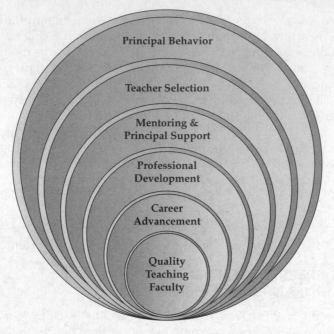

quality of the faculty will come into question requiring the principal to make personnel decisions.

PROGRAM ASSESSMENTS   The assessment of the instructional program often begins with making a determination as to whether instructional programs are being implemented in the manner they were designed to be implemented. In addition, program assessments are conducted to determine if the programs are producing the achievement results they were implemented to achieve. The results from these assessments may surface a need for a change in programs which might also require a change in the teaching faculty.

Teachers should be selected for the purpose of teaching and learning. With an understanding of each faculty member and the students served, principals can foster the creation of a vision of what the school needs to become and acquire knowledge of the type of faculty that will allow that vision to become a reality. For example, if a school with a large percentage of special education students attempts to implement a program of inclusion, a select group of teachers will be needed. Another school with the same percentage of special education students may choose to use a different instructional model, requiring a different select group of teachers. Thus, the instructional program being implemented will determine, to a large extent, faculty needs.

STUDENT ASSESSMENTS   Student assessments are most often conducted by analyzing student test data. Student test data can be analyzed in several ways. The data may be disaggregated by grade level, subject area, teachers, students, and classes. The assessment also considers diversity, special needs students, advanced students, and underachieving students. The assessment of student progress may also surface a need for a program change, which may require a change in existing personnel or the addition of new personnel. In addition, it may surface a need for the reassignment of one or more teachers.

ONGOING PERSONNEL ASSESSMENT   As was discussed in Chapters 2 and 3, it is important for principals to understand the people with whom they work. Having this knowledge affords the principal an opportunity to make internal personnel changes to address program needs, desires, and preferences of individual faculty members. Using a systematic plan to collaborate with the faculty on an ongoing basis, principals can determine their strengths and weaknesses, preferences, and desires. Principals need to be knowledgeable of the values, beliefs, preferences, desires, and goals of the existing faculty, prior to contacting human resources to fill a vacancy or to address a program need. It is good practice for them to determine if the need can be met internally, or if some internal moves would enhance program effectiveness. When a vacancy occurs, or a program change is warranted, this is an excellent opportunity for the principal to engage the existing faculty in collaborative dialogue to reach agreement on the plan and to determine if there are individuals who would like to fill that vacancy. It would also be beneficial for the school leader to determine if some previously expressed needs, desires, and goals of current faculty members can be met.

RECRUITING TEACHERS IN A TIMELY MANNER   It is important for school leaders to recruit and employ teachers in a timely manner, as all schools and school districts are interested in selecting and employing quality teachers. If the selection is not made in a timely manner, the person most qualified to fill the position may have been selected earlier by another school or school district, leaving individuals in the selection pool who will not fully meet the assessed needs of the school. The effects of selecting an individual who is not a match with the culture of the school or who is not equipped to implement an approved program, can become very problematic and disruptive. For example, if the program design is team teaching, and the individual the principal wants to assign does not favor the concept or is inexperienced in the concept, placing that individual in the team teaching program could become problematic. It would be in the best interest of the program to assign that individual to another position and bring in someone who is interested and capable of teaching as a part of a team. Tom Collins (2001) advises that it is better to leave a position vacant than to fill it with an inadequate person.

Budgetary accountability is another reason information has to be communicated accurately and in a timely manner. If the information communicated to the human resources office is not accurate or is not presented in a timely manner, the consequences could be severe. For example, if the projected personnel needs of the school are above what is actually needed, central administrators may contract and assign more individuals to a school than required, negatively impacting the budget. Conversely, if the projections are below what are required, individuals with the knowledge, skills, and attributes needed for program implementation may not be available. Assessing and reporting the personnel needs of the school are critical parts of the teacher recruitment process and the beginning stages of acquiring a quality teaching faculty.

Teacher Selection

After the personnel needs of the school are communicated to the human resources administrator, candidates will be sent to the school from the district pool, and a school team of individuals at the building level will need to interview those candidates and make a selection. The interview team may consist of teachers, administrators, parents, students, and community stakeholders. The team should work from a position description, raising a set of questions that will ascertain whether or not the individual is a match for the school. The concern for the selection of an individual to join the faculty should far exceed subject area certification and academic knowledge. In fact, it should include an assessment of whether or not the personal qualities of the individual are a match with the culture and climate of the school. In making this determination, the selection team should use a predetermined rating scale based on position qualifications and expectations. The process, if conducted in an ethical manner, should identify a person who will best fit the position.

CHARACTERISTICS OF EFFECTIVE TEACHERS   In the interview process, the interview team will want to look for certain qualities. There is no one best way to determine if the teacher selected will be a great success or even align with the faculty. However, the team can establish some guidelines to follow. First, the team should determine if the candidate is certified and has a major in the subject area needed. One might assume that a candidate sent to the school for an interview by the district's human resources officer is certified in his/her field of study and has a major in the area requested; however, this is not always the case. Therefore, to ensure the selection of a candidate that will add to the quality of the teaching faculty, the committee will want to verify the candidate's teaching credentials, as there is a positive relationship between teacher certification and student achievement (Darling-Hammond, 2000).

A second area of focus for the committee might be the actual presentation made by the candidate. It is not uncommon for selection committees to ask candidates to teach a lesson. If this is not a requirement of the committee, another alternative is to focus on the manner in which the candidate presents ideas, gives thought to questions, organizes thoughts, and relates responses to questions, not only to the person on the committee that raised the question, but to all committee members. When a candidate makes a clear thought-provoking presentation to the committee, providing explanations for answers given, the same is likely to occur in the classroom. This type of behavior increases the potential that all students will be given attention through classroom instruction, which will enhance academic achievement (Ball, Lubienski, & Mewborn, 2001; Land, 1987).

A third area of consideration could be the personal presence of the candidate. Personality is very important in the classroom. The candidate must be able to relate to the students he/she will be assigned to teach, the student's parents, members of the community, and certainly other members of the faculty. A candidate who is warm, friendly, and enthusiastic is more likely to become an effective teacher than one who does not exhibit these behaviors (Murray, 1983).

SELLING THE SCHOOL TO THE CANDIDATE   The principal should keep in mind that the interview is a two-way process and if a quality person is to be selected, the selection committee might need to sell the school to the candidate. Following is a list of items that might be considered when the committee is selling the school:

- Describe the unique characteristics of the school
- Advise the candidate as to why this school would be a good place to work
- Inform the candidate of individuals already on the faculty and share their qualities
- Speak to the culture, climate, and structure of the school
- Speak to the positive interaction that occurs among faculty members
- Provide examples of why the school is a safe place to work
- Share the vision of the school
- Inquire about the candidate's career aspirations and share how current teachers have been assisted in reaching their career goals
- Explain life in the school
- Explain to the candidate the teacher leadership possibilities
- Describe the support he/she will receive:
  - mentoring support
  - support from the principal
  - support from parents

In the final analysis, it is imperative that the committee select an individual who will add to the collective capacity of the faculty to meet the needs of all students served.

Teacher Induction

The induction process can be critical to the success of the teacher selected. Teachers need to feel supported and a part of the school family, and this should occur within the first week of the teacher's arrival. A preplanned orientation to the school might consist of some of the following:

- a reception
- a tour of the school community
- presentation of the faculty handbook
- a tour of the building, including an introduction to all teachers, administrators, and staff, with emphasis on individuals who are responsible for certain areas of authority (i.e., grade chairs, department chairs, team leaders, PTA presidents)

- a description of materials and services that are available
- a description of how materials and services are ascertained
- general operational processes and procedures
- an explanation of the teacher appraisal process
- an explanation of how business is conducted in the school

Teacher Placement

Once the teacher is selected and inducted, the principal must make sure the teacher has the appropriate assignment (Collins, 2001), and the skills and attributes of the teacher must be aligned with the needs of the school. A principal makes great strides in promoting student success by ensuring that a quality teacher is in every classroom and that every teacher has the resources needed to address the academic achievement of the students served. The research literature is clear; when a quality-teaching faculty is in existence, the developmental evidence points to three factors: (1) establishment of a formal mentoring program; (2) the behavior of the principal, and (3) having a formal support system in place for all teachers. Each of these factors will be discussed later in the chapter. First, we discuss instructional supervision.

INSTRUCTIONAL SUPERVISION

To maintain a quality faculty, a process must be in place to ensure that teachers have the skills needed to move current conditions to the vision. The Collaborative Observation Relationship Evaluative Response model (C.O.R.E.) is recommended for 21st-century school leaders to use in that process.

The Collaborative Observation Relationship Evaluative Response Model

In the previous chapters, we have discussed school leaders using a facilitative style and distributing leadership throughout the organization. In keeping with those inclusive leadership practices, we present C.O.R.E. for use in supervising the instructional program. The importance and benefits to be derived from collaborating, building relationships, and providing feedback have also been addressed in earlier chapters. Using C.O.R.E., we add observation and illustrate how an instructional leader puts the four concepts into practice for the enhancement of the instructional program.

C.O.R.E, a collaborative supervision model, is an approach that moves instructional supervision from a perceived evaluative assessment tool to a process that provides mentoring and support. A close examination of the literature reveals several approaches for collaborative supervision (Glanz, 2005; Glickman, 2002; Peterson, 2000; Ponticell, 2004; Sergiovanni, 2005). This model combined the best of those approaches to formulate a four-step circular process that addresses the relationship between principals and teachers advocated by the current reform movement. The components of C.O.R.E. include: (1) collaborative dialogue; (2) observation in the classroom;

EXHIBIT 6.2 A Collaborative Supervisory Model

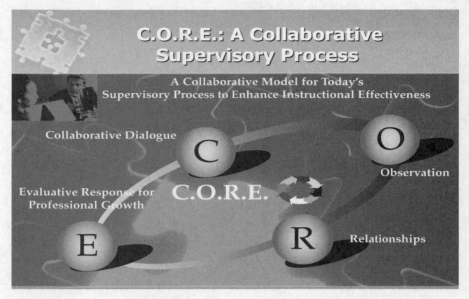

Source: Exhibit 6.2 was designed and developed by Dr. Sharen Cypress. Dr. Cypress is the co-designer of the C.O.R.E. model.

(3) relationships between principal and teacher, and (4) evaluative feedback from the principal to the teacher (see Exhibit 6.2).

In order to begin the collaborative supervisory process, the principal has to establish rapport with each teacher. This rapport building has to occur in the type of trust-based culture discussed in previous chapters, as it requires the principal to become knowledgeable of the teacher's background experience, areas of expertise, and the culture and climate of his/her classroom. Once the principal establishes rapport with each member of the faculty, he/she can enter the classroom in a non-threatening, non-evaluative manner for the purpose of observing the teaching and learning process. In essence, the principal becomes a critical friend prepared to engage the teacher in collaborative dialogue. The following is a description of how the circular process works.

Collaborative Dialogue

In order to engage the teacher in collaborative dialogue, the principal must become the lead learner, conducting inquiry into best practices. Having conducted inquiry into best practices, the principal and the classroom teacher can discuss strategies for use in resolving challenges or simply enhancing classroom instruction. The principal's role is nondirective as the teacher retains ownership for seeking best practices for instructional enhancement. The principal acquires information sufficient to facilitate collaborative dialogue, first with the classroom teacher and then, if necessary, with a team of lead teachers who serve as mentors. The team also works collaboratively to explore strategies that can be used to enhance instruction in both the assisted teacher's classroom, as well as classrooms of other faculty members.

Observation

Having previously reviewed lesson plans for the day, the principal enters the classroom and conducts a formative assessment, observing the teaching and learning process. After the completion of the assessment, the teacher is provided feedback on what was observed by the principal, and the two individuals engage in collaborative dialogue for the purpose of identifying any instructional skills or activities that need to be enhanced. During the process, the teacher is provided an opportunity to reflect on his/her practices and to assess his/her weaknesses and strengths. Once the principal and teacher reach an agreement regarding areas that need to be strengthened, the overall expectations for future observations are clearly communicated. Both the teacher and principal leave the session to conduct inquiry into best practices for the purpose of identifying strategies that can be used to enhance classroom instruction.

As a result of the discussion, it may be determined that the teacher needs to participate in a series of professional development activities. A frequent outcome of the collaborative discussion is the identification of appropriate professional development activities for the teacher. Once teachers have acquired the necessary professional development to enhance their skills or identified strategies to enhance instruction, the principal makes a second observation to assist the teacher in refining strategies and utilizing best practices for instructional improvement.

Relationships

Throughout the process, principals are encouraged to enhance the trust-based culture. The school culture has to perpetuate a true learning environment wherein trust is embedded and positive relationships are maintained between the principal and teachers, teachers and teachers, and teachers and students. Unless a trust-based culture is maintained and positive relationships are sustained, teachers and principals will not be able to engage in open dialogue regarding the teaching and learning process. As a result, classroom observation will return to an evaluative process that is focused on what is not occurring, as opposed to what needs to occur.

The principal must be able to enter the classroom for the purpose of enhancing instruction, rather than evaluation. Ryan and Oestreich (1998) proposed that satisfying relationships are present when employees, regardless of position, pose a mutual understanding and helpfulness, serving as reality checks and providing feedback for each other.

Evaluative Response

Following each visit, the principal provides the teacher with evaluative feedback concerning the observation. This includes the review of lesson plans, the effectiveness of professional development activities, program strategies implemented, and comments received from mentoring teachers. Appropriate appraisal records may be discussed at this time; however, most critical in the process is maintaining the connection that has been made between the school leader and the teacher. Maintaining the connection enables the principal to continue to encourage the teacher to make decisions regarding his/her instructional processes. Additional visits should be made as required, and the process should provide effective feedback and ongoing support.

When collaborative supervision exists, a professional learning community emerges. Teachers are empowered to make effective decisions; cohesive relationships are established, and each individual is respected and valued as a major part of the organization. Principals and teachers benefit from the process through enhanced trust and collaboration. The confidence of the faculty is enhanced, and classroom practices are improved. There is enhanced teacher satisfaction and, most importantly, there is an increase in student achievement.

A MENTORING PROGRAM FOR TEACHERS

Not every teacher who enters the schoolhouse is ready to teach; therefore, principals desirous of developing and retaining a quality faculty must provide the novice, as well as senior teachers, with an effective support system. An effective support system for teachers includes a variety of strategies, among which are a formal mentoring program, common planning time for teachers to share and engage each other in discussions that lead to problem solutions, and a positive relationship with the principal.

Formal Mentoring

It is clear that mentoring is a positive factor in building a quality-teaching faculty, as an effective mentoring program assists novice teachers in becoming acclimated to the school and faculty they are joining, as well as the teaching and learning process and their role in that process. It also provides services in the areas of instruction, data analysis, classroom management, community relations, fiscal management, and building school capacity for change to enhance student achievement.

The major focus of the mentoring program is learning, and the mentor takes full responsibility for the mentee's learning. During this process, the responsibility for establishing the learning setting is shared; priorities and activities are developed, and the needed resources are secured (Zachary, 2000). The mentor/mentee relationship should be a collaborative partnership with the mentor facilitating a process that affords the mentee an opportunity to acquire strategies to use in organizing and managing classroom instruction. For example, Ms. Williams, a first-year teacher just exiting a teacher preparation program, is deeply ingrained in the learning process and now must convert her activities to the teaching process. Whereas she has experience in developing lessons plans at the university, they were plans of a general nature and, at best, plans done during her student teaching experience.

Now, she must develop plans for a specific group of students in a full- time capacity, in a specific subject area, using a specific set of rules and procedures. Thus, she is likely to welcome assistance in analyzing student test data, developing lesson plans informed by that data, and obtaining the resources and materials needed to implement the plans. Given that managing student behavior is a major challenge for the novice teacher, support in that area would also be helpful.

There are models from which principals can select to establish a mentoring program in their school. Some of the most noted ones are the mentoring groups, mentoring circles, peer mentoring, and mentoring teams. Regardless of the model selected, learning of the mentee must remain the major focus. In addition, biweekly meetings should be held including the mentor and mentee. The meetings can be conducted through face-to-face conferencing, questions and answer by e-mail, or through collaborative classroom engagement. The main foci of the meetings should center on problem solving, minimizing challenges, and enhancing the teaching and learning process.

Common Planning Time

Once the mentoring relationship is established, the principal can schedule common planning times for the mentor and mentee to meet and discuss difficult issues. Allocating time for common planning yields positive results and serves as a vehicle for use in facilitating collegiality among faculty members (Bingham, 1997). During the common planning time, teachers can collaborate, share information, discuss instructional methods, identify teaching strategies, select intervention programs, and engage in other activities to enhance the instructional process. In addition, a formal process can be outlined for teachers to observe and/or critique one another.

Discussions should center on data collected regarding student progress, including both formal and informal assessments done in the classroom. Common planning time also gives teachers the opportunity to talk about the results and share reasons why some students are achieving high results or suggest intervention strategies for use with underachieving students. In either case, suggestions that lead to enhanced teaching and learning can be shared. A good practice is to allot at least three days of common planning time per week. One can be used for data-driven discussions about instructional strategies and interventions to use with underachieving students, and the other two days can be used to discuss general instructional matters, make decisions about professional development needs, work on school-wide projects, and identify best practices. Principals may vary time for common planning and observations based on the grade levels of the school and the activities to be addressed.

Mentoring is not restricted to novice teachers. Principals can also utilize team-building activities to develop interpersonal relationships among all teachers. In instances where senior teachers are experiencing challenges, a mentor can be assigned, and special sessions can be held between the assigned mentor and senior teachers. The issue that is of primary importance is the need for the principal to build interpersonal relationships between and among all faculty members and establish a receptive climate for mentoring to occur among the entire faculty.

When the mentoring program is effectively implemented, both the mentor and the mentee benefit from the experience, but more importantly, the quality of the teaching faculty is increased, and the instructional program is enhanced.

Retaining a Quality Faculty

There is compelling evidence in the literature that supports the argument that the behavior of the school principal is a critical factor that must be considered when selecting and retaining quality teachers (Bullough, 2007; Colley, 2002; DuFour, 2007; Elmore, 2003; Johnson & Birkeland, 2003; Tye & O'Brien, 2002;). Principals affect the daily life of teachers and greatly influence their decision to remain in the classroom. The major influencing factors regarding teacher satisfaction and ultimately retention are support from the school principal, higher salaries, flexibility to influence decision making, improved discipline, quality of working conditions, and significant on-the-job training, and support. All except one of these factors, in one way or another, are influenced by principal behavior. The converse is also true, as when these elements are not evident, teachers become dissatisfied, find reasons to leave the school, and, in some instances, the profession (Charlotte Advocates for Education, 2004). Therefore, a major issue for consideration in building a faculty of quality teachers is the influence of the principal's behavior on the faculty.

The Behavior of The Principal

From a number of studies, it is evident that the establishment of effective interpersonal relationships between principals and teachers leads to a quality-teaching faculty (Barth, 1990; Ingersoll, 2001; Marzano, Waters, & McNulty, 2005). Principals who support and encourage teacher growth and development characterize successful schools. They construct messages in ways that empower teachers, rather than overwhelm them. Inclusive phrases, such as "our school", and statements, such as "We have to come up with a plan." can invite and sustain collaborative thinking among teachers, enabling the principal to build the kinds of relationships that are needed to sustain a quality teaching faculty for effective teaching and learning.

Another strategy principals can use to influence teacher retention is to improve working conditions to the extent that teachers view themselves as empowered, competent professionals who have a desire to grow professionally and reach self-actualization. Teachers who are empowered tend to commit to the organization and its goals, exercising the flexibility and freedom to teach the curriculum using their preferred teaching style within the parameters of teaching best practices (Bogler & Somech, 2004).

PROFESSIONAL DEVELOPMENT AND CAREER ADVANCEMENT

One of the most important resources a principal can provide a faculty is focused professional development informed by an ongoing assessment of the needs of students and the ability of the faculty to meet those needs. In some instances, the professional development program emerges out of self-assessment activities, principal and teacher interaction, principal observations, the formal appraisal process, and mentoring relationships. The program should have, as its major purpose, the strengthening of quality faculty and staff, both instructionally and professionally. Ultimately, it is the responsibility of the principal to make sure a quality program is planned and implemented.

The program should also equip the faculty with updated instructional strategies and provide them with material resources to implement those strategies. As students' needs change, the strategies teachers use to address those needs necessarily have to change, and the process that informs the change is professional development. In general, some common ways to ascertain information to inform professional development program content and activities are:

- surveying the faculty to ascertain their desires regarding the planning and development of the professional development program for the year;
- holding meetings with individual teachers to discuss their needs;
- observing classroom instruction and assessing teacher needs, and
- acquiring suggestions from mentors.

A quality faculty needs to be aware of the latest methods and techniques in the field. The principal can facilitate the acquisition of that knowledge through faculty meetings, one-on-one conferences, and processes for instructional change, all of which should be a part of a comprehensive professional development program.

Faculty Meetings

Weekly faculty meetings should be a part of the professional development program and should enhance the professional learning community, resulting in the growth of the entire faculty. Rather than general announcements that the principal can distribute by e-mail or memoranda, emphasis should be placed on such activities as grade level collaboration to coordinate students' progress from grade to grade and school-wide issues that ensure faculty cohesiveness. In addition, the principal can conduct trust-building sessions to enhance relationships. Through the process of sustaining trusting relationships and hosting quality faculty meetings, principals increase their interaction with the faculty, enhance the faculty's knowledge of teaching strategies and secure buy-in from them (Brower & Balch, 2005).

One-on-One Conferences

A one-on-one conference gives the principal an opportunity to explore the strengths and weaknesses of a faculty member in a confidential manner. The principal cannot take for granted that a faculty member knows how to perform specific activities. They have to spend time with individuals, getting to know them personally and professionally. If a faculty member has personal problems, this is a time when the principal can address them and establish rapport. Problems that affect people personally can also affect the organization professionally.

One-on-one conferences also give the principal an opportunity to support individuals regarding sensitive matters and show genuine concern for their welfare through open lines of communication. In one-on-one conferences, principals can review progress reports, bring clarity to issues, establish timelines, and set clear expectations. Of primary importance, they can enhance the self-efficacy of the teacher by conveying to him/her that an unsuccessful activity is not failure, rather an impediment which provides him/her an opportunity to begin again using new strategies and ideas.

Instructional Change

Implementation of instructional first or second order change will require some type of change in the behavior of teachers. When either of the two types of change occurs, often teachers attend program-training sessions to learn the new instructional processes and procedures. The sessions may last a half-day, a day, and sometimes two days. In some instances, teachers leave the session, having heard presentations but feeling a great deal of discomfort regarding engaging in the implementation of the new concept. Therefore, prior to implementing any new program concept, a part of the school's professional development plan should be assessing the readiness level of faculty members to implement the new concept. The process should entail some type of assessment activity, other than simply asking teachers about their readiness level, as professional modesty is certain to play a role in their response.

Career Advancement

Teachers' readiness and developmental levels as educators vary according to how well their biological and psychological needs are satisfied. Psychologist Abraham Maslow designed a model of a hierarchy of need indicating individuals are initially motivated by the basic need for survival and safety. Accordingly, individuals tend to seek to satisfy higher needs when their basic needs have been adequately met, the highest of which is self-actualization—the desire to use one's talents, abilities, and potentialities to the fullest (Maslow, 1962). For example, a first-year teacher is likely to be concerned with adjusting and learning how to function in a clean, comfortable, safe work environment, and meeting the needs of his/her students. Once these needs are met, a different set of needs comes into focus, and the process continues through various levels, which may include becoming teacher of the year, grade level chairperson, and ultimately principal—which may be self-actualization.

A part of the principal's role is to assist teachers in moving from one level to another—advancing their career. An excellent starting point is to provide them with experience as teacher leaders, providing services to the school and their colleagues. Allowing time and facilitating attendance at workshops and seminars can also enhance the career of teachers. However, in some instances, teachers will need assistance in simply retaining their current position. For example, if a teacher is teaching on an alternative license, he/she will need assistance in converting that license to a permanent license. This support not only builds relationships between the principal and the teacher, but it enhances the teacher's preparation and thus, the academic program.

Another form of professional career enhancement for teachers is acquiring assistance from the principal in obtaining an advanced degree and securing information concerning career opportunities that are available in the district. Teachers can engage in one of a variety of leadership programs to acquire skills in leadership. During this development activity and after the activity is completed, they can assume responsibility for leading school programs and activities. In many instances, they provide valuable instructional assistance as workshop presenters, program coaches, general mentoring, team leaders, and developers of professional enhancement plans.

Principals influence teacher quality and retention in the learning community when they focus their attention on teacher needs, providing them with quality mentoring, and making instructional support available. When this type of support is provided, teachers function at a quality level; they tend to be committed to goal attainment and utilize best practices to enhance student achievement (Feiman-Nemser, 1996; NEA, 2005). In summary, assisting teachers in reaching their career goals is a plus for the principal.

■ ■ ■

Implications for Leadership

- Twenty-first-century school leaders need to understand the importance of conducting assessments for the purpose of acquiring knowledge of the existing conditions in the school.
- Twenty-first-century school leaders need to recruit, employ, and retain a quality-teaching faculty.
- The behavior of the school leader influences the behavior of the faculty.
- School leaders need to acknowledge the contributions teachers make to leadership effectiveness.
- A focused professional development plan is a critical element in effective 21st-century schools.
- Principals have to establish a foundation for effective teaching and learning.
- Principals have to create a forum for the faculty to weave new learning into their existing knowledge base.
- Principals have to create a forum for the faculty to broaden their understanding of the teaching and learning process.

- Collaboration must be an ongoing part of the teaching and learning process.
- Effective teaching and learning is a team effort.
- Effective mentoring programs are essential in the retention of a quality teaching faculty.

Reflective Practice

1. What are some procedures you would use to select a teacher leadership team?
2. What is your vision of a quality-mentoring program?
3. Explain how you would put the strategies presented in this chapter into practice.
4. What are some additional strategies that you deem appropriate for use in recruiting, selecting, and retaining a quality-teaching faculty?
5. What would you identify as critical elements in a focused professional development program?
6. Outline the ideal leader behavior for the retention of a quality-teaching faculty.

Chapter Essentials

Interstate School Leaders Licensure Consortium Standards, and Leadership Core Competencies

Three of the six ISLLC Standards and five of the 13 Core Competencies combine to inform leadership behavior for the selection and retention of a quality teaching faculty for 21st-century schools.

The Role of 21st-Century School Leaders

The role of school leaders has expanded to include a larger focus on teaching and learning, professional development, data driven decision making, and accountability for student learning. The shift is from school leaders taking an authoritarian top-down role to an inclusive facilitative role with teachers, parents, and other stakeholders participating in making decisions that affect the school and student achievement.

Principle

By building leadership capacity in others, school leaders can foster the attainment of a shared vision.

Dichotomy
From Production-Centered to People-Centered

The leadership style of principals must focus on people, not production. It is our position that if the focus is truly on people, production will be a natural occurrence.

References

Ball, D. L., Lubienski, S. T., & Mewborn, D. S. (2001). Research on teaching mathematics: The unsolved problem of teacher's mathematical knowledge. In V. Richardson (Ed.), *Handbook of research on teaching* (4th ed. pp. 433–456). Washington, D.C.: American Educational Research Association.

Barth, S. R. (1990). *Improving schools from within: Teachers, parents, and principals can make the difference.* San Francisco, CA: Publishers. Inc.

Bingham, C. (1997). *Scheduling for grade team planning in the elementary school: A formative evaluation.* Retrieved January 10, 2008, from Web site: http://www.serve.org/UCR/pdfs/UCR9Steveblocksch.pdf

Bogler, R., & Somech, A. (2004). Influence of teacher empowerment on teachers' organizational commitment, professional commitment, and organizational citizenship behavior in schools. *Teacher and Teacher Education. 20*(3), 277–289.

Brower, R. E., & Balch, B. V. (2005). *Transformational leadership and decision making.* Thousand Oaks, CA: Corwin Press.

Bullough, R. (2007). Professional learning communities and the eight-year study. *Education Horizons, 85*(32), 168–180.

Charlotte Advocates for Education (2004). *Role of principal leadership in increasing teacher retention: Creating a supportive environment.* Retrieved from Web site: http://www.advocatesfored.org/principalstudy.htm

Colley, A. C. (2002). What can principals do about new teacher attrition? *Principal, 81*, 22–24.

Collins, J. (2001). *Good to great.* New York: Harper Collins Publishers Inc.

Darling-Hammond, L. (2000). Teacher quality and student achievement: A review of state policy evidence. *Educational Policy Analysis Archives, 8*, 1–48. Retrieved from Web site: http://epaa.asu.edu/epaa/v8nl/

DuFour, R. (2007) Professional learning communities: A bandwagon, an idea worth considering, our best hope for high levels of learning. *Middle School Journal, 39*(1), 4–8.

Elmore, R. (2003). *Knowing the right thing to do: School improvement and performance-based accountability.* Washington, D.C.: NGA Center for Best Practices.

Feiman-Nemser, S. (1996). *Teacher mentoring: A critical review.* Washington, D.C. (ERIC Document Reproduction Service No. ED397060).

Glanz, J. (2005). Action research as instructional supervision: Suggestions for principals. *National Association of Secondary School Principals Bulletin, 89*, 17–27.

Glickman, C. D. (2002). Leadership for learning: How to help teachers succeed. Alexandria, VA: Institute for Schools, Education, and Democracy.

Ingersoll, R. (2001). Teacher turnover and teacher shortage: An organizational analysis. *American Educational Research Journal, 3*(38), 499–534.

Johnson, S. M., & Birkeland, S. E. (2003). The schools that teachers choose. *Educational Leadership, 60*(8), 20–24.

Land, M. L. (1987). Vaguenesss and clarity. In M. Dunkin (Ed.). *The international encyclopedia of teaching and teacher education* (pp. 392–397). New York: Pergamon.

MacDonald, J. (2008). *10 choices: A proven plan to change your life forever.* Nashville, TN: Thomas Nelson, Inc.

Maslow, A. (1962). *Toward a psychology of being.* New York: Basic Books.

Marzano, R., Waters, T., & McNulty. B. (2005). *School leadership that works: From research to results.* Alexandria, VA: Association for Supervision and Curriculum Development.

Murray, H. G. (1983). Low influence classroom teaching behavior and student ratings of college teacher effectiveness. *Journal of Educational Psychology, 75*, 138–149.

National Education Association, (2005). Attracting and keeping quality teachers. Retrieved on April 23, 2005, from Web site: http://www.nea.org/index.html

Peterson, K. D. (2000). Teacher evaluation: A comprehensive guide to new direction and Practices (2nd ed). Thousand Oaks, CA: Corwin Press.

Ponticell, J. A. (2004). Confronting well-learned lessons in supervision and evaluation. *The National Association of Secondary School Principals Bulletin*. Retrieved July 1, 2005, from Web site: www.nassp.org/publications/bulletin/bltn_0904_ponticell.cfm

Ryan, K. D., & Oestriech, D. K. (1998). Driving fear out of the workplace: Creating the high-trust, high-performance organization. San Francisco, CA: Jossey-Bass Publishers. Inc.

Schlechty, P. (2002). *Working on the work: An action plan for teachers, principals, and superintendents*. San Francisco, CA: Jossey-Bass Publishers. Inc.

Sergiovanni, T. J. (2005). *Strengthening the heartbeat: Leading and learning together in schools*. San Francisco, CA: Jossey-Bass Publishers. Inc.

Tye, B. B., & O'Brien, L. (2002). Why are experienced teachers leaving the profession? *Phi Delta Kappan, 84*, 24.

Zachary, L. J. (2000). *The mentor's guide: Facilitating effective learning relationships*. San Francisco, CA: Jossey-Bass Publishers. Inc.

PART FOUR

Dimension 3
Building Bridges Through Relationships

Principal/ Teacher	Teacher/ Teacher
Teacher/ Student	School/ Community

Chapter 7 Developing Relationships for Effective Leadership in Schools

DIMENSIONAL CONCEPTS

The primary focus of this dimension is the benefits to be derived by school leaders who establish and nurture relationships between and among individuals in the internal and external environments of the schoolhouse. These relationships include, but are not limited to, the following: Principal/Teacher; Teacher/Teacher; Teacher/Student, and School/Community.

Building on the concepts presented in the first two dimensions, the content addresses the importance of school leaders being aware of how people are treated. This includes how they feel about working in particular school situations and how they respond to the leadership relative to making a commitment to goal attainment. The intent is for the reader to gain insight into how effective leaders remove fear and intimidation from the workplace, free the human spirit to be creative, and build a capacity for self and others to lead. This dimension is fundamental to an individual desirous of becoming the type of leader who develops collegial relationships and builds a professional learning community within a school. In such a community, all stakeholders are dedicated to continuous school improvement and share accountability for student success.

7

Developing Relationships for Effective Leadership in Schools

(Standards 4, 5, and 6)

"Give me the courage of a lion, the skin of a hippopotamus, and the heart of an angel, and I will lead you from current reality to the vision."

"The most important single ingredient in the formula of success is knowing how to get along with people."

THEODORE ROOSEVELT

Enabling Relationships

Hindering Relationships

INTRODUCTION

In leading one of today's schools, school leaders will need to make connections with many entities inside and outside of the schoolhouse. The bridges that make these connections will have to be built through relationships, for success in school organizations can only become a reality when relationships are built between and among stakeholders. Whereas individuals standing alone might be seen as capable of making a contribution to student achievement, it is only when individuals establish productive relationships with other individuals that the true essence of the school as a whole is revealed.

Relationships begin with the selection of individuals to join the faculty team. In selecting faculty members, school leaders must realize that the faculty can only be as strong as the strength of individuals who make up the team. If individuals who have values and beliefs that are not aligned with established goals and objectives and the culture of the school organization are selected, the possibility exists that they will be unwilling to commit to the manner in which the teaching and learning process occurs. Thus, the true strength and effectiveness of the school as an organization will be compromised. Conversely, if the appropriate individuals are selected, through the building of relationships, they can ultimately be acculturated into a strong faculty that will not disintegrate over time.

Organizational effectiveness is enhanced by the combined skills, strengths, and unique attributes that exist as a result of the building of solid relationships between and among members of a faculty. When individuals in the schoolhouse build relationships with each other, they form a connection that strengthens the work of each individual, as well as the total teaching and learning process. They bond together, and the connection provides support, not only for each individual, but also for the establishment of a common purpose and shared goals, which leads to positive outcomes for students and the community at large.

Another important realization is that over time, established relationships between and among faculty members can encounter challenges that will weaken them, threatening to negatively impact the entire teaching and learning process. In the best of schools, conditions and circumstances that cause disconnect between or among faculty members can surface. In such instances, the school leadership must be at its most actualized level, prepared to step in and be creative, motivational, and resilient enough to reconnect faculty members. If such action is not taken, organizational effectiveness will be inhibited.

In this chapter, we explore the types of relationships needed to foster goal attainment in 21st-century schools. Approaches that school leaders use to build and sustain those relationships are also explored. The primary focus of the chapter is to review the responsibility of school leaders relative to establishing and nurturing relationships between and among individuals in the internal and external environments of the schoolhouse. The reader should gain insight into processes school leaders can use to build and/or enhance relationships by identifying the enabling effects of positive relationships and the hindering effects of negative ones.

RELATIONSHIPS DEFINED

It is not uncommon when reading about leadership in today's schools to read repeatedly about the need for school leaders to build relationships. The importance of building relationships has been stated or written about so frequently that it should be an accepted practice. In today's schools, effective leaders accept the notion that relationships are important, and they understand that they have to build bridges to goal attainment through relationships. However, in the context of human behavior, one might ask "What is a relationship?" and, "What are the elements that comprise quality relationships in the schoolhouse?"

A relationship is a connection between people, enabling them to engage in some sort of exchange. It is a feeling or sense of emotional bonding, "a catalyst, an enabling dynamism in the support, nurture, and freeing of people's energies and motivations toward solving problems and using help" (Perlman, 1979). If the behavior, emotions, and thoughts of two individuals are mutually and casually interconnected, the individuals are interdependent and a relationship exists" (Clark & Reis, 1988).

The purpose of the relationship will largely determine its nature and qualities—how individuals relate to one another in any given setting or situation. For instance, in the schoolhouse, a connection or bonding may occur because of a required interaction that is needed in order for members of a faculty to fulfill their roles and to perform identified functions. The interdependent nature of tasks necessarily requires that there be a connection between the individuals who must perform them. Interdependence centers on the process of giving and accepting benefits in a relationship. People in relationships give to each other the feeling and connections that they both desire. These connections may be verbal, emotional, physical, or intellectual, and often involve all of these (Goetschius & Tash, 1967). They are not individual interactions; rather, they are a form of communal life in which dialogue, practical discourse, and judgment are strongly embodied in everyday practices in the schoolhouse.

THE IMPORTANCE OF ESTABLISHING POSITIVE RELATIONSHIPS IN SCHOOLS

Upon entering the schoolhouse as lead learner, the school leader must facilitate the establishment of relationships between and among all constituents. In essence, effective leadership is tantamount to the existence of positive relationships, as they are essential in establishing and maintaining the foundation needed to acquire the desired outcomes of school programs and activities. Some theories informing the importance of building positive relationships appear in Table 7.1.

TABLE 7.1   Theories, Theorist(s), Definitions, and Implications for Leadership

Theories	Theorist(s)	Definitions	Implications for Leadership
Equity Theory	John Stacy Adams	Individuals expect to experience a fair balance between what they put into their job and what they receive for doing their job.	Leaders must be aware of the input that individuals contribute to a relationship, so as to provide adequate returns.
Expectancy Theory	Victor Vroom	In order for individuals to be motivated to complete a task, they must believe that they can complete the task to the specified standard of excellence, and the reward to be received must be valued by the individual.	En route to building effective interpersonal relationships, school leaders should develop an in-depth understanding of faculty members, make assignments giving consideration to their skills and attributes, and reward them based on what they value.
Power Theory	French	Leaders have four sources of power: position power, personality power, reward power, and expert power.	In building relationships, leaders should give strong consideration to using personality power as often as possible.
Situational Leadership	Hersey and Blanchard	In various situations, work performance will differ based on the leader's style, the maturity level of followers, and environmental factors.	Responsibilities (tasks) should be assigned to followers based on their readiness level and the situation: then, the school leader can use a leadership style that is appropriate for that situation.
Moral Leadership	Thomas Sergiovanni	Relationships are developed within an organization based on the values and beliefs of a leader.	School leaders must be prepared to address moral dilemmas as they occur. They should be servants, coaching, influencing, and empowering followers to participate in building learning communities.

Source: The content of this table was developed using material from Practicing the Art of Leadership: A Problem-Based Approach to Implementing the ISLLC Standards.

After positive relationships are established, school leaders must constantly inspect the stability of those relationships to ensure that there are no weak links. If, at any point, one of the relationships begins to weaken, the leader must quickly take action to reestablish that base of support. By continuously building, nurturing, and reinforcing positive relationships, the leader is able to maintain an efficient and effective organization.

TYPES OF RELATIONSHIPS NEEDED TO FOSTER GOAL ATTAINMENT

There are various types of relationships within a school community, and the quality of those relationships can enhance or hinder organizational effectiveness. These relationships can be professional, social, business, or personal, and they can exist in the internal or the external environment of the schoolhouse. Regardless of the type of relationships or where they exist, the school leader has to build bridges to goal attainment through them. There must be a bridge between the leadership of the school and the faculty; the school and the community; the building administration and central administration; the school and political constituents, and several other entities. Therefore, establishing and nurturing quality relationships must be one of the leader's top priorities. In the following section, we explore relationships in the internal and external environments of the schoolhouse that are likely to positively or negatively influence the teaching and learning process.

Internal School Relationships

In the internal environment of the schoolhouse, three important types of relationships must exist. They are principal/teacher relationships; teacher/teacher relationships, and teacher/student relationships. The importance of each of these relationships is discussed in the following section.

PRINCIPAL/TEACHER RELATIONSHIPS   A critical element of effective leadership is the relationship that exists between school leaders and members of their faculty. According to R. Barth (1990), the most important relationship in the schoolhouse is the relationship that exists between the principal and teachers. To enhance the academic achievement of all students, the school leadership and the faculty must work together, striving to gain an understanding of the needs of every student and identifying research-based programs that will address those needs. For this relationship to be effective, teachers have to perceive that their leader is competent, honest, committed, possesses integrity, and will lead using processes that are fair, affording dignity and respect to all followers.

To determine the extent of the relationship that exists between school leaders and members of their faculty, we developed the Leadership Behavior Inventory for Principals. This inventory is based on the 13 core competencies listed in Chapter 1. The assumption tested by the inventory

Standard 5

An education leader promotes the success of every student by acting with integrity, fairness, and in an ethical manner.

Functions
  a. Ensure a system of accountability for every student's academic and social success
  b. Model principles of self-awareness, reflective practice, transparency, and ethical behavior
  c. Safeguard the values of democracy, equity, and diversity
  d. Consider and evaluate the potential moral and legal consequences of decision making
  e. Promote social justice and ensure that individual student needs inform all aspects of schooling

is that school leaders who successfully display behavior informed by the 13 competencies will experience positive relationships with members of their faculty. The inventory was administered to one thousand ninety-three (1,093) teachers in elementary, middle, and high schools to measure teachers' perceptions of the behavior of their principals. The results revealed that teachers in each of the schools in the study perceived that their principal exhibited behaviors informed by the 13 core competencies to varying degrees. The Purdue Teacher Opinionaire was also administered to the same one thousand ninety-three (1,093) teachers to measure their expressed job satisfaction with their work assignments. The results of a comparative analysis of data from both instruments revealed that the greater teacher perception regarding the behavior of his/her principal as informed by the 13 core leadership competencies, the greater was their expressed satisfaction with their working environment (Ivy, 2007). Thus, we concluded that the quality of the relationships between principals and teachers makes a difference in the job satisfaction of teachers.

TEACHER/TEACHER RELATIONSHIPS   Another set of relationships that is important to school effectiveness is the relationship that exists between teachers. The interdependent nature of their work assignments requires a level of interpersonal relations that must exist if they are to complete tasks in an effective manner. The connecting factor is the attainment of a common vision. Therefore, their relationship should be professional, collegial, and collaborative.

Teachers have to care enough about their students to build the kind of relationships with each other that foster approaches that meet student needs. For a number of reasons, those types of relationships are not developed. Among those reasons is a lack of trust, caring, and support. A lack of trust breaks the close relationship between teachers and hinders their effectiveness. In such instances, school leaders must intervene and assist teachers in building trust and making a connection. Often, faculty members build positive relationships working on projects. For example, a negative relationship might exist between a veteran teacher and her new colleague fresh out of the local university. The factor that fosters this negative relationship is a difference in point of view regarding the teaching and learning process. Each has had experiences that cause them to have different expectations for the process of teaching and learning. With the appropriate intervention from the school leadership, establishing norms of behavior and working together, the level of trust between the teachers may change.

TEACHER/STUDENT RELATIONSHIPS A third type of relationship that must exist in the schoolhouse is the relationship between teachers and students. This relationship should be professional and ethical, as the nature of the relationship can make a difference in teaching and learning (Salzberger-Wittenberg et al., 1983). In schools, a fundamental source of learning is the ability to develop good and satisfying interpersonal relationships. In particular, the quality of the relationship deeply influences the hope that is required for students to remain curious and open to new experiences. It can also affect their capacity to see connections and discover meanings (Salzberger-Wittenberg et al. 1983).

Assessing Teacher/Student Relationships Three instruments that have proven to be very effective in assessing the relationship between teachers and students are the Nurturing School Inventory for Teachers; The Nurturing School Inventory for Students, and The My Voice Student Aspiration Survey.

The Nurturing School Inventory consists of thirteen (13) characteristics that cluster into four themes: (1) student-teacher relationships; (2) professionalism among administration, faculty, and staff; (3) environment of the school and classroom, and (4) students' feelings about themselves. The Nurturing School Inventory for Teachers measures the teachers' perceptions of students on these four themes. The Nurturing School Inventory for Students measures the students' perceptions of their school life on three of the aforementioned themes: (1) student-teacher relationship; (2) environment of the school and classroom, and (3) students' feelings about themselves. The results of these inventories have proven to be quite useful for school leaders, as they attempt to determine the extent to which teachers and students perceive the aforementioned characteristics to be important in their school life, as well as the extent to which they are perceived to exist in their school.

The *My Voice Student Aspiration Survey* assesses student aspirations relative to eight conditions that make a difference in the school life of students. The eight conditions are belonging; heroes; sense of accomplishments; fun and excitement; curiosity and creativity; spirit of adventure; leadership and responsibility, and confidence to take action.

Student scores on these eight scales allow school leaders to acquire a picture of how students feel about their school life. Specifically, it provides school leaders with a tool to acquire an understanding of what motivates and inspires students to achieve and how well students believe those objectives are being met by their school (Quaglia Institute for Student Aspirations).

When used effectively, these instruments provide school leaders with an empathetic understanding of how teachers feel about students and how students feel about themselves and their school environment. An empathetic understanding will aid school leaders in developing solid interpersonal relations between teachers and students. This is important, as empathetic understanding establishes a climate for self-initiated experiential learning (Rogers, 1967). The benefit derived is teachers having a sensitive awareness of the way students view the process of teaching and learning. Additionally, students feel deeply appreciated when they are simply understood—not evaluated, not judged, rather, just simply understood from their own point of view, not the teacher's point of view (Rogers, 1967).

Establishing Relationships in the External Environment of the Schoolhouse

In addition to building relationships with individuals in the internal environment of the schoolhouse, relationships must be built with the external public. In order for the school leader to bridge the gap between current conditions of the school and the vision, relationships must be established with parents, central office administrators, business leaders, and political elements in the community.

RELATIONSHIPS WITH CENTRAL OFFICE ADMINISTRATION Establishing relationships with central office administrators is a critical bridge between the school and an essential entity in the external environment of the school. For it is through relationships with central office administrators that school leaders position themselves to obtain the necessary approvals, support, and resources to move the school forward.

Through our work with school districts in West Tennessee, we have found that many of the challenges faced by school leaders occur because of a disconnect between school leadership teams and district level administrators. To assess the extent of this disconnect and its effect on schools, we developed the *Leadership Behavior Inventory for Central Office Administrators*. The same 13 core competencies used to comprise the *Leadership Behavior Inventory for Principals* were used to comprise the *Leadership Behavior Inventory for Central Office Administrators*. The results from the administration of this in-

Standard 4

An education leader promotes the success of every student by collaborating with faculty and community members, responding to diverse community interests and needs, and mobilizing community resources.

Functions
a. Collect and analyze data and information pertinent to the educational environment
b. Promote understanding, appreciation, and use of the community's diverse cultural, social, and intellectual resources
c. Build and sustain positive relationships with families and caregivers
d. Build and sustain productive relationships with community partners

ventory revealed that the major causes of the disconnect between central office administrators and school-based personnel are the lack of visits to schools by central administrators, lack of exposure to and understanding of everyday school practices, lack of autonomy of school principals, and no input sought by central office administrators from school-based leadership teams. In essence, the disconnect is caused by a lack of a deep understanding on behalf of central office administrators regarding what is occurring in schools on a day-to-day basis. When the two groups of administrators came together and participated in a series of seminars designed to foster a deep understanding of the work of each group, the disconnect dissipated, and positive working relationships were developed.

RELATIONSHIPS WITH THE LARGER COMMUNITY The school leader has to establish relationships with every facet of the community, as every facet is important and can contribute, in one way or another, to the success of the school. Therefore, the leader has to understand the culture of the school community, become knowledgeable of policies, rules and regulations, and be politically astute. He/she must know when to aggressively pursue an issue and when it is necessary to pull back, regroup, reassess, and challenge the issue from a different perspective.

School leaders who have positive relationships with community stakeholders do not acquire those relationships accidentally, nor are they guaranteed to last once they have been established. Furthermore, school leaders have to engage in strategic planning, implement the outcome of the planning process, and facilitate a sustained effort to foster the success of those plans (Hooper, 2001).

The community feels a part of the educational process when the school leader and individuals inside of the schoolhouse communicate with them and participate in community activities. This type of involvement demonstrates a sense of caring to parents, community organizations,

Standard 6

An education leader promotes the success of every student by understanding, responding to, and influencing the political, social, economic, legal, and cultural context.

Functions

  a. Advocate for children, families, and caregivers

  b. Act to influence local, district, state, and national decisions affecting student learning

  c. Assess, analyze, and anticipate emerging trends and initiatives in order to adapt leadership strategies

and business leaders and provides them with an opportunity to see the progress the school is making. It also gives them insight into the many needs of the school and how community resources might be used to foster school goal attainment. When the community has a clear picture of the school—the commitment of the faculty, the progress of students, and the work ethic that drives efforts- they are generally more than willing to lend a helping hand. Consequently, school leaders should work cooperatively with their faculty and staff to develop a strategic plan that fosters positive school-community relationships.

After the relationships have been established, the leader has to nurture the relationships, as the leading cause of alliance failure is the inability of leaders to manage relationships (Linden, 2003). Leaders can nurture relationships with followers by focusing on being considerate, communicating openly, and respecting individual differences. In addition, they must recognize the expertise of individuals, invite their participation into the decision-making process, and celebrate their successes (House, 1971).

APPROACHES TO BUILDING EFFECTIVE SCHOOL RELATIONSHIPS

Quite clearly, healthy relationships between school leaders and their constituents contribute greatly to the success of school leaders and organizational effectiveness, most specifically, the academic success of all students. Therefore, a discussion on how to develop and maintain positive and lasting relationships should prove extremely beneficial.

Some school leaders possess skills and attributes that exude a certain "magnetic chemistry" that invites individuals to bond with them with little or no effort. For others, bonding with individuals takes considerable effort. However, the effort is worthwhile and quite beneficial, as it contributes greatly to bridging the gap between the existing conditions of the school and the vision that everyone involved is attempting to achieve.

An extensive review of the literature reveals several approaches that school leaders might utilize to establish effective and lasting relationships (Ciancutti & Steding, 2001; Covey, 1989; Gladwell, 2002; Maeroff, 1993; Maxwell, 2003; Miler, 2005; Sieler, 1998). Of those reviewed, the following five approaches seem to be extremely important for developing relationships in schools: (1) establishing trust; (2) fostering effective communication; (3) encouraging commitment; (4) fostering collaboration, and (5) reaching closure on organizational issues. School leaders who incorporate these five approaches into their leadership behavior have established and sustained effective relationships with their stakeholders (see Exhibit 7.1).

ESTABLISHING TRUST: A FOUNDATION FOR RELATIONSHIPS In order to establish healthy relationships, school leaders must first lay a foundation upon which relationships can be developed: Trust is that foundation (Ciancutti & Steding, 2001). Individuals in schools engage in relationships by choice and when there is a level of trust, they engage in those relationships willingly, conducting themselves openly while participating in a wide array of activities (Sieler, 1998).

Because of the interdependent nature of work in schools, individuals need the assistance of others. In fact, the quality of the outcome produced by one individual is often dependent on the type of assistance they receive from other individuals. The level of trust determines how individuals relate to one another, and the greater the risk to the individuals who are interacting, the greater the need for trust. Consequently, trust becomes an important element in developing relationships, and trusting relationships are enhanced in the schoolhouse when individuals feel valued, respected, and appreciated for the contributions they make to organizational goal attainment (Sieler, 1998). Conversely, when there is a lack of trust, there is a lack of confidence in the

EXHIBIT 7.1 Approaches for Building Effective School Relationships

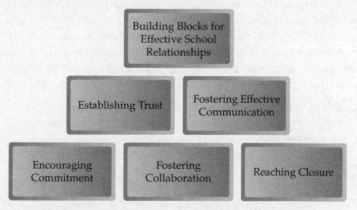

Source: This exhibit was designed and developed by Dr. Sharen Cypress.

action of individuals, and the interaction between them is limited (Covey, 1989; Sieler, 1998). Therefore, reliability is a critical element in the trust building process.

Reliability: A Trust Building Element A trustworthy school leader is reliable, fostering a sense of security, support, care, and acceptance between and among all faculty members. In schools, individuals seek and acquire information from one another and openly discuss successes and failures to learn from each other. For that reason, making and keeping agreements become important. The faculty and staff have to believe that individuals with whom they work are dependable and will do what they say they will do when they say they will do it. Thus, school leaders have the responsibility to point out to all stakeholders the need to be reliable. They have to create a trust-based culture wherein they convey to all stakeholders that they will be fair in their actions. Then, they have to foster the same behavior among others. As a result, trust becomes the foundation upon which relationships are built and the glue that holds individuals together in relationships. Having established a trust-based culture, the stage is set for the school leader to acquire effective relationships with and among all stakeholders.

FOSTERING EFFECTIVE COMMUNICATION A second approach to building relationships is through effective communication (Brickman, 2002). When an effective system of communication is in place, the entire climate of the school is positively affected (Halawah, 2004). What is said, how it is said, how it is perceived, and its underlying meaning contribute or detract from relationships. Therefore, school leaders must consider both verbal and non-verbal communication cues, as the most effective communication occurs when school leaders remove the surprise factor, and there is synergy, which is created through verbal and non-verbal messages (Miler, 2005). Two proven practices school leaders can use to enhance effective communication in relationships are removing the surprise factor and establishing rapport.

Removing the Surprise Factor School leaders can remove the surprise factor by becoming active listeners, acquiring feedback, displaying empathy, and bringing ethics to conversations held with and among stakeholders (Green, 2005). When these qualities are embedded in conversations, positive relationships are enhanced, as individuals listen to one another without making judgments. Conversations are governed by reason, and participants are willing to provide evidence for their position and yield to the better argument (Grant, 1996).

Establishing Rapport Another positive aspect of effective communication is the establishment of rapport. Individuals establish rapport by developing an in-depth understanding of others, being cognizant of their viewpoints, feelings, and styles of communication (Greenberg & Baron, 2003). To build rapport, school leaders have to take a personal interest in individuals who make up the faculty and staff and demonstrate that their opinions are valued. Through this process, individuals develop an in-depth understanding of one another (Greenberg & Baron, 2003).

Conversely, when a system of effective communication is not in place, rapport is not likely to be established, and situations that adversely affect the entire faculty are likely to occur. Serious disconnect will occur, as individuals will lose trust in one another and will not collaborate and empower each other. Because of lost trust, the organization stands to lose opportunities to use information and/or resources. For that reason, school leaders have to have a systematic communication process in place, and that process must be shared through a well-planned professional development program on effective communication. Using clear, concise communication strategies, school leaders can foster and sustain positive relationships.

Encouraging Commitment

Providing support to faculty and staff, considering their ideas, and assisting them in achieving their personal goals are approaches that school leaders can use to encourage faculty and staff to commit to organizational goal attainment. What is significant relative to encouraging and gaining commitment is giving consideration to everyone's opinions and ideas, which fosters a sense of belonging.

Commitment signals positive interpersonal relationships, which forms a bridge between the leadership of the school, the faculty, and other stakeholders. It is a reciprocal process; relationships exist as a result of support, encouragement, and engagement of stakeholders by the leadership of the school. Positive relationships foster commitment; the more school leaders support and encourage faculty, staff, and other stakeholders, the greater the possibility that they will have commitment to school goal attainment.

In encouraging commitment, school leaders are pursuing a connection with and between others, and a supportive attitude plays a critical role in that process. Through their behavior, school leaders display their thoughts, feelings, moods, and expectations. It is through their behavior that they gain the respect of stakeholders. Having conducted team-building workshops in over a hundred schools, we have observed that the value that surfaces most often among faculty and staff is respect. Stakeholders want to be respected and are willing to give respect in return. Respect is a critical factor relative to school leaders making the desired connection with stakeholders and gaining their commitment.

Individuals may be respected for their knowledge, position, disposition, leadership style, or for any number of other factors. Regardless of the reason, when individuals develop respect for one another, they work collaboratively to find solutions to organizational challenges (Heap, 2001). Therefore, it is beneficial for school leaders to examine their attitude towards others, as one's attitude toward others will determine the manner in which they behave and the type of relationship they develop (Urban, 2003). The leader's role is to take the necessary actions to create the type of climate wherein all individuals develop a caring attitude, one that encourages stakeholders to commit, not only to the school organization, but also to respecting the needs and feelings of others.

Fostering Collaboration

A fourth approach to building relationships in schools is through the establishment of collaborative teams. It is a widely advocated practice that many school leaders use to respond to faculty and student needs as they distribute leadership throughout the school organization (Bauer & Lange, 1993; Liontos, 1994). It is a powerful tool, as through the process, faculty members have freedom and flexibility and are provided an opportunity to exercise their expertise by participating in decision making, sharing responsibility, and assuming accountability for goal attainment (Bennis & Nanus, 1985).

To initiate the process in effective 21st-century schools, school leaders conduct inquiry into the strengths and values of individuals and use that information to establish collaborative teams and form work groups. These school-based decision-making teams consist of teachers, parents, and other stakeholders who are instrumental in day-to-day school operations.

Social interaction and the involvement of people depend on what individuals bring to the situation. Again, it is important for school leaders to understand faculty members and become knowledgeable of the skills and attributes that they bring to the faculty. According to Gladwell (2002), school leaders can select individuals with at least three distinct skills. These individuals fall into three categories: connectors, mavens, and salesmen. He refers to connectors as individuals who know a large number of people in a variety of settings. They have a unique personality, are self-confident, have energy, are sociable, and have the capability of bringing together many different groups of people. Mavens are individuals who accumulate knowledge. They are passionate about figuring things out and passing that information on to others. The third group called salesmen are individuals who have mastered the art of persuasion and have a tremendous ability to influence other individuals (Gladwell, 2002).

The success of activities in the schoolhouse is largely attributed to the nature of the relationships between and among individuals (Woodbury, 2005). If school leaders can identify individuals on the faculty who fall into the three previously mentioned categories, they can use their skills and attributes to foster the type of collaboration needed for organizational goal attainment. When individuals do not feel that their relationship with the leader or other faculty members is positive, they tend to act in an independent manner, and the work requiring collaboration is not completed in an effective manner. Consequently, rather than allowing individuals to develop a negative attitude, school leaders have to build bridges to problem solutions through the establishment of positive and effective relationships. As relationships develop, new experiences are acquired, and resolutions to old conflicts are achieved. When faculty members engage in positive relationships, they grow as individuals, become socially responsible and willing to share responsibility for goal attainment (Flora, 1994). They will see that relationships are decisive in determining how well they can adjust to the daily stresses of school life and will appreciate how conflict can be resolved using a variety of methods (Wheeler, 1994).

Some Negative Aspects of Collaboration. Along with the many positive aspects of collaboration, which can be extremely advantageous to school leaders, there are some impediments, as some relationships can have a negative effect on school goal attainment. Negative relationships are fostered by a lack of trust and a culture wherein individuals cast blame and fail to assume responsibility for their behaviors, which can cause conflict (Gore, 2002).

Conflict in schools is a natural occurrence and can contribute to or hinder goal attainment. When individuals express different opinions, thoughts, or ideas without fear of reprisal, conflict becomes a contributor to goal attainment. However, when individuals resort to actions that negatively affect the relationship between individuals and among groups, conflict hinders goal attainment (Wheeler, 1994).

In order for the process of collaboration to work effectively, individuals have to believe that collaborating to achieve a common vision is more effective than working individually (Katzenbach & Smith, 1993). Relationships between and among individuals have to be assessed; all participants have to be comfortable as team members and display a win-win attitude. Most importantly, the process must ensure that every voice is heard and valued, and that competition is minimized.

REACHING CLOSURE ON ORGANIZATIONAL ISSUES The fifth approach to building and sustaining effective relationships is closure. Ciancutti and Steding (2001) define closure as ending an interaction with a promise. They offer that every interaction should end with a promise of, "Who will do what? And when?" In reaching closure, school leaders create a climate wherein individuals can avoid the ambiguity of not knowing what activities will be completed by whom. For example, a principal might say to the faculty, "I will deliver the English books to the English faculty by Thursday at 2:00 P.M." With this statement, closure is reached as to when the English books will be delivered and by whom. Conversely, the school leader might state to a faculty, "I am working on the delivery of English textbooks." This statement leaves uncertainty in everyone's mind as to when the textbooks will be delivered.

Closure can be reached, regardless of whether the response is positive or negative. For example, a principal might say, "We are not going to be able to deliver English textbooks this year." Closure is reached; as a result, the English faculty members can invest their energy in developing lesson plans around existing materials, rather than delaying the development of plans waiting on new books.

Trust is at the core of closure, as it enhances the level of confidence that individuals have for each other and the consistency in which stated behavior becomes reality. This consistency enhances trust and strengthens relationships. However, as easy as reaching closure may seem, there are a number of roadblocks that prohibit individuals from reaching it. Ciancutti and Steding (2001) identified the following as possible roadblocks to reaching closure:

- Faculty members may have hidden agendas, either personal or departmental.
- Some members of the faculty may not be able or willing to tell the truth.
- There may be individuals who participate in gossip and talk behind peoples' backs.
- A competitive spirit might divide faculty members into groups of them vs. us.
- The downward flow of communication may be inadequate.
- Individuals may cast blame that results in interdepartmental conflicts.
- There may be a lack of commitment to vision attainment on the part of select individuals.
- The rude and demanding behaviors of some individuals create roadblocks.
- The tendency of some individuals to procrastinate is problematic.
- The desire on the part of some individuals to avoid conflict creates problems.
- Some individuals may be unwilling to admit that a problem exists.

In general, closure incorporates the previously mentioned four approaches that lead to effective relationships in schools, enhancing their quality and sustaining their existence. Once these approaches are operating simultaneously, the school organization is positioned to reap a number of benefits.

BENEFITS DERIVED FROM ESTABLISHING EFFECTIVE RELATIONSHIPS

There is sufficient evidence to substantiate what most educators believe to be true: Quality relationships contribute to leadership effectiveness in schools, and the benefits to be derived are many (Brewster & Railsback, 2003; Ciancutti & Steding, 2001; Collins, 2001; Green, 2005; Linden, 2003; Maxwell, 2003; Sergiovanni, 1992).

When quality relationships exist, there is a connection between school leaders and individuals and groups inside and outside of the schoolhouse, and this connection is necessary for school goal attainment. Building bridges through relationships, school leaders develop credibility, and once they acquire credibility, they can demonstrate a genuine interest in individuals and the desire to address the needs of all students. In addition, with credibility, the door is open for collaboration, and the greater the collaboration between school leaders and members of the school community, the greater the possibility for school goal attainment.

When positive and stable relationships exist between school leaders and the faculty, there is open communication, mutual respect and learning, real creativity, and genuine support for vision attainment. If individuals are engaged in positive relationships and perceive their positions to be equitable, they grow and become more socially responsible, tend to be more confident about the relationship, and work to maintain that relationship (Clark, 1988; Flora, 1994). Equally important, the leadership capacity of teachers can be developed and with the development of their leadership capacity, teachers feel that they own their work. As a result, they put forth their best efforts, as they feel empowered and are willing to take risks and try new ideas (Maeroff, 1993).

Another benefit derived from establishing effective relationships is the link school leaders can establish between the school and the community. Through positive external relationships, they can acquire and sustain external stakeholder commitment to the attainment of the vision of the school. Positive relationships with community stakeholders promote continuous growth and change through influence, rather than authority. As stakeholders in the community feel a part of the educational process, they are able to see the needs of the school and gain insight into how they can support vision attainment.

Relationships, whether impersonal or personal, negative or positive, essentially exist as a result of choices that are made by the individuals involved. More importantly, relationships cannot be forced. The critical factor for consideration by the school leader is not whether a faculty member decides to actively seek a relationship or to avoid creating a lasting foundation for growing one. The pivotal point is whether the decision will have a significant effect on how that person will interact with others socially or professionally.

To transform a school from one state to another, the school leader must bridge the gap between current conditions and the shared vision, and that bridge has to be built through relationships. Through the establishment of positive productive relationships with individuals in the internal and external environments of the schoolhouse, the journey to vision attainment can be considerably easier.

■ ■ ■

Implications for Leadership

- To provide effective leadership, school leaders must make a connection with individuals inside and outside of the schoolhouse.
- The tasks that individuals perform in schools are interdependent and should not be attempted in isolation.
- Schools function as a part of a larger system, and no part of a school is an entity in and of itself. Each part depends upon another part to sustain its existence.
- It is vital for a school leader to exhibit behavior that fosters a connection between and among individuals.
- Largely, it is the depth of the relationship that exists between and among individuals that contributes to their success in schools.
- The focus must be on the faculty as a body, individuals who make up the faculty, and the relationship that exists between and among them.

Reflective Practice

1. Describe the approach you would use to develop effective interpersonal relationships with members of a faculty.
2. What has been your experience with developing a trust-based culture?
3. Describe how you feel about sharing your leadership role with members of a leadership team.
4. How would you describe the characteristics of an effective relationship?
5. What are some reasons you might offer for building bridges to goal attainment through relationships?
6. Describe your most effective relationship and share the process you use to maintain its positive effects.

Chapter Essentials

Interstate School Leader Licensure Consortium Standards 4, 5, and 6

An education leader promotes the success of every student by collaborating with faculty and community members, responding to diverse community interests and needs, and mobilizing community resources.

An education leader promotes the success of every student by acting with integrity, fairness, and in an ethical manner.

An education leader promotes the success of every student by understanding, responding to, and influencing the political, social, economic, legal, and cultural context.

Principle

Building a solid support system—interpersonal relationships foster creativity and generative thinking; both assist school leaders in building a capacity to lead.

Dichotomy

Enabling Relationships or Hindering Relationships

School leaders must constantly seek to identify ways to establish and maintain relationships that enhance organizational goal attainment.

References

Barth, R. S. (1990). Improving schools from within: Teachers, principals can make the difference. San Francisco: Jossey-Bass.

Bennis, W., & Nanus, B. (1985). *Leaders: The strategies for taking charge*. New York: Harper & Row.

Brewster, C., & Railsback, J. (2003, September). *Building trusting relationships for school improvement: Implications for principals and teachers*. Retrieved September 25, 2006, from Web site http:www.nwrel.org/request2003sept/trust.pdf

Brickman, C. (2002, November). *Positive parent contact logs: An invaluable addition*. Retrieved from Web site: http://teacher.net/gazette

Ciancutti, A. & Steding, T. (2001). *Built on trust: Gaining competitive advantage in an organization*. Chicago: Contemporary Books.

Clark, M., & Reis, H. (1988). *Interpersonal processes in close relationships*. Annual Review Inc. Retrieved September 23, 2006, from Web site: http://web.ebschost.com. ezproxy.uu.edu:2048

Collins, J. (2001). *Good to Great: Why some companies make the leap . . . and others don't*. New York: Harper Collins.

Covey, S. (1989). *The 7 habits of highly effective people*. New York: Simon & Schuster.

Flora, C. (1998). *Community building for a healthy ecosystem*. ERIC Clearinghouse on elementary and early childhood education. Retrieved September 25, 2006 from Web site: http://www.eric.ed.gov

Gladwell, M. (2002). *The tipping point: How little things can make a difference*. Boston, MA: Little Brown and Company.

Gore, W. G. (2002). *Navigating change: A field guide to personal growth*. Memphis, TN: Team Trek.

Grant, R. (1996). The ethics of talk: Classroom conversations and democratic politics, fearless cause. *Teacher College Record, 97*(3), 470–482.

Green, R. L. (2005). *Practicing the Art of Leadership*. Upper Saddle River, NJ: Pearson Education, Inc.

Greenberg, J., & Baron, R. (2003). *Behavior in organizations*. Upper Saddle River, NJ: Prentice Hall.

Halawah, I. (2004). The relationship between effective communication of high school principals and school climate. *Education, 126*.

Heap, N. (2001). Building effective relationships that work. *Training Journal, 45*(2), 16–20.

House, R. (1971). A path-goal theory of leader effectiveness. *Administrative Science Quarterly, 16*, 331–333.

Interstate School Leader Licensure Consortium (ISLLC). (1996). *Standards for school leaders*. Washington, D.C.: Council of Chief School Officers.

Ivy, S. (2007). *School leaders' behavior informed by thirteen core leadership competencies and the relation to teacher job satisfaction*. (Unpublished Dissertation). Memphis, TN: University of Memphis.

Katzenback, J. R., & Smith, D. K. (1995). *The wisdom of teams: Creating the high performance organization*. Boston: Harvard Business School Press.

Liontos, L. (1994). Shared decision making. *Eric Digest, 87*.

Linden, R. (2003). The discipline of collaboration. [Electronic Version] *Leader to Leader, 29*, 41–47.

Maeroff, G. I. (1993). *Team building for school change: Equipping teachers for new roles*. New York: Teachers College Press.

Maxwell, J. C. (2003). *Relationships 101: What every leader needs to know.* Nashville, TN: Thomas Nelson, Inc.

Miller, P. (2005). Body language in the classroom. *Techniques: Connecting Education and Careers, 80*(8), 28–30.

My Voice Student Survey. (2008). Quaglia Institute for Student Aspirations. Portland, ME.

Perlman, H. H. (1979). *Relationship. The heart of helping people.* Chicago: University of Chicago Press.

Salzberger-Wittenberg, I., Henry, G., & Osborne, E. (1983). *The Emotional Experience of Learning and Teaching,* London: Routledge and Kegan Paul.

Sergiovanni, T. (1992). *Moral leadership: getting to the heart of school improvement. San Francisco: Jossey-Bass.*

Sieler, A. (1998). *Trust and relationships.* Newfield, Australia: Pty. Ltd.

Urban, H. (2003). *Life's greatest lessons: 20 things that matter.* New York: Fireside.

Woodbury, L. (2005). *Relationships.* Retrieved September 24, 2006 from Web site: http://www.strugglingteens.com

Wheeler, E. (1994). *Peer conflict in the classroom.* ERIC Clearinghouse on elementary and early childhood education. Retrieved September 25, 2006 from Web site: http://www.eric.ed.gov

PART FIVE

Dimension 4
Engaging in Leadership Best Practices

Change	Decision Making
Conflict Management	Change

DIMENSIONAL CONCEPTS

Effective school leaders identify and utilize best practices to transform school organizations from one level to another. Through this dimension, the power of effective communication is illustrated, as well as the essence of quality decision making. The benefits derived by school leaders from using data to identify strategies for use in managing conflict and making organizational change are also discussed. Throughout Chapter 8, the 13 core competencies and ISLLC Standards validate school leaders' use of best practices as they relate to the areas of communication, decision making, conflict management, and change. In Chapter 9, we present a model for instructional improvement, putting into practice the concepts discussed in the previous chapters of the text. The presentation illustrates how school leaders can develop and implement a school improvement plan that addresses the needs of all students.

Utilizing Leadership Practices for Educational Renewal

(Standards 1 through 6)

"The new model of school reform must seek to develop communities of learning grounded in communities of democratic discourse."

LINDA DARLING-HAMMOND

"How humans learn and how they can best be taught are subjects of great importance and profound complexity."

JOHN GOODLAD

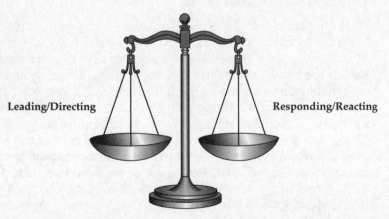

Leading/Directing   Responding/Reacting

INTRODUCTION

Of the four dimensions presented in this text, utilizing best practices is fast becoming one of the major topics of conversation. It is a powerful tool used by 21st-century school leaders to guide them through the myriad of challenges they face in addressing the needs of all students. Leaders of highly effective schools are confident, and they acquire much of that confidence because of their knowledge of best practices. Not only do they have knowledge of best practices, they are astute in identifying situations that are appropriate for their use. There is no one best way to educate all children. However, there are proven practices that have worked effectively in select school situations. If school leaders become astute in identifying them, they can pursue their vision of educational excellence, using practices that have proven to be successful in transforming a school or school district from one state to another.

Our goal, in this chapter, is to investigate leadership best practices and present examples of how 21st-century school leaders might use them to implement change, make decisions, communicate with stakeholders, and manage conflict. In an earlier work, *Practicing the Art of Leadership: A Problem-Based Approach to Implementing the ISLLC Standards (3rd ed.)*, we illustrated how leaders lead by acquiring knowledge of theories that underpin these leadership practices. In this chapter, those practices are aligned with 13 core competencies that leaders must master in order to effectively implement them.

The underlying tenet of the chapter is that in order for school leaders to effectively promote the success of all students, they must exhibit behaviors informed by the 13 core competencies outlined in Chapter 1. Additionally, they must have knowledge and understanding of best practices advocated for use by 21st-century school leaders. Once they master the competencies and become knowledgeable of related best practices, they will be able to meet the challenge of transforming schools or school districts from one state to another.

UNDERSTANDING BEST PRACTICES

Leadership best practices consist of programs, activities, or behaviors that are research-based and have proven to generate specific outcomes in a variety of settings. They are supported by longitudinal data and when implemented as designed, the results produced are consistent. Therefore, we offer that practices most appropriate for use in addressing challenges in 21st-century schools are those that fit into this category.

Identifying Best Practices

Three approaches were utilized to identify the best practices described in this chapter. We conducted an extensive literature review and consulted with more than sixty (60) principals who have completed *Center for Urban School* leadership programs at the University of Memphis and received principal or other leadership assignments in various school districts. Many of the

EXHIBIT 8.1   Competencies Informing Leader Behavior

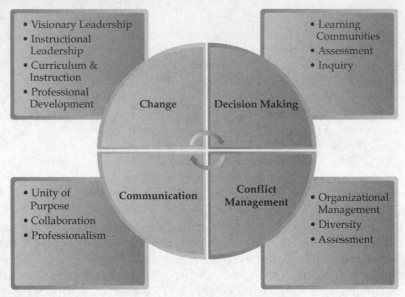

- Visionary Leadership
- Instructional Leadership
- Curriculum & Instruction
- Professional Development

Change

Decision Making

- Learning Communities
- Assessment
- Inquiry

- Unity of Purpose
- Collaboration
- Professionalism

Communication

Conflict Management

- Organizational Management
- Diversity
- Assessment

individuals receiving principal assignments were appointed principal of a low-performing school and have used these practices to successfully transform those schools. In addition, our work in school districts in state corrective action status revealed evidence regarding the effectiveness of these practices. Our work in these three areas suggests that the areas of most impact in school leadership are: (1) developing unity of purpose around a shared vision; (2) engaging stakeholders in shared decision making through collaboration; (3) developing instructional leaders through focused professional development; (4) using data to inform curriculum and instructional decisions; (5) assessing teachers' and students' needs, and (6) facilitating the development of a professional learning community (Green, 2009; Leithwood & Jantzi, 2005; Walters, Marzano, & McNulty, 2003). See Exhibit 8.1.

Best practices, in each of the aforementioned areas, relate directly to one of the 13 core competencies discussed in Chapter 1. Therefore, we discuss best practices in conjunction with a competency. The complex nature of leading a 21st-century school requires mastery of all 13 core competencies and possibly a number of others. For that reason, we discuss best practices as they relate to each of the 13 core competencies.

THE THIRTEEN CORE COMPETENCIES AND RELATED BEST PRACTICES

To transform a school or school district from one state to another, school leaders must be able to examine ideas, concepts, and practices that best fit the culture, climate, and readiness level of their respective school organization. Skills to perform these tasks can be acquired through mastery of the 13 core competencies. Having mastered the competencies, school leaders are positioned to identify and remove roadblocks to school goal attainment.

Visionary Leadership

Visionary leaders have a mental picture of what they want the school organization to become; they influence the faculty and other stakeholders to share that vision. They are generative thinkers who model a standard of behavior that conveys to stakeholders that they know where the school should go and have the knowledge and skills to take it to that place.

The ultimate responsibility of school leaders is to enhance the academic achievement of all students who enter the schoolhouse door. In fulfilling that responsibility, visionary school leaders collaborate with stakeholders to develop a plan for the future of the school with the goal of meeting the needs of all students. Additionally, they communicate that plan to others in a manner that captures their attention and secures their trust to the point that they become committed to providing both human and material resources for implementation of the vision.

Visionary leaders collect and utilize data to develop unity of purpose and foster that purpose through a system of effective communication. They relate to other individuals, providing guidance, encouragement, and support. Some of the practices used by central office administrators and principals interviewed and observed are listed below.

1. *Establish Advisory Teams*—They establish parent advisory teams and host a dinner meeting for the team once a month; occasionally, all parents are invited. During these monthly meetings, the teams foster school goal attainment.
2. *Monday Memo*—Each Monday of the school year, they send out a memo to all faculty members. Through the Monday memo, they distribute the calendar for the week, outline activities, review goals, convey

Standard 1

An education leader promotes the success of every student by facilitating the development, articulation, implementation, and stewardship of a vision of learning that is shared and supported by all stakeholders.

Functions
  a. Collaboratively develop and implement a shared vision and mission
  b. Collect and use data to identify goals, assess organizational effectiveness, and promote organizational learning
  c. Create and implement plans to achieve goals
  d. Promote continuous and sustainable improvement
  e. Monitor and evaluate progress and revise plans

expectations, and offer tips for the involvement of individuals inside and outside of the schoolhouse.

3. *Outreach*—A faculty member or community stakeholder is identified as a spokesperson for the school, and that person speaks at local community group meetings, updating the community on school-related issues.

4. *Parents' Place*—They provide a place in the schoolhouse for parents and community stakeholders and ensure that the main entrance to the building is welcoming. They also provide a lounge area for seating and a convenient place for parents to park.

5. *Morning Walkthroughs*—Each morning before the opening bell, they become highly visible by walking through the school, stopping to speak to teachers who are preparing for the day, welcoming individuals who have been absent, and addressing various concerns that may surface. Through this practice, they build relationships and gain trust, as they show genuine concern for faculty and staff members. In addition, interruptions during the day are decreased because faculty members anticipate the morning visits and utilize that time to address concerns when no students are present.

6. *School/Business Partnerships*—They contact business leaders in the community and offer to provide them services, in addition to soliciting their services. Having a detailed plan of what the school can offer and what the school would like to receive is important to vision attainment.

7. *The Parent Link*—They establish an online link that allows parents access to their children's grades, attendance records, transcripts, and other student information.

8. *Key Communicators*—They identify individuals throughout the community and provide them with important information regarding school events, as well as information regarding unexpected occurrences. All individuals in the community know who the key communicators are, and school/community relations are fostered through them.

Visionary leadership is fundamental to organizational change, as it incorporates an assessment of current conditions and a desired educational outcome that meets the needs of all students. Processes, procedures, and methodology that can be used to effectively move the school or school district from its current condition to a desired outcome are also incorporated.

Establishing Professional Learning Communities

There is a growing body of literature suggesting that school leaders have a greater chance of meeting the challenges they face if they are functioning in a professional learning community where the primary focus is on curriculum and instruction, and there is a built-in culture of collaboration (Burden, 2003; Leithwood, Seashore-Louis, Maxwell, 2003; Ormrod, 2003). In a professional learning community, the focus is on curriculum and instruction; there is an air of professionalism among all teachers as they participate on effective learning teams and share basic norms and values relative to students, as well as teaching and learning. They participate in reflective dialogue about instructional challenges and work cooperatively to identify teaching strategies that positively address them. This type of interaction fosters collaboration across grade levels and among departmental groups, generating data that inform revisions that need to be made in the instructional program.

Effective 21st-century school leaders can be confident that creating learning teams in a professional learning community increases student achievement (DuFour, DuFour, Eaker, & Many, 2006). Some benefits derived from creating professional learning communities are:

1. a warm, safe, and nurturing school environment wherein students are engaged in the instructional process;
2. a climate of trust wherein teachers feel comfortable in collaborating with one another;
3. a climate wherein individual differences are respected;
4. advocacy of inclusive decision-making processes;
5. encouragement of teachers to become self-directive;
6. flexibility for teachers to be experimental, innovative, and creative, and
7. empowerment of students to become actively involved in their education (DuFour, DuFour, Eaker, & Many, 2006).

Another important reason for creating a professional learning community is the focus it provides for teachers. In this type of environment, teachers have the opportunity to focus on renewing their skills, enhancing their content knowledge, and expanding their areas of expertise. In essence, teachers increase their knowledge of the instructional process, and the more teachers know about the instructional process, the more effective they become in addressing student needs. School leaders must create a professional learning community and exhibit behaviors informed by standards of excellence. It is also imperative that they develop a quality faculty committed to teaching and learning and place them in the correct assignment. This lays the foundation for their becoming instructional leaders who facilitate the academic achievement of all students.

Instructional Leadership—Teaching and Learning

In this period of standards-based accountability, instructional leadership has been elevated to the top of the school leader's agenda. There is heavy pressure for school leaders to be accountable for the development and implementation of the school's academic program, complete with practices that maximize student and adult learning. They are being asked to set high expectations for student performance, align content and instruction with standards, create a culture for learning, and use multiple sources of data to enhance student progress (National Association of Elementary School Principals, 2001).

Standard 2

An education leader promotes the success of every student by advocating, nurturing, and sustaining a school culture and instructional program conducive to student learning and staff professional growth.

Functions
   a. Nurture and sustain a culture of collaboration, trust, learning, and high expectations
   b. Create a comprehensive, rigorous, and coherent curricular program
   c. Create a personalized and motivating learning environment for students
   d. Supervise instruction
   e. Develop assessment and accountability systems to monitor student progress
   f. Develop the instructional and leadership capacity of staff
   g. Maximize time spent on quality instruction
   h. Promote the use of the most effective and appropriate technologies to support teaching and learning
   i. Monitor and evaluate the impact of the instructional program

In many instances, if not most, in order to meet these new standards and accountability measures, school leaders are required to engage in some type of change, and there are best practices that can be used in making that change. For example, as this text goes to press, a complete redesign initiative is underway in the state of Tennessee. The purpose of that initiative is to ensure that school leaders in the state are equipped to provide instructional leadership and lead change. Some of the best practices advocated by that change initiative are discussed in the following section.

Leading Change in 21st-Century Schools

To effectively lead change, the process of change must be conceptualized, and there must be a clear purpose for the change. The purpose might fall into one of two categories, first order change or second order change (Green, 2009; Meyer, Brooks, & Goes, 1990). With first order change, the existing teaching process is not substantially altered. No new strategies or techniques are employed, and the way teachers perform is not altered. Existing teaching practices are only modified in an effort to enhance their effectiveness (Conley, 1997).

The other category of change is second order change. With second order change, the underlying assumptions are challenged. There is a shift in values, beliefs, and practices of stakeholders, and a transformation occurs in the original program or activity. This type of change requires greater capacity and a deeper commitment from stakeholders (Conley, 1997).

Regardless of whether the change is first order or second order, stakeholders must understand that change is necessary and how it is aligned with the vision and purpose of the school. If they do not understand, they are not likely to commit to participating in the change process or assuming responsibility for the outcome of the change. Therefore, instructional leaders have to engage stakeholders in the process which includes providing them with evidence that the change initiative selected is the right one for the school, and that they will benefit from its implementation. Identifying appropriate practices in making the selection requires being knowledgeable of the change process and highly skilled in the implementation of that process. School leaders must also be able to conceptualize ideas and transform them into action steps that the school organization has the capability to implement.

Several agencies, including state departments of education, leadership preparation programs, school districts, and other organizations, have generated debate over competing perspectives relative to what school leaders need to know and be able to do to enhance their instructional programs. Based on our research and work with school leaders, we have designed a model entitled "A Proactive Model for Instructional Leadership." A number of school leaders report success using this model to make instructional change. The components of the model are listed in Exhibit 8.2.

This model recognizes the use of standards as the foundation for leading instructional improvement. The structure of the model aligns assessments with standards and establishes expectations for individuals receiving service, as well as individuals providing service. In addition, the model follows trends in educational leadership that advocate conducting assessments, establishing unity of purpose, and using data to inform instructional change. The components of the model are fully developed in Chapter 9. (See Exhibit 8.2).

In the type of learning community previously described, leading effective change requires interaction between the leader and elements in the environment of the school (DuFour, DuFour, Eaker, & Many, 2006). Instructional leadership is evolving quickly, and there are new theories and new approaches informing the way school leaders should attend to the academic needs of the students they serve. In Chapter 5 of the companion text, *Practicing the Art of Leadership: A Problem-Based Approach to Implementing the*

EXHIBIT 8.2   A Proactive Model for Instructional Leadership

> - Define Excellence for the School—the School Vision
> - Develop a Plan to Achieve Excellence
> - Create a System of Effective Communication Inside and Outside of the Schoolhouse
> - Create a Climate for Effective Teaching and Learning
> - Structure the School for Effective Teaching and Learning
> - Pool all Resources
> - Place Innovative Leadership in Every Facet of the School
> - Put a System of Assessment in Place
> - Generate Data That Informs Change in the Teaching and Learning Process

ISLLC Standards (3rd ed.), readers can review the change process and the theoretical framework that supports that process.

ASSESSMENT In this era of accountability for student achievement, instructional change needs to be data driven; the data informing change should speak to the vision, current conditions, and any discrepancies that lie between the vision and current conditions. To acquire this data, effective school leaders conduct assessments and identify the needs of students, as well as the strengths and weaknesses of teachers. Using the data collected, they make decisions to improve the teaching and learning process.

A best practice in this area that school leaders might find helpful is the creation of a comprehensive school-based instructional leadership team. The team consists of the principal, a professional school counselor, an instructional data coach, and the lead special education teacher. The responsibility of the team is to work with each faculty member to assist him/her in developing a deep understanding of student achievement data. When achievement test data are returned to the school, the team working with each teacher disaggregates the data to reflect the scores of individual students by subjects, grade levels, and skill sets. The data are further refined by grouping the results in subsets and categories, such as underachieving students, students who score above the established standard, socio-economic categories, boys, girls, and different race and ethnic groups. Once teachers develop a comprehensive understanding of the data, the team provides them assistance in identifying instructional strategies to use in enhancing the academic achievement of the students they serve.

UNITY OF PURPOSE Creating unity of purpose is one of the most important elements in the instructional process. If school leaders do not unify the faculty and staff around a purpose, raising student achievement can be extremely difficult. To acquire unity of purpose, school leaders must first develop an understanding of the needs, beliefs, and values of faculty members and other stakeholders. Then, they must collaborate with stakeholders to create a vision of the school that they can share. Collaboration is a critical element in the process of instructional improvement and will be discussed in some detail in the next section of this chapter. However, first, we continue our discussion of unity of purpose.

Unity of purpose requires school leaders to acquire the commitment of a faculty around a single focus and align their behavior with activities that foster goal attainment. One practice school leaders can utilize to acquire unity of purpose is *The Appreciative Inquiry Summit*, a methodology for positive change.

The Appreciative Inquiry Summit Using the principles and practices of *Appreciative Inquiry*, school leaders can build relationships and establish partnerships for conducting strategic planning that leads to system-wide positive change. The school leadership, all faculty members, and other stakeholders come together; representatives of the entire school are in the meeting. All stakeholders are provided an opportunity to gain an appreciation for the

Standard 6

An education leader promotes the success of every student by understanding, responding to, and influencing the political, social, economic, legal, and cultural context.

Functions
  a. Advocate for children, families, and caregivers
  b. Act to influence local, district, state, and national decisions affecting student learning
  c. Assess, analyze, and anticipate emerging trends and initiatives in order to adapt leadership strategies

needs of the school and to strategize on how to address those needs (Cooperrider & Whitney, 1999).

The summit occurs over a two to five-day period during which time participants engage in personal reflection, informal dialogue, and whole group synthesis. It is designed around four principles: *discovery, dream, design*, and *destiny*. During the discovery phase, participants focus on who makes up the organization; their core competencies; hopes and dreams for the future; the resources they bring to the table; the macro trend impacting the organization, and the ways that can be imagined going forward together.

The second phase is the dream phase. During this phase, participants engage in dialogues around the future of the organization ten (10) years or more hence. The dialogue might center around such questions as:

  • How do you see the organization ten years from now?
  • What is happening in the community?
  • How is the school different?
  • What do stakeholders need?

During phase three, the design phase, participants focus on constructing an organization in which positive change comes alive through strategies, processes, systems, decisions, and collaboration.

The final phase, referred to as the destiny phase, is the time when participants focus on what will be done. Individual participants are invited to foster personal and group initiatives and become self-organizing. The goal is to get the large group's commitment and support for those who choose to move forward, working on behalf of the whole group to attain goals that surfaced through the process (Cooperrider & Whitney, 1999).

From hosting an *Appreciative Inquiry Summit*, school leaders can anticipate enhanced trust, a group of individuals willing to focus on a purpose greater than their own, the elimination of false assumptions, the development of a sense of community among stakeholders, and greater collaboration for vision attainment (Cooperrider & Whitney, 1999).

Shared Decision-Making Another practice school leaders are using to establish unity of purpose is shared decision making. Some researchers view the premise of shared decision making as the more effective and efficient practice for use by 21st-century school leaders (Covey, 1991; Fullan, 2001; Maxwell, 2003). When school leaders effectively implement this practice, they increase commitment and enhance decision quality and acceptance (Covey, 1991; Green, 2005).

Ideally, school leaders should nurture the school environment to the extent that shared decision making becomes the norm. In such an environment, before decisions are made, individuals consider the nature of the decision—if the decision should be made by an individual or involve a group of individuals. Other factors to be given consideration are the degree of change influenced by the decision—first order or second order change and the effects of the change—the people directly affected by the change and those who will implement the change. Because of the importance of these best practices, we provide a brief discussion of each.

Autocratic vs. Democratic Decision Making Every day in an attempt to enhance teaching and learning, school leaders face the challenge of selecting best practices to use in making decisions. The critical factor they face is whether to make decisions autocratically or in a participatory manner. Using an autocratic style, leaders select the decision alternative without the involvement of others and assume full responsibility for the outcome. Conversely, when leaders use a participatory style of leadership, they invite followers to share their ideas and opinions and collaborate in the selection of the decision alternative. Determining the appropriate level of involvement, school leaders must take into account a number of factors, among which are the leader's level of expertise, time constraints on the decision, and the importance of having stakeholder support (Vroom, 1993). Regardless of the style of leadership utilized, decision quality and acceptance are major factors in decision effectiveness.

Utilizing Processes to Ensure Decision Quality When school leaders elect to make decisions using either approach, quality becomes a major factor. The difference between decisions of quality and non-quality is the degree of uncertainty that lies between selecting, from among alternatives, one that will achieve the desired outcome. The quality of the decision depends on the decision alternative selected, and selecting the best alternative depends on the quality of the data used in making the selection. Failure to have good data can prove detrimental to the quality of the decision. With good data, school leaders reduce the likelihood of choosing the wrong alternative and avoid having to address unanticipated consequences. To ensure quality decisions, school leaders will want to acquire the most accurate and appropriate data possible. In some instances, the leader will have the necessary data; in other instances, to acquire the necessary data, they will have to assemble various individuals and engage then in collaborative dialogue. The best practice is to involve individuals who have expertise in the area of the problem and are most knowledgeable of the situation or issue.

Utilizing Processes to Ensure Decision Acceptance To ensure decision acceptance, school leaders have to develop an understanding of people and come to realize what is important to them. This knowledge must become a part of the decision-making process. Best practice suggests that if a decision is in an individuals' zone of concern, then the leader should involve that individual in the decision-making process. A decision is in an individual's zone of concern when that individual will be affected by the decision or will have to participate in implementing the decision (Green, 2009). When school leaders make decisions with little or no involvement of faculty or stakeholders, contingent on the situation, acceptance can be problematic. People best understand a decision and are more likely to accept the consequences of a decision when they are involved in reaching that decision.

COLLABORATION   In today's schools, there is an underlying theme focusing on the need to build significant relationships. If this is true, collaboration is a best practice that must prevail. Through collaboration, school leaders can change traditional practices, shift the attention of stakeholders to goals that focus on student learning, and begin to build relationships that will open the door for new ways of working together to profoundly affect the achievement of students.

Individuals in effective 21st-century schools work in concert with each other to enhance student achievement. Even though they may have diverse interests, they share ideas, resources, and accountability for meeting the goals of the organization. Every member of the faculty assumes responsibility for the academic achievement of every student. More importantly, faculty members have regard for one another, trust one another, and respect each other's opinion.

The challenge for school leaders is creating a climate wherein faculty members develop collaborative relationships, as there are instances when individuals will prefer to work independently. In fact, they will find it beneficial to work alone. However, when tasks dictate that it is mutually beneficial for individuals to collaborate, school leaders will have to demonstrate the benefits of collaboration.

Standard 4

An education leader promotes the success of every student by collaborating with faculty and community members, responding to diverse community interests and needs, and mobilizing community resources.

Functions
 a. Collect and analyze data and information pertinent to the educational environment
 b. Promote understanding, appreciation, and use of the community's diverse cultural, social, and intellectual resources
 c. Build and sustain positive relationships with families and caregivers
 d. Build and sustain productive relationships with community partners

An assessment process that school leaders can use to identify student needs and the strengths and weaknesses of faculty has been described. This was followed by a process that can be used to establish unity of purpose and create a culture of collaboration; now, we proceed to a discussion of best practices for use in improving the school curriculum.

INQUIRY It is important for school leaders to examine current research to identify best practices to use in responding to specific instructional situations. Conducting inquiry is a way to keep the school alive and keep student achievement moving in a positive direction. Through a consistent practice of conducting inquiry, school leaders can challenge stakeholders inside and outside of the schoolhouse to think positively, be creative, and seek to find new and better solutions to complex problems.

One practice that has become extremely successful in conducting inquiry is the questioning technique. School leaders do not have to have all the answers, but it is imperative that they have the right questions. If school leaders ask the right questions, stakeholders can assist them in acquiring answers to those questions. For example, in one school system, we observed use of the Self-Directed Improvement System (SDIS). Using this system, the proficiency target is set; teachers analyze data, and data analysis generates questions. Some questions that surfaced were:

- What are the students' strengths and weaknesses?
- What are the individual teachers' strengths and weaknesses?
- How can we best utilize our teachers to improve student achievement?
- How can we work together to nurture, inspire, and successfully promote student achievement?

This type of inquiry occurs repeatedly, producing strategies for execution to reach the proficiency targets, as effective school leaders are constantly seeking answers to help clear the path for students, teachers, and staff to obtain their goals. The cycle of inquiry never ends because the question, "Now what?" is always in the minds of members of the leadership team, as the team is always in search of strategies that can be used positively to affect change that enhances student performance.

School leaders can also acquire information on best practices by attending conferences, searching the Web, becoming involved in focused professional development activities, reading the latest journals in select subject areas, and talking to colleagues who are successfully working in comparable situations. Of primary importance is having a system in place to identify the problem and conducting inquiry into solutions to address the problem. When such a system is in place, members of the faculty and staff become lifelong learners and resources to one another.

CURRICULUM AND INSTRUCTION Another important competency for school leaders to master is facilitating the implementation of the curriculum and the instructional program in a manner that meets the needs of individual students. In high performing schools, to make this practice a reality, school leaders build a capacity for instructional improvement using data (Blankstein, 2004). Through the collection and analysis of data, they identify the positive and negative factors of the curriculum and instructional program and use the results to inform instructional change.

How a school leader decides to implement the process of using data to inform instructional change is less a critical factor than having a process in place to create data. Failure to use data is one of the major difficulties in producing change in schools (Blankstein, 2004). An effective first step in determining how to get where you want to be is determining where you are, and data assist school leaders in making that determination. The model presented in Chapter 9 provides examples of how school leaders effectively use data to drive instructional change.

PROFESSIONAL DEVELOPMENT The fundamental purpose of educational leadership is the enhancement of academic achievement. To achieve that purpose, instructional leaders must engage in educational initiatives designed to keep professionals energized, motivated, informed, and inspired to perform at high levels. To that end, they have to conduct a comprehensive assessment of the needs of the individuals they lead, identify the strengths and weaknesses of those individuals, and design professional development programs that enhance their strengths and eliminate their weaknesses.

The importance of professional development cannot be overstated. Because of its importance, it has been previously mentioned in sections of several chapters. When a focused professional development program is in place, the quality of the faculty can be continuously enhanced. Considering the research on professional development, it is our position that professional development programs for 21st-century schools should address the following four areas: (1) the individual's area of assignment; (2) the vision, programs, and goals of the school in which the individual works; (3) the vision, programs, and goals of the district in which the individual works, and (4) the profession of education in general.

The Individual's Area of Assignment Each individual is assigned a specific area in the schoolhouse; if the individual is to be effective in that area over time, he/she needs to constantly enhance his/her skills and attributes in that area. To that end, professional development becomes a process of building and maintaining the capacity of individual faculty members to enhance teaching and learning, reflecting changes that occur in their assigned area. The role of the instructional leader is to assist individual teachers in identifying new approaches and trends in their subject area. The supervisory process outlined in Chapter 6 is a recommended best practice that can be used for that purpose.

The School in Which the Individual Works The new accountability movement is requiring all teachers to become a part of the learning community, conducting inquiry into strategies that build organizational capacity to enhance teaching and learning. In the previous section, professional development was offered as a series of activities designed to enhance the skills and attributes of teachers, positioning them to perform effectively in their assigned area. Traditionally, for classroom teachers, this would mean professional development in an instructional area, such as Mathematics, English, Reading, or Social Studies. However, in 21st-century schools, where distributive leadership and life-long learning are advocated for all educators, professional development programs should be a standard of practice. This includes activities that enable individuals to enhance their leadership skills, as well as instructional skills, both of which may be required for them to participate in organizational goal attainment.

If leadership is to be distributed throughout the school organization, school leaders must clearly articulate the vision of the school to all instructional personnel and clear any roadblocks or pitfalls that may hinder them from participating in its attainment. When attainment of the vision requires elements of instructional excellence unfamiliar to teachers, the school leader has a professional responsibility to provide the necessary professional development to enable teachers to acquire the skills to implement those elements of excellence with confidence.

In addition, professional development that addresses school-wide issues enables the faculty to develop an understanding of the big picture, the total school program. Rather than focusing only on their individual assignments, they can develop an understanding of school-wide programs and activities, their purpose, the resources being used to implement them, and the benefits to be derived from their implementation. Through this type of professional development, conflict is minimized, morale increased, and collaboration enhanced.

Specific types of professional development activities that we have found to be effective in this area include:

1. *Collaborative Dialogue*—Allowing time for teachers to engage in dialogue with colleagues in their building, as well as with colleagues in other buildings.
2. *Faculty Cohesiveness*—Allowing teachers time to engage in problem-solving activities with members of the department in which they are assigned or forming cooperative groups with members of comparative departments in other schools, facilitating the identification of solutions to school challenges.
3. *Faculty Leadership Skill Development*—Making available opportunities for teachers to acquire leadership skills through formal leadership preparation programs.
4. *Using Innovative Practices*—Fostering the creativity of the faculty by providing teachers an opportunity to conduct inquiry into new practices and strategies.
5. *Enhancing Self-Efficacy*—Providing opportunities for faculty members to participate in activities that will enable them to gain confidence in delivering services in their assigned area.

The District in Which Individuals Work Individuals serving in a particular school in the district need to understand the vision of the school district and how the district's vision relates to the vision of their school. To that end, district-wide meetings are necessary to foster a sense of community among all stakeholders. They also serve the purpose of connecting all schools, enhancing unity of purpose and facilitating support for the attainment of district-wide goals. In addition, the position of the district regarding policies and procedures that affect all stakeholders can be reviewed, allowing stakeholders to make suggestions for revisions. Through district-wide professional development activities, all stakeholders become aware of how their job relates to the goals of the school system and how they can grow as professionals. In essence, through a formal district-wide professional development program, a purposeful community is created.

The Professionalism of the Individual Professional development is a life-long process. All professionals, regardless of their position or level of experience or expertise, need to engage in programs and activities that will keep them abreast of the latest trends in their field. To fulfill this need, individuals may attend classes at a university, attend state and national conferences, read journal articles, and travel. They may also conduct action research, engage in reflective practice, conduct inquiry into best practices, and engage in journal writing. These activities enable individuals to become self-sufficient learners, thus, enhancing the school's potential of becoming a learning organization.

REFLECTION Leaders of today's schools must take time to think about their professional practices with a focus on improvement. Reflective practice is an approach school leaders can use to assess various areas of their professional, personal, and social lives. Through self-reflection, school leaders proactively build the capacity to identify what works, what does not work, and how they can make improvements in their performance.

For school leaders, time for self-reflection may be the most important time of the day. This is time when they focus and reflect on aligning their actions with the goals and vision for the school. It is a time when they can close the door to their office, focus on challenges of the day, and identify ways of renewing their energy and passion for task completion. Such reflection keeps one's daily actions focused and aligned with the vision of the school.

Reflective practice is not only an approach used by school leaders for self-reflection; it can be beneficial for their work with faculty members. Engaging in collaborative dialogue with the faculty should cause teachers to reflect on their teaching strategies. Conversations with teachers can reveal issues that call for action on instructional practices, procedures, thoughts, and beliefs. For example, Rosalind Martin, a graduate of the Memphis Leadership Fellows Program and principal of Georgian Hills Middle School, uses the *Exit Interview* as a practice of dialoging with teachers to encourage them to reflect on their teaching practices, as well as her style of leadership. The exit interview is a practice that allows both the school leader and the teaching faculty to reflect on the school year. At the end of each school year, Principal Martin holds a thirty (30)-minute conference with each teacher to reflect on general school procedures, teaching strategies, and upcoming professional development activities to get feedback from them. Both Principal Martin and each teacher assess the current situation to determine if there are positive or negative trends developing, or if requests have been made that need to be addressed immediately. The conversation allows teachers to have a voice in the management of the school, as well as setting directions for mission and vision attainment. More specifically, the exit interview allows teachers to assist in shaping academic plans for the next school year.

When issues are approached honestly, reflection is a powerful practice that school leaders can use to build a better self, as well as a better faculty, and it works best when it is preplanned and executed selflessly.

ORGANIZATIONAL MANAGEMENT In today's society, school leaders must be skilled in outlining practices to govern the workflow. These practices consist of effective planning, organizing, coordinating, communicating, and collaborating. They also include community building, vision development, risk taking, change management, and effective use of resources. In essence, the entire school organization must be managed. With these skills and a participatory leadership style, school leaders can effectively manage their school organization by managing the culture, the staff, working environment, change, and conflict (Hoy, Sabo, & Barnes, 1996). Of these five areas, the one that deserves special note is conflict, as conflict is inevitable, and school leaders must be knowledgeable of best practices that can be used to manage it.

A conflict is more than a disagreement; it is a social phenomenon that is heavily ingrained in human relations and expressed and sustained through communication. Conflict in schools often occurs as a result of individuals feeling threatened with a loss of power or status. Because of the interdependent nature of the work in schools, it is a frequent occurrence. Leaders who effectively manage conflict use established procedures that enable them to focus on issues, rather than people. They review the different perspectives, consider proactive behavior, as opposed to reactive behavior, and identify a

Standard 3

An education leader promotes the success of every student by ensuring management of the organization, operation, and resources for a safe, efficient, and effective learning environment.

Functions
  a. Monitor and evaluate the management and operational systems
  b. Obtain, allocate, align, and efficiently utilize human, fiscal, and technological resources
  c. Promote and protect the welfare and safety of students and staff
  d. Develop the capacity for distributed leadership
  e. Ensure teacher and organizational time is focused to support quality instruction and student learning

solution that all parties can endorse. When school leaders meet in a neutral area, listen, refrain from making assumptions, gather information, and avoid using an authoritarian demeanor, they tend to be successful in reaching a solution that all parties can endorse (Goleman, Boyatzis, & McKee, 2002). Although it is natural and inevitable for conflict to exist, engaging in proven practices will minimize its disruptive effects. By minimizing the disruptive effects of conflict, school leaders empower themselves and their followers to produce extraordinary results (Brock & Grady, 2004).

DIVERSITY   Most schools have a diverse population, consisting of students with varied backgrounds who exhibit a wide range of knowledge and talent. To meet the needs of a diverse student population, effective school leaders create an environment wherein inequities and inequalities are recognized and eliminated. The leadership behavior is two-fold; in one instance, school leaders enforce a no tolerance policy for the display of inequities between individuals and eliminate the inequalities. In a second instance, they recognize differences and celebrate them. For example, each year at Freed-Hardeman University, Drs. Sharen and Karen Cypress, Associate Professors of Education, orchestrate an Ethnic Cultures Day for over twenty-three hundred (2300) students and the faculty. During this spectacular, cultural event, approximately fifty (50) students representing over thirty-two (32) countries share their values, attitudes, and beliefs though music, energizing speeches, visual arts, dance, and flag presentations. In addition, the University Chef collects recipes from each of the cultural groups and prepares an international feast for the entire student body, faculty, and staff.

Through this experience, students not only embellish a sense of security within their own cultural groups, but they obtain a deeper understanding and appreciation of the world view of other cultural groups and recognize the similarities and differences between and among them. Consequently, the entire Freed-Hardeman University community is enriched.

We live in a highly diverse society, and that diversity is increasing. Effective school leaders become knowledgeable of the differences that exist in society and enact inclusive practices that exhibit respect for all of them. The rewards that come from eliminating inequalities and celebrating diversity are

Standard 5

An education leader promotes the success of every student by acting with integrity, fairness, and in an ethical manner.

Functions
  a. Ensure a system of accountability for every student's academic and social success
  b. Model principles of self-awareness, reflective practice, transparency, and ethical behavior
  c. Safeguard the values of democracy, equity, and diversity

numerous, as culturally diverse students are able to make their own contributions to the school community.

PROFESSIONALISM Identifying practices that can be used to exhibit professional behavior can pay huge dividends for school leaders. In fact, professionalism is a practice that will enhance the work of school leaders in the other twelve competency areas. Best practice as a professional requires school leaders to display behavior that conforms to the technical and ethical standards of the educational professional, and there is no substitute for a display of fair and ethical leadership behavior.

Most individuals consider professionalism to be consistent with a strong work ethic, courteous, friendly behavior, and a dedication to fulfilling the demands of one's job description. These are elements of professionalism; however, true professionalism has a much greater meaning. School leaders who are true professionals are knowledgeable of the ethical standards that underpin the profession and are diligent in implementing those standards. Through their daily activities, they convey an image that commands respect for their leadership, the school as an organization, and education as a profession. They lead by a professional code of ethics, demonstrating values and beliefs that inspire members of the faculty to commit to school goal attainment. Integrity, fairness, dignity, and respect are consistently demonstrated through their behavior.

School leaders who are true professionals attend state, local, and national conferences, mentor others, and become advocates for the profession. Through their behavior, they uphold the principles upon which the profession is built, and they expect that other people in the internal and external environments of the school will exhibit behavior that demonstrates integrity and respect for diversity.

The school is a place most noted for the service it renders to members of the greater community. Perhaps the individuals who stand to reap the greatest benefits are the students the school seeks to serve. Young minds are impressionable and vulnerable. Therefore, it is imperative that individuals working in the schoolhouse set examples for students by displaying professional behavior. True professionals are knowledgeable of the purpose of education and the role they should play. Through their behavior, they demonstrate a willingness to subordinate their own interests for the good of the school and community (ISLLC Standard 5). Simply put, they demonstrate values, beliefs, and attitudes that inspire students and others to high levels of performance.

PUTTING BEST PRACTICES INTO ACTION

Effective school leaders must pursue their vision of educational excellence in a way that moves the school from one state to another. While pursuing that goal, they must remain conscious of the effects of their actions on the faculty, staff, students, and community associated with the school. To that end, they must concentrate on utilizing best practices in the areas of change, decision making, communication, and conflict management. When leaders employ practices in these areas, using behaviors that are informed by the 13 core competencies, providing leadership in these areas is much easier, as they create a culture of innovation that rewards creativity. School leaders become less directive and more responsive in their daily practices. The use of best practices can also bring together employees with divergent viewpoints, as individuals can see the connections between current conditions and the vision (Kanter, 1984).

■ ■ ■

Implications for Leadership

- Effective school leaders foster a shared vision for student learning.
- The leader's ability to gain the trust of stakeholders, as well as market and implement change, is critical to the success of the change.
- Effective 21st-century school leaders develop teacher leaders, lead instruction in a professional learning community, and engage parents and members of the community in the educational process.
- Effective school leaders engage teachers in collaborative dialogue, facilitate action research, and provide teachers with meaningful feedback regarding their work.
- School leaders of high performing schools make changes in the curriculum and instructional program based on data.
- Effective school leaders foster a program of professional development for self and others.
- Distributive leadership is becoming a standard practice, as 21st-century school leadership is so challenging that no one individual single-handedly can meet the challenge.
- Perception is reality, and it is a good representation of who an individual really is when he/she functions as a school leader.
- To enhance academic achievement, effective school leaders seek to reach a predetermined level of competence, find innovative ways to increase student achievement, and utilize best practices.
- School leaders tend to be most effective when they afford individuals throughout the organization the flexibility to participate in problem solving that leads to organizational goal attainment.

Reflective Practice

1. What are some practices that you would use to establish an effective professional development program?
2. What are some practices that you would use to ensure that as a 21st-century school leader, you have mastered the 13 core competencies and have the capacity to implement the best practices informed by each competency?

3. What practices would you use to enhance your leadership behavior through reflective practice?
4. What strategies would you use to assess the climate of a school to identify and remove barriers to student learning?
5. What are some practices that you would use to structure a school for effective teaching and learning?
6. How would you determine stakeholder perception of your professional leadership behavior?
7. How would you identify best practices for use in a practical school situation? First, describe the situation, then, describe the process you would use in addressing that situation.

Chapter Essentials

Interstate School Leader Licensure Consortium Standards 1–6

An education leader promotes the success of every student by facilitating the development, articulation, implementation, and stewardship of a vision of learning that is shared and supported by all stakeholders.

An education leader promotes the success of every student by advocating, nurturing, and sustaining a school culture and instructional program conducive to student learning and staff professional growth.

An education leader promotes the success of every student by ensuring management of the organization, operation, and resources for a safe, efficient, and effective learning environment.

An education leader promotes the success of every student by collaborating with faculty and community members, responding to diverse community interests and needs, and mobilizing community resources.

An education leader promotes the success of every student by acting with integrity, fairness, and in an ethical manner.

An education leader promotes the success of every student by understanding, responding to, and influencing the political, social, economic, legal, and cultural context.

Principle

It is important for school leaders to know and understand the expectations others hold for them.

Dichotomy
Leading/Directing or Responding/Reacting

Individuals must recognize the need to change, be able to lead the change, and in the process, influence stakeholders to accept and respond to the change.

References

Blankstein, A. (2004). *Failure is not an option: Six principles that guide student achievement in high performing schools.* Thousand Oaks, CA: Corwin Press.

Brock, B., & Grady, M. (2004). *Launching your first principalship: A guide for beginning principals. Thousand Oaks, CA: Corwin Press.*

Burden, P. R. (2003). *Classroom management: Creating a successful learning community.* (2nd ed.) New York: John Wiley & Sons, Inc.

Conley, D. T. (1997). *Roadmap to restructuring: Charting the course of change in American education.* Eugene, OR: University of Oregon (ERIC Clearinghouse on Educational Management).

Cooperrider, D. L., & Whitney, D. (1999). *Appreciative inquiry.* San Francisco: Berrett Koehler.

Covey, S. R. (1991). *Principle-centered leadership.* New York: Simon & Schuster.

Darling-Hammond, L. (1993). Reforming school reform agenda. *Phi Delta Kappan,* 74, 761.

DuFour, R. DuFour, R., Eaker, R., & Many, T. (2006). Learning by doing: A handbook for professional learning communities at work. Bloomington, IN: Solution Tree.

Fisher, K., Rayner, S., & Belgard, W. (1994). Tips for Teams: A Ready Reference for Solving Common Team Problems. New York: McGraw-Hill.

Fullan, M. (2001). *Leading in a culture of change.* San Francisco: Jossey-Bass Publishers, Inc.

Goleman, D., Boyatzis, R., & McKee, A. (2002) *Primal Leadership-Learning to Lead with Emotional Intelligence.* Boston: Howard Business School.

Goodlad, J. (1994). *Educational renewal: Better teachers, better schools.* San Francisco: Jossey-Bass Inc., Publishers.

Green, R. L. (2005). *Practicing the art of leadership: A problem-based approach to implementing the ISLLC standards.* (2nd ed.). Columbus, OH: Merrill Prentice Hall.

Green, R. L. (2009). *Practicing the art of leadership: A problem-based approach to implementing the ISLLC standards* (3rd ed.). Columbus, OH: Merrill Prentice Hall.

Hoy, W., Sabo, D., & Barnes, K. (1996). Organizational health and faculty trust: a view from the middle. *Research in Middle Level Education Quarterly* (Spring), 21, 39.

Interstate School Leader Licensure Consortium (ISLLC). (1996). *Standards for school leaders.* Washington, D.C.: Council of Chief School Officers.

Kanter, D. (1984). Change is everyone's job: Managing the extended enterprise in globally connected world. In J. S. Osland, D. A. Kolb, & I. M. Rubin (Eds.). *The organizational behavior reader.* (pp. 562–576). Upper Saddle River, NJ: Prentice Hall.

Leithwood, K., & Jantzi, D. (2005). *A review of transformational school leadership research 1996–2005.* Paper presented at the annual meeting of the American Educational Research Association. Montreal, Canada.

Leithwood, K., Seashore-Louis, K., & Wahlstrom, K. (2004). *How leadership influences student learning (Learning From Leadership Project Executive Summary).* New York: The Wallace Foundation.

Maxwell, J. C. (2003). *Thinking for a change. Eleven ways highly successful people approach life and work.* Nashville, TN: Center Street.

Meyer, A. Brooks, G., & Goes, J. (1990). Environmental jobs and industrial revolution: Organizational responses to discontinuous change. *Strategic Management Journal,* 11, 93–110.

National Association of Elementary School Principals. (2001). *Leading learning communities: Standards for what principals should know and be able to do.* Alexandria, VA: Author.

Ormrod, J. (2003). *Educational psychology: Developing learners.* (4th ed.). Upper Saddle River, NJ: Pearson.

Sergiovanni, T. J. (2005). *Strengthening the heartbeat: Leading and learning together in Schools.* San Francisco: Jossey-Bass Publishers, Inc.

Vroom, V. (1993). Two decades of research on participation: Beyond buzz words and management fads. In J. S. Osland, D. A. Kolb, & I. M. Rubin (Eds.). *The organizational behavior reader.* (pp. 429–436). Upper Saddle River, NJ: Prentice Hall.

Walters, J. T., Marzano, R. J., & McNulty, B. A. (2003). *Balanced leadership: What 30 years of research tells us about the effects of leadership on student achievement.* Aurora, CO: Mid-continent Research for Education and Learning.

CHAPTER

9

Putting Instructional Leadership into Practice: A Model for Instructional Improvement

(Standards 1 through 6)

"When starting the process of school improvement, having insights into the conditions of the school that are grounded in facts, and making decisions that are data driven, will enhance your success potential."

"Simply importing practices that work well in one place doesn't necessarily lead to greater student learning. Each local school has to think through the principles of what it wants to see in students, and then let the practices emerge from those principles."

CUSHMAN

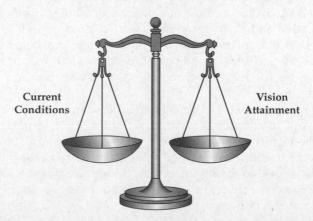

Current Conditions   Vision Attainment

INTRODUCTION

Each of the previous chapters was written to assist the reader in acquiring a deep understanding of the role of 21st-century school leaders, their purpose, and the processes they use to achieve a desired outcome, as informed by the standards, competencies, and accountability movement. In this culminating chapter, we bring the content of the previous chapters together in a model that can be used to put instructional leadership into practice. The focus is on the role of school leaders in developing and implementing a plan for school improvement.

We begin the chapter by setting the stage for change. Then, we discuss a systematic process for instructional improvement with the intent of sharing with readers, practices recommended by contemporary scholars for use in leading instructional change. The process for planning and implementing change for instructional improvement is outlined in the following phases: (1) defining and communicating the vision; (2) assessing current conditions; (3) identifying the discrepancy; (4) assessing the cause of the discrepancy; (5) identifying the needed change and/or modifications; (6) assessing the school's capacity for change; (7) building the capacity for change; (8) implementing the identified change, and (9) conducting evaluations (see Exhibit 9.1). Through an analysis of the dynamics of each phase, readers can gain an understanding of how school leaders develop and maintain effective instructional programs within their schools.

SETTING THE STAGE FOR CHANGE

Before school leaders attempt to engage in the change process, they must first seek and acquire an understanding of the complexity of the school organization they serve, inclusive of its culture, climate, and the interaction of individuals. These areas were addressed in some detail in Chapter 4. Additionally, school leaders must realize that the effectiveness of the change initiative is contingent on the extent to which they establish relationships with stakeholders inside and outside of the schoolhouse. The types of relationships needed and their importance were delineated in Chapters 5 and 6. The underlying theme is that school improvement must emerge from and be central to the individuals being served and what needs to be accomplished in order for them to thrive in a social and political democracy (Sergiovanni, 1996).

One practice that sets the stage for the change process and works extremely well in planning and implementing school improvement is allowing the faculty to serve as a committee assuming responsibility for the development and implementation of a plan for school improvement. School leaders develop faculty teams and assign each team a component of the plan. A coordinating team is formed, and a member from each of the component teams serves on the coordinating team, which frequently reports

EXHIBIT 9.1 A Model for Instructional Improvement

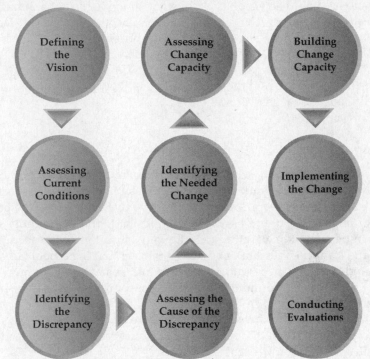

to the entire faculty. This planning structure, based on the Delphi Technique, involves the entire faculty and empowers all faculty members to utilize their creativity. In addition, it fosters a school-wide commitment to the development and implementation of a plan that is designed to enhance academic achievement.

A comprehensive school improvement plan has a number of components. However, tantamount to its success is its occurrence in a professional learning community where (1) leadership is distributed; (2) a culture of mutual respect exists; (3) ideas are shared; (4) common values are created, and (5) bridges that lead to cooperation and participation in the change process are built (Hargreaves & Fink, 2003). Having given these prerequisites consideration, the stage is set for change and renewal of the instructional program.

CREATING AND COMMUNICATING THE VISION

Twenty-first century school leaders are being asked to assume responsibility for the development and implementation of an academic program that is complete with strategies for maximizing both student and adult learning.

Consequently, they must be able to create a compelling vision of what the school is to become. The vision is a realistic, attractive idea of an image of a more desirable future for the school. It guides the change process, leads to norms of behavior, and places the focus on student learning (Hord, 1997; Nanus, 2002). When a shared vision is in existence, a standard of excellence is established; interpersonal skills and content knowledge among faculty members are enhanced, and the faculty is more likely to commit to working toward organizational goal attainment.

Creating the Vision

In order to create a vision, school leaders must first develop a deep understanding of the school organization and establish positive interpersonal relationships with stakeholders. Additionally, they must understand the process of school improvement and assist the faculty, staff, and community stakeholders in understanding that process. Equally important is the need for the faculty and staff to understand and accept the fact that the school faces challenges, and change is necessary to provide and sustain a solution to those challenges. With this foundation in place, the process of establishing a shared vision can begin.

Systems thinking and shared visioning are cornerstones of the school improvement process. In that regard, the key questions for school leaders to answer in collaboration with the faculty are:

• What are our core beliefs, values, and goals?
• What do we want the school to look like in five years?
• What are our strengths and areas needing improvement?
• What changes need to occur in order for us to meet the needs of all the students we serve?

With answers to these questions, the vision becomes clear and concise, and all stakeholders will acquire an awareness of the leader's purpose and expectations (Blankstein, 2004). This becomes the blueprint for structuring the school for effective teaching and learning, giving focus and purpose to the school and faculty, as well as guiding their behavior relative to enhancing the academic achievement of all students.

The school leader's primary responsibilities during the visioning phase are to direct and empower faculty teams as they begin to mold their understandings about the school's instructional process, the change process, and approaches to school improvement (Seikaly & Thomas, 2004). In essence, the leader is the "keeper of the vision" and responsible for leading the school to its attainment. In order to fulfill that role, he/she will need to be aware of his/her beliefs and values, be able to process information, assess data in an objective manner, and facilitate the interaction of individuals who work in the schoolhouse. In essence, the school

EXHIBIT 9.2 Structuring the School for Effective Teaching and Learning

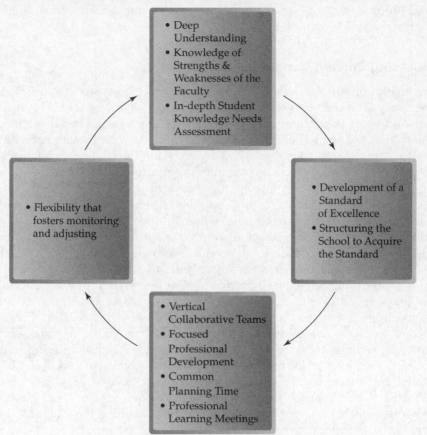

leader has to structure the school for effective teaching and learning (see Exhibit 9.2).

Communicating the Vision

After school leaders have completed the developmental process, it is vital that they communicate the vision to all stakeholders. All stakeholders need to know the school's vision, understand the reasoning behind the process of school improvement and be knowledgeable of the desired results of goal attainment. Therefore, school leaders must take the proper steps to communicate the vision to all stakeholders. Through modeling, symbols, multi-media, and school activities, teachers and students can assist in communicating the vision throughout the school and community. In addition to the initial sharing of the vision, school leaders should implement a plan for the continuous communication of the vision so that it gains power and does not lose its momentum over time. Real organizational change occurs when stakeholders, inside and outside of the schoolhouse, acquire new understanding about what the change means, and new meanings are negotiated socially through a shared vision (Miron, 1997).

Assessing Current Conditions

The second phase of the school improvement process involves the collection and analysis of data that will provide the faculty and staff with a clear understanding of the current condition of the school's instructional program. The role of the school leader in this phase is to conduct a thorough data analysis of the instructional program and provide the faculty and staff with data that will afford them an opportunity to acquire an in-depth understanding of any voids that exist in student achievement. This phase is critical in the process of instructional renewal, as school leaders cannot effectively enhance the instructional program in a way that affects the achievement of all students without assessing current conditions. Utilizing data received from this phase, they can communicate to the faculty and community strengths and weaknesses that exist in the instructional program.

To determine the change initiative and set goals for improving teaching and learning, successful school leaders use pre-existing data in the areas of demographics, culture, and climate. They also assess the behavior of teachers and students, as well as teacher and student attendance records, report cards, achievement test results, state assessment measures, criterion-referenced tests, and community interests and expectations (Maxwell, 2001; O'Neill & Conzemius, 2006; Schmoker, 2006). Analyzing data in these areas gives the leader a sense of purpose as the purpose of the renewal effort is embedded in the data. In collecting and communicating this data, two essential tasks school leaders must facilitate are aggregating and disaggregating data to the extent that the faculty can make a determination of the needs of students and teachers, individually and collectively. The disaggregation of data will also reveal instructional needs by students, grade levels, and subject areas.

Once the data analysis reveals areas of strengths and weaknesses in the instructional program, this information should be shared with faculty and staff in a manner that enables them to fully appreciate the condition of the school's instructional program and its effect on student achievement. Instruction can be maximized when school leaders use data about student and teacher performance to make adjustments in the curriculum and instructional program. Additionally, helping the faculty and staff understand the significance of data analysis directly affects their ability to personalize student instruction.

Assessing current conditions is a major phase in the change process as it provides school leaders an excellent opportunity to distribute leadership and enhance the teacher team concept. The probability of influencing teachers to collaborate for the purpose of embracing instructional change is greater when they understand the data and what it reveals about their performance and current student achievement (Seikaly & Thomas, 2004). Once leadership is distributed and leadership teams are formed, the teams can use the data provided them to create short and long-term goals for the purpose of addressing identified areas of the instructional program that need strengthening.

IDENTIFICATION OF THE DISCREPANCY

Having developed a shared vision and determined the current conditions of the instructional program, school leaders will want to identify what lies in between the vision and current conditions, often called the discrepancy. Conducting a discrepancy analysis is an important part of the school improvement process, as accuracy in the identification of the discrepancy enhances the likelihood that the strategies chosen will close the gap between existing conditions and the vision, resulting in improved student performance. Therefore, the entire faculty and staff should be involved in this phase of the process. Different researchers and writers offer suggestions as to how school leaders can approach this phase.

Seikaly and Thomas (2004) propose that school leaders might lead the faculty through this phase by raising and addressing the following questions:

1. Is there evidence to suggest that there is a problem?
2. What is the problem?
3. Is the problem a serious one?

Using a different approach, Green (2009) offers that school leaders might:

1. seek to identify root causes and contributing factors to the discrepancies revealed.
2. collect evidence to prove or disprove conclusions reached.
3. discuss the causes of the discrepancies with major stakeholders, instructional supervisors, and/or consultants.
4. identify a small number of high-impact causes to address in the school improvement effort.

Using a third approach, based on the situation, Gainey and Webb (1998) offer that school leaders can take one or more of the following actions:

1. Leaders can formulate a statement of what is to be achieved and describe the situation in the school environment that will be addressed by the effort.
2. If rectifying a problem, the team should indicate what is wrong and how it will be addressed.
3. If intervention is seen as an opportunity to improve some aspect of the school operation, leaders can frame the opportunity in the form of questions.

4. An introductory statement can be developed, followed by a list of questions that would be addressed in the action plan.
5. The opportunity can be stated in one or two sentences; if trouble is experienced, there is a possibility that the focus of the effort has not been crystallized.
6. The leader can raise a question: Is this a serious problem, or is this a good opportunity? If so, is the faculty likely to be able to do anything about it? If the answer to either question is no, find another opportunity.

Regardless of the approach used, collaboration among the faculty during this phase is important, as the skills and knowledge of teachers enhance the accuracy of determining areas that need to be changed or modified. Their involvement will pay dividends in selecting and implementing the program strategy; the greater the unity among faculty, the greater the possibility the program strategy selected for implementation will eliminate the discrepancy and reach the vision that is shared by the entire school community.

SELECTING THE PROGRAM STRATEGY

Selecting the program strategy to be implemented is the third phase of the school improvement effort. In a number of situations, best practices that have worked in other schools are chosen for implementation. Either the school leader or members of the planning team read about a strategy, participated in a seminar where a strategy was demonstrated, or visited a particular school that was experiencing success with a particular strategy. However, a red flag of caution is raised concerning using these practices for strategy identification and selection. The planning team is ill advised to simply import a strategy or practice that worked well in another school (Cushman, 1999). Practices that have worked well in one school do not necessarily lead to greater student learning in another school. Each school is unique and even though the challenges may appear to be similar, the climate, culture, and characteristics surrounding the challenges are different. Therefore, the school improvement team in each local school has to analyze its discrepancy, think of what their students need to know and be able to do, and then select a program strategy that is best suited for their situation.

It is important to note that the program strategy selected should be research-based and proven to eliminate the discrepancy identified in the discrepancy analysis phase of the planning process. The strategy selected could be (1) "Reading First"; (2) "Looping"; (3) "Small High Schools"; (4) "The Paideia Proposal"; (5) "School-Within-A-School", or any number of other program concepts. What is most important is selecting a program concept or making a program modification that is aligned with the identified discrepancy, supported by the faculty, and accepted by the school community. Then, the school leader can facilitate the setting of priorities and establishing goals that will guide the implementation of that strategy.

Establishing Short and Long-Term Goals

Having selected the program strategy, in order to facilitate its implementation and maximize the quality of teaching and student achievement, school leaders must create a set of short and long-term goals that clarify and redefine the relationship between the program strategy and efforts of the faculty (Schmoker, 2006). Marzano, Waters, and McNulty (2005) found a strong correlation between achievement and goal setting. They state that the impact of setting instructional goals for student achievement ranges from a low of eighteen (18) percentile points to a high of forty (40) percentile points. Consequently, if a student who starts at the fiftieth (50th) percentile has a teacher who functions with clear instructional goals, that student can achieve anywhere from the sixty-eighth (68th) to the nintieth (90th) percentile. By facilitating the development of a goal-oriented action plan, school leaders can ensure that appropriate accountability measures are in place to drive the implementation of the selected program strategy.

ASSESSING THE SCHOOL'S CAPACITY FOR CHANGE

One of the leadership tasks associated with implementing a school improvement plan is ensuring that the school has the capacity to implement the identified change initiative. Change capacity refers to the faculty's ability to implement the change and sustain it when key individuals leave. Equally important, the change has to be systematic, rather than personality driven. Additionally, it has to be vision-driven, and stakeholders have to share the vision. With systematic change, the change process is connected to the vision and not to the change agent. However, school leaders have to position the organization for the change, and therein lies another major responsibility of school leaders.

The Effects of Change Capacity

Change capacity fosters the success potential of the change. Consequently, to make effective and sustained change, producing the least amount of conflict, the school's capacity for that change must be determined (Green, 2009). A successful discrepancy analysis will surface the cause of the discrepancy, positioning the school leader to conduct inquiry into best programs and practices to use in eliminating the discrepancy. This may mean a program change or modification and/or a personnel change. In either case, the faculty and staff must have the capacity to make the change. For example, if a new program is selected, members of the faculty will need to be knowledgeable of the purpose of the program, the process of implementing the program, and the outcome the program is designed to produce. A concern, at this stage, is the discomfort the change is likely to cause individuals who will be affected by the change or who will have to implement the change. Also, the need for faculty members to engage in new learnings, fear of failure, and the time and energy necessary for them to make the change are three of the reasons faculty members might resist the change, lessening the school's capacity to make the change (Green, 2009).

Let's assume that after the discrepancy analysis, the faculty planning team decides that to improve academic achievement in the area of reading, the existing reading program that is phonetic based will have to be replaced with a new reading program that is whole language based. With this decision, the faculty can identify the focus of the change and begin the change process with a clear understanding of its purposes, processes, and the desired outcomes. However, the school has to have the capacity to make the change; essential to the success of any change is the school's capacity to make that change (Green, 2009). To determine if the school has the capacity to make the change, the school leader might take the following actions:

1. He/she should determine if the culture inside the schoolhouse, as well as in the community, will accept the change. The school leader should inform the school and community of the desired change and make the determination as to whether the faculty, parents, and other stakeholders will be receptive to the new method of teaching reading.
2. The leader needs to determine the extent to which members of the faculty have the skills needed to teach reading, using the whole language methodology. If a large percentage of the faculty is skilled in the whole language methodology, the change will likely be smoother. If not, it will be necessary for the school leader to plan and implement a focused professional development program. As was discussed in an earlier chapter, asking teachers to implement a concept that they do not have the skills to implement can become problematic.
3. Leaders must assess the human and material resource needs and determine if the budget will accommodate the change in terms of adding additional resources, if they are needed.
4. A facet of the leader's role is to determine if the new program strategy aligns with district, state, and national standards.
5. He/she must determine if the new program aligns with the vision of the school.

Addressing the aforementioned issues, school leaders can begin the process of determining if the school has the capacity to make the change from teaching reading using a phonetic method to a whole language instructional method. Two theories, worthy of note in this area, are Fullan's (1993) Change Agency Theory and Kurt Lewin's (1951) Force Field Analysis Theory. Both of these theories are discussed in Chapter 7 of the companion text. After making the assessment, if it is determined that the school does not have the capacity to make the change, it is advisable that before proceeding with the change process, the school leader establish a plan to build the capacity for change. Four practices that have proven to be successful in building change capacity in schools are: (1) communicating the change initiative to stakeholders; (2) acquiring internal and external support for the change; (3) pooling the resources of the school and community, and (4) enhancing teaching skills. Each of these practices are briefly discussed in the following section.

BUILDING THE CAPACITY FOR CHANGE

In building the capacity for change, school leaders will want to first determine areas to be addressed, and conducting a force field analysis would enable them to identify driving and restraining forces of the change initiative. After the analysis, the capacity building process can begin, as school leaders will want to convert restraining forces into driving forces (Lewin, 1951).

Communicating the Change Initiative to Stakeholders

Schools do not operate in isolation; rather, they are part of a larger social system. The change capacity can be enhanced if stakeholders inside and outside of the schoolhouse endorse and support the change initiative. Therefore, school leaders will want to communicate the change initiative to stakeholders and describe how they will benefit when the change initiative is implemented. Communicating openly and honestly concerning the conditions of the instructional program and the challenges faced in addressing the needs of all students, the leadership can work to secure the endorsement and support of stakeholders.

It is not uncommon for stakeholders to have a misconception regarding the state of the school organization and be unwilling to acknowledge the need for change. When individuals do not acknowledge the need for change and/or do not realize the benefit they will derive from the change, they tend to resist the change. In other instances, some individuals simply are unwilling to accept reality; they will not admit a lack of effectiveness in the instructional program. Therefore, to build capacity for change, school leaders have to be skilled in communicating the condition of the instructional program and facilitating stakeholder understanding of the need for change, as well as the change initiative.

Acquiring Internal and External Support

The change process in 21st-century schools is far too complex and consists of too many variables for any one individual to lead a change initiative. Therefore, one of the key elements in building capacity for instructional improvement is acquiring the expertise, commitment, and support of faculty and staff. Also, external support from central office personnel, specialists, and community leaders is vital to the successful implementation of the change initiative. Additionally, school leaders should address contractual agreements. In the change process, contractual agreements with unions or professional organizations can be a restraining force or a driving force. If it is a restraining force, before the change process begins, the restraining force will need to be converted to a driving force.

Pooling the Resources of the School and Community

Still another way to build change capacity is to pool the resources of the school and community. In building change capacity, school leaders will want to assess the material and human resource needs of the new program concept. Then, they must proceed to pool the resources of the school and community to acquire what is needed to effectively implement the change in a manner that will produce the desired outcome. Aligning the budget with the vision of the school and setting budgetary priorities are critical to a school having the capacity for change. For example, if the budget and the change initiative it supports are aligned with the shared vision, as well as state and district standards, resources for use in the implementation will be easier to justify. Whenever funds are allocated for a purpose for which there has been a prior agreement, the faculty is more likely to be receptive to the allocation because they realize that priorities have been set, and funds are being allocated in accordance with those priorities.

Enhancing Teaching Skills

A fourth approach school leaders can use to build change capacity is to enhance the skills of members of the faculty so that teachers can effectively implement the new initiative. School leaders should plan and conduct workshops addressing the innovation and provide ongoing support throughout the year to facilitate the transition from the previous instructional approach. The plan should provide teachers with multiple instructional strategies and multiple forms of assessments. A best practice for use in enhancing the skills of teachers relative to the use of a new instructional strategy is the "Trainer-of-Trainer Model." It has been my experience that teachers are more receptive to receiving information when that information is provided by a colleague. Therefore, instead of a large number of teachers attending professional development sessions on a topic outside of the building, the trainer-of-trainer model can be used. One or two teachers attend the workshop, become skilled in the concept, return to the school, and plan sessions to impart that information to the entire faculty. The greatest benefit lies in the fact that one or two teachers on the faculty have in-depth knowledge of the new strategy and can serve as a resource to other teachers on a daily basis. By enhancing the skills and attributes of teachers, school leaders build the capacity to provide true instructional improvement.

IMPLEMENTING THE IDENTIFIED CHANGE

After the vision has been established, and data have been analyzed, the discrepancy must be determined and the change initiative selected. Then, the school leader, in facilitating the change capacity, is ready to move to the next phase, implementing the change. In implementing the change initiative, school leaders will want to determine distributive leadership responsibilities, establish a monitoring system, and provide ongoing professional development for the faculty and staff.

Distributive Leadership

A theory that links directly to implementing instructional improvement initiatives in today's schools is Distributed Leadership Theory. Often used interchangeably with "shared leadership", "team leadership", and "democratic leadership", the elements of distributive leadership are consistent with the leader behavior being advocated by the standards, competencies, and accountability movement. Thus, in implementing a change initiative in 21st-century schools, school leaders should consider distributing leadership throughout the school organization.

Spillane (2005) explains that distributive leadership is about leadership practices, rather than leaders or their roles. Functions, routines, and structures are viewed as products of the interactions of school leaders, followers, and situations. Leadership practices typically involve multiple leaders, including those with formal and informal positions. The leader-follower approaches of the past have been chiefly concerned with the skills, abilities, and capabilities of one person, the school leader. This type of model is severely limited in bringing about school and classroom-level change (Fullan, 2001). No longer is it effective for school leaders to single-handedly provide leadership for school improvement. Instructional leadership practices for today's schools are a distributed entity that is facilitated through human interaction. It must occur at the level of the school, rather than the level of the individual, and it is the appropriate approach for implementing instructional change in 21st-century schools (Harris, 2002). Key people who will share the responsibility of instructional leadership-along with the school leader-must be identified. Sharing responsibility for instructional improvement will most likely lead to maximizing and increasing the academic achievement of all students.

Monitoring and Adjusting

After the change strategies are put into practice and leadership responsibilities have been successfully distributed, the implementation process must be monitored to ensure that the school is progressing toward the desired outcome. If necessary, adjustments must be made. To that end, school leaders must facilitate the implementation process and frequently review all program components. Some of the ways they can monitor the process are conducting walkthroughs; one-on-one classroom visits; assessing student progress reports; facilitating individual self-assessments by teachers; acquiring parent feedback, and conducting grade level or subject area meetings. It is important for school leaders to monitor the process as data collected from assessment activities (formative assessments) can be use to clarify problems, make program adjustments, and collect evidence that is acceptable as measures of goal attainment. The monitoring and adjustment process is also a viable accountability measure.

Providing Ongoing Professional Development

The final component of the implementation phase is professional development, which is key to the success of the change process. Over the last five years, all of the school leaders with whom I have worked have said repeatedly that the most important resource in their school is the classroom teacher and that a quality faculty is the linchpin in developing and implementing an effective change initiative. Therefore, school leaders should demonstrate their commitment to the faculty and staff by supporting them through planned professional development. The strengths and weaknesses of the faculty and staff should be identified, and professional development activities should be planned, giving consideration to their strengths and weaknesses. The activities should also be consistent with the goals and objectives of the change initiative and sufficient to meet new needs of individuals as they surface.

In planning professional development activities, Girvin (2002) offers the following suggestions for school leaders:

- survey the staff to solicit input on topics
- find the best resources to address the topics
- determine the cost of the training and follow-up activities and establish a budget
- establish the timeline for the training sessions
- publish the professional development calendar
- send written reminders to all participants a few days before each activity
- adhere to the designed times and agenda
- create an appealing environment for the training
- provide teachers with all relevant print materials
- provide door prizes for incentives

When school leaders are well versed in what is actually occurring in the instructional program and have a good understanding of what teachers need to accomplish on a daily basis, then, the potential of success is greatly enhanced (Israel, 2003). In addition to the data-driven school-wide plan, each teacher should have an individual plan; student achievement data sufficient to support the ability of an individual teacher to address his/her students' success potential should inform the development of the plan.

THE EVALUATION PHASE

Throughout the school improvement process, school leaders will want to guide the school improvement planning team in assessing the quality of the overall process and the progress the school is making toward goal attainment. The two types of assessments that school leaders should consider are program and pupil, and the two forms of assessments are formative and summative. Additionally, the performance of teachers should be appraised, keeping in mind that the purpose of all forms of assessments and appraisals is to enhance the school improvement process.

Pupil and Program Evaluation

School leaders might conduct program assessments to determine if the program or change initiative is being implemented as it was designed and if the program is producing the results that it was implemented to produce. In regard to pupil evaluation, the determination has to be made as to whether or not students are meeting the established standards and mastering the skills and concepts advocated. These two assessments can be made in two forms, formative and summative.

FORMATIVE EVALUATION   The formative evaluation is an ongoing process designed to assess program and teacher effectiveness, as well as and student achievement. It is a process that school leaders can use to guide the work of the school improvement teams, facilitating their actions in assessing all major components of the plan. By facilitating the formative assessment process, school leaders can assist the school improvement planning team in making adjustments to the program as it is being implemented. Techniques can be included to evaluate program effectiveness, student achievement, and teacher effectiveness. As the program is being evaluated, the team will want to determine if all program components are implemented as they were designed and if each program component is producing the intended results.

In regard to assessing student performance, the assessment is conducted to make a determination as to whether student achievement is increasing and the discrepancies initially identified are being eliminated. Benchmarks can be established, and assessments can be conducted to determine if the benchmarks are being reached. Some of the assessments that may be used are interim tests, classroom observations, teacher feedback, and student feedback.

Being able to manage change during the implementation phase is critical to successful goal attainment. Therefore, a process for assessing program and student achievement en route to goal attainment should be in place at the beginning of program implementation and conducted at frequent intervals. During the planning stage, the assessment or curriculum committee should identify the assessment instruments that will be used and determine the administration intervals at which program effectiveness and student progress will be evaluated. The procedures that will be used to collect and analyze data, determine intervention strategies that will be utilized for remedial and enrichment needs, and the kinds of comparisons that will be made should also be predetermined.

In some instances, the formative assessment will inform school leaders of changes that are needed in specific areas or in the program in general. The more frequently a formative evaluation is conducted, the more likely the planning team will be able to identify areas of the plan that are not effectively contributing to goal attainment. Data collected and the changes and modifications regarding student learning that are informed by data should be communicated to all stakeholders on a frequent basis.

SUMMATIVE EVALUATIONS   Summative evaluations should occur at a predetermined stage of program implementation, which may happen in one, two, three, or five years. Through the summative assessment process, the school leader is attempting to determine if the program design has achieved the established goals. Therefore, summative assessments should be designed to reach conclusions about the merit or worth of the program initiative, strengths and weaknesses of the instructional strategies, interventions being used, or the entire change process. In essence the question becomes, "Is student growth occurring, and if so, what is the extent of the growth and the contributing factors?" If student growth is not occurring, the leader must ask why not and what additional changes are needed?

Using data from these assessments, school leaders can make determinations as to whether programs should be retained, altered, or eliminated. Information collected can also inform the next redesign initiative. When assessments are complete and decisions are made regarding revisions to the plan, that information should be communicated to school personnel and members of the community as soon as possible.

TEACHER APPRAISAL   An additional step in the assessment process is the appraisal of teachers. This process might consist of classroom observations, teacher self-assessments, student benchmark assessments, individual teacher conferences, and mentor feedback. Each of these processes can generate information regarding teacher effectiveness and modifications that are needed in the area of instruction. The supervisory process described in Chapter 6 is strongly recommended as a tool for use in enhancing teacher performance and, ultimately, student achievement. In sum total, school leaders should understand that the school improvement process is continuous, and the assessment phase should inform the next redesign initiative.

In summary, implementing the change model presented in this chapter, or any change model, school leaders are well advised to make change that is informed by a shared vision, and ensure that the program plan is developed based on solid theoretical principles and a conceptual framework that is easily understood. Change is not likely to be sustained if the change initiative is not shared by the faculty and other stakeholders. Therefore, school leaders can ill afford to assume that the faculty and stakeholders are in agreement with the change initiative; they must acquire evidence of their agreement. Once the model is implemented, school leaders must stay connected and know what is occurring in the schoolhouse at all times.

Implications for Leadership

- The personal beliefs of school leaders affect their approach to instructional improvement.
- Leadership effectiveness, to some extent, is the result of interaction between the style of the leader and the characteristics of the environment in which the leader works.
- The experience level of teachers, demographics of students and their families, and curriculum offerings must be taken into consideration as school leaders plan the redesign of the instructional program.
- School leaders must be committed to understanding the unique complexities of the entire school and community, not just the elements contained in the schoolhouse.
- With an in-depth knowledge of the characteristics of the community being served, school leaders are poised to design and implement instructional programs containing motivational strategies that are effective in enhancing student achievement in that community.
- Sharing responsibility and leadership for instructional improvement will likely increase and maximize change capacity.
- If the instructional program is to be improved to the extent that the needs of all students are addressed, school leaders will have to effectively function in a dual role. They will have to have knowledge of instruction and do the right things as instructional leaders; then, they must have leadership skills and do the right things while practicing the art of leadership.
- Focused professional development is a necessary component in the school improvement process.
- School leaders can remove some obstacles and clear the path to vision attainment by providing ample and ongoing professional development for teachers in research-based instructional strategies.
- Adequate resources must be provided to teachers and other school personnel so they can fulfill their assigned responsibilities.
- By involving all faculty and staff in the practice of leadership and providing them with the needed resources, school leaders build a capacity to implement the change initiative.
- Distributing leadership responsibilities facilitates the school becoming a whole. Through this oneness, people continually seek to enhance the whole.
- Instructional improvement is a result of planning, implementation, and evaluation on a consistent basis.
- Preparing and sharing data on the progress of the school improvement process provide valuable information to the school and community. Additionally, school leaders can use it as they plan next steps for enhanced student achievement.

Reflective Practice

1. What are some procedures you would use to set the stage for school improvement?
2. What is your personal standard of excellence?
3. What are three theories that you would use to inform the change process? Explain why you selected those theories and how they inform your leadership practices.
4. What are some procedures that you would use to clearly and concisely communicate a change initiative to the school and community?
5. What is your concept of an impacting school?
6. Explain how you would share with a faculty the analysis of data that revealed that forty (40th) percent of the students in all grades were functioning below the fiftieth (50th) percentile in mathematics, and all of those students are of a particular minority group.

Chapter Essentials

Knowledge of Self and Others + Knowledge of Effective Leadership Strategies = Effective Practice

When school leaders have an understanding of themselves and others, and understand the needs of teachers and students, they can lead, making a connection between teacher effectiveness and student achievement.

The Role of 21st-Century School Leaders

An in-depth analysis of effective 21st-century school leaders who make and sustain instructional change that impacts the academic achievement of all students reveals that they are academically inclined. In addition, they associate with and constantly seek the mentorship of other effective leaders, are proactive, innovative risk-takers, generative thinkers, and engage themselves and their faculty in instructional activities at all times.

Principle

Student achievement is optimized when school leaders connect alternative courses of action with the student's current state of existence and transform it into conditions that positively affect their lives.

Dichotomy

From current conditions in the schoolhouse to vision attainment in the schoolhouse

In effective 21st-century schools, leaders assess current condition relative to student achievement, facilitate the creation of a vision for the future, and utilize research-based practices in leading the school to vision attainment.

References

Blankstein, A. (2004). *Failure is not an option: Six principles that guide achievement in high performing schools*. Thousand Oaks, CA: Corwin Press.

Cushman, K. (1999). Essential school structure and design: Boldest moves get the best results. *Horace. 15*, 5.

Fullan, M. (1993). *Change forces: Probing the depths of educational reform*. Philadelphia: The Falmer Press.

Fullan, M. (1996). Leadership for change. In K. Leadwood, J. Chapman, D. Carson, P. Hallinger, & Hart (Eds.), *International handbook of educational leadership and administration: Part 2* (pp. 701–721). Dordrecht, The Netherlands: Kluwer Academic Publishers.

Fullan, M. (2001). *The new meaning of educational change* (3rd ed.). New York: Teachers College Press.

Gainey, D. D., & Webb, L. D. (1998). *The education leader's role in change: How to perceive*. Reston, VA: National Association of Secondary School Principals.

Green, R. L. (2009). *Practicing the art of leadership: A problem-based approach to implementing the ISLLC Standards* (3rd ed.). Upper-Saddle River, NJ: Prentice-Hall.

Girvin, N. (2001). *The principal's role in K-12 professional development. Strategies for K-12 professional development*. Retrieved June 10, 2004 from Web site: http://www.askasia.org/for_educators/professionaldevelopment

Hargreaves, A., & Fink, D. (2003). Sustaining leadership. *Phi Delta Kappan, 84*(9), 693.

Harris, A. (2002). *Distributed leadership in schools: Leading or misleading*. Paper presented at the 2002 British Educational Leadership, Management, and Administration Annual Conference. Retrieved June 10, 2006, from Web site: http://www.shu.ac.uk/bemas/harris2002.html

Hord, S. M. (1997). *Professional learning communities: Communities of continuous inquiry and improvement*. Austin, TX: Southwest Educational Development Laboratory.

Israel, M. (2003). Effective strategies for staff development: A wire-side chat with Angela Peery. Education World. Retrieved June 14, 2004 from Web site: http://www.educationworld.com/a_admin/admin307.shtml

Lewin, K. (1951). *Field theory in social sciences*. New York: Harper & Row.

Marzano, R. J., Waters, T., & McNulty, B. A. (2005). *School leadership that works*. Alexandria, VA: ASCD Publications.

Maxwell, J. C. (2001). *The 17 Indisputable Laws of Teamwork*. Nashville, TN: Thomas Nelson, Inc.

Miron, L. F. (1997). *Resisting discrimination: AYrmative strategies for principals and teachers*. Thousand Oaks, CA: Corwin Press, Inc.

Nanus, B. (2002). *Visionary Leadership: Creating a compelling sense of direction for your organization*. San Francisco: Jossey-Bass.

National Association of Secondary School Principals. (2004). *Breaking ranks II: Strategies leading high school reform*. Reston, VA: Author.

O'Neill, J., & Conzemius, A. (2006). *The power of SMART goals*. Bloomington, NJ: Solution Tree.

Schmoker, M. (2006). *Results now: How we can achieve unprecedented improvements in teaching and learning*. Alexandria, VA: Association for Supervision and Curriculum Development.

Seikaly, L., & Thomas, R. (2004). *Leading your school through a school improvement process*. Retrieved June 10, 2004, from Web site: http://www.mdk12.org/process/leading/leading.html

Sergiovanni, T. (1996). *Leadership for the schoolhouse*. San Francisco: Jossey-Bass.

Spillane, J. (2005). *Distributed leadership*. The Educational Forum. Retrieved June 10, 2006, from Web site: http://www.findarticles.com/p/articles/mi_qa4013/is_200501/ai_n9473825

Concluding Thoughts

When an individual assumes the role of principal of a 21st-century school, that individual is actually assuming the role of instructional leader charged with the responsibility of enhancing the academic achievement of all of the students the school serves. To fulfill that responsibility, school leaders must first develop a strategic plan. Then, they must implement that plan using principles of open social system and motivational theories. Principles of these theories inform the need for school leaders to establish an empowering, collaborative school culture. Enhancing academic achievement is not a single event conducted by a single individual. Rather, it requires a faculty working together, striving to understand the complexities of the school organization, identifying goals that need to be achieved, and building bridges to the attainment of those goals through relationships.

It should be clearly noted that establishing and working in an empowering, collaborative culture is not as simplistic as one might think. The dynamics of working with a faculty of individuals with multiple backgrounds and values make establishing an empowering, collaborative culture a challenging endeavor. Therefore, school leaders must identify the skills and attributes of individuals, assign and clarify roles and functions, and involve them in tasks that they have the capacity to complete, meeting a pre-determined standard of excellence. The tasks assigned necessarily have to be identified at the beginning of the change process, so as to convey total inclusion and value for the expertise and creativity of the individuals receiving the assignments.

Making significant instructional change brings certain challenges which require school leaders to be synergistic, balancing tasks and relationships. They have to begin with the end in mind, learn the culture of the school, have a perception of people, research the need for change, and structure the process. Then, they must approach tasks with passion, be persistent in seeking task completion, and focus on results, utilizing data to identify and inform the facts. The faculty and staff have to be valued, and they must feel a sense of purpose. The underlying purpose must be teaching and learning, and that requires knowledge of what students need to know and be able to do to live and work in a social and political democracy.

School leaders must keep in mind that self-awareness and socialization are critical issues that can inhibit successful implementation of any plan, regardless of how well it has been developed. Being the instructional leader in name is not sufficient; rather, through the interaction with individuals, school leaders have to radiate positive energy. They cannot be content with average progress; far too many school leaders have failed to meet the needs of all students because they accepted average success, met the needs of large numbers of students, became complacent, and failed to conduct inquiry into strategies that lead to educational excellence for of all students.

In the schools and school districts where we have worked, it has been our experience that the potential of achieving effective change comes as a result of having definitions for each stage of the process and each concept in the process, knowing the outcome being sought, and using pre-determined group decision-making techniques. Using the four dimension of leadership, Understanding Self and Others; Understanding the Complexity of Organizational Life; Building Bridges to Goal Attainment Through Relationships, and Utilizing Leadership Best Practices, school leaders effect change in schools and school districts that leads to enhanced academic achievement for all students. They develop a process that is based on solid theoretical principles, trust the process, and let the process work.

APPENDIX A

Relating Phases of Instructional Change to the 13 Core Competencies

Steps for Instructional Change	Relation to Core Competencies	Description
Phase 1: Creating the Vision: A Standard of Excellence	*Visionary Leadership*	The principal facilitates the staff's understanding of the need to establish a clear sense of purpose—the vision and/or goals of the school. A determination is made of the standard of excellence the school staff desires to reach.
	Unity of Purpose	The principal's primary responsibilities during this phase are to direct and empower teams as they begin to mold their understandings about the school's instructional process, the change process, and approaches to school improvement.
Phase 2: Assess Current Conditions	*Instructional Leadership*	Student data must be collected, both individually and collectively, by grade, subject, and skill sets.
	Curriculum and Instruction	Teacher data must be collected, both individually and collectively, by grade, subject, and skill sets.
	Diversity	Sample data to assess include report cards, attendance, retention rate, graduation rate, dropout rate, Terra Nova, and ACT scores.
Phase 3A: Identification of the Discrepancies	*Instructional Leadership*	A determination is made of the difference between current conditions and the established standard.

(continued)

Steps for Instructional Change	Relation to Core Competencies	Description
	Collaboration	The results of the data analysis conducted in Phase 2 can be used to facilitate the identification of instructional areas that will receive priority. Collaboration with the faculty during this phase is vital, as the skills and knowledge of teachers enhance the accuracy of findings.

Phase 3B: Assess the Causes of the Discrepancies	*Instructional Leadership*	The principal leads the faculty through this process by raising and addressing the following questions:
		 1. Is there evidence to suggest that there is a problem?
		 2. What is the problem?
		 3. Is the problem a serious one?
		   a. What does the achievement data say to us?
		   b. What skills do students most often fail to master?
		   c. Where are those skills taught?
		   d. Who teaches those skills?
		   e. What resources are being used?
		
		 As discrepancies are identified and analyzed, principals might
		 • seek to identify root causes and contributing factors to the discrepancies revealed by the data.
		 • collect evidence to support conclusions reached.
		 • identify a small number of high-impact causes to address in the school improvement plan effort.
		
		 To assess the cause, principals might also
		 • assess the internal and external culture.
		 • assess the internal and external climate.
		 • review teacher readiness levels.

(continued)

Steps for Instructional Change	Relation to Core Competencies	Description
Phases 4 and 5: Identify the Needed Change and/or Modifications, Selecting Program Strategies, and Goal Setting	*Instructional Leadership*	School goals and/or objectives that relate to the needed change and/or modifications must be established. Principals in effective schools facilitate this process by taking the following actions: • Review district long-term goals • Identify annual objectives for the new school improvement plan • Identify evidence that is acceptable as a measure of goal attainment • Hold open discussions about how teachers will monitor the progress of each of their students (Marshall, 1992; McEwan, 2003) There are three questions that might be used in facilitating this process: **(1)** What approach does the faculty currently use to address instructional needs of students who are having difficulty in achieving identified learning outcomes? **(2)** Have teachers developed an appropriate criteria to be used in assessing the work of students? **(3)** What information will assist us in making an accurate assessment of student needs? Principals must also lead the faculty in identifying the evidence of goal attainment that will be acceptable, as well as the data they will collect throughout the year to monitor progress toward the objective.
Phase 6: Assessing the Capacity for Change and/or Modification	*Instructional Leadership*	Change capacity refers to the faculty's ability to conduct and sustain that change when key individuals leave. To assess change capacity, principals must consider the following: • Level of dissatisfaction • Short and long-term costs • The extent to which the faculty understands the vision

(continued)

Steps for Instructional Change	Relation to Core Competencies	Description
		• The consequences of the change • The degree of difficulty in making the change • The amount of extra time and attention that will be required to implement the new program
Phase 7: Build the Capacity If It Does Not Exist	*Collaboration*	If a school does not have the capacity for a desired change, the leader can build that capacity by reversing existing conditions. Other effective strategies include: • Establishing effective lines of communication between the school leader and the community • Securing community support for the change concept • Acquiring expertise in the new program concept • Driving fear out of the school • Working out collective bargaining regulations that facilitate change • Acquiring necessary approvals from the State Department of Education • Identifying sources of the necessary resources • Utilizing effective change strategies
Phase 8: Implementing the Change	*Professional Development* *Inquiry*	Pool the resources of the school and community to implement the plan Implement a professional development plan that addresses teacher needs Implement an assessment model that will continuously provide data on both teacher and student needs Effective Instructional Approaches • Small Group Instruction • Cooperative Groups • Project-based Learning • Coaching • Interdisciplinary Units

(continued)

Steps for Instructional Change	Relation to Core Competencies	Description
Phase 9: Conducting a Formative and Summative Assessment	*Assessment*	Conduct pupil and program assessments The following guiding questions can be used by principals in conducting the formative assessments of pupils: • What assessments will be used to evaluate progress and at what pre-determined intervals? • What procedures will be used to analyze formative assessment data? • What intervention strategies will be utilized for remedial and enrichment needs revealed by the data? • What kind of comparisons will be made with this data?
Phase 9A: Formative Assessment		When conducting program assessment, principals should raise two guiding questions: **(1)** Was the program implemented as it was designed? **(2)** Did the program produce the results that it was designed to produce? Conducting a formative program evaluation allows the leader to acquire and use information about the program before it is fully implemented or during the refinement stage. This type of evaluation is conducted to ensure that there are no flaws in the program design and that the program is appropriate for the area of change under consideration. In conducting formative pupil evaluations, principals can improve student performance by measuring at frequent intervals during the learning process.

(continued)

Steps for Instructional Change	Relation to Core Competencies	Description
Phase 9B: Summative Assessment	*Assessment*	Summative evaluations address the totality of the program responding to the questions: (1) Did the program do what it was designed to do? (2) How effective was the program in achieving the goals for which it was implemented? In general, this type of evaluation is undertaken after the program has been operational for a specific period of time. It occurs annually and is designed to present conclusions about the merit or worth of a strategy, intervention, or program. Data from these assessments can be used to make recommendations regarding whether strategies, interventions, or programs should be retained, altered, or eliminated.

APPENDIX B

Suggested Readings

Chapter 1

Collins, J. (2001). *Good to great: Why some companies make the leap . . . and others don't.* New York: Harper Collins Publishers Inc.

Gore, W. G. (2002). *Navigating change: A field guide to personal growth.* Memphis: Team Trek.

DuFour, R., & Eaker, R. (1998). *Professional learning communities at work.* Alexandria, VA: Association of Supervision and Curriculum Development.

Goleman, D. (1997). *Emotional intelligence: Why it can matter more than IQ.* (2nd ed.) New York: Bantam Dell Publishing Company.

Marzano, R. J., Waters, T., & McNulty, (2005). *School leadership that works: From research to results.* Alexandria, VA: ASCD.

Chapter 2

DuBrin, A. J. (1996). *Human relations for career and personal success.* (4th ed.) Upper Saddle River, NJ: Prentice Hall.

Glickman, C. Gordon, S., & Gordon, J. (2004). *Supervision and instructional leadership: A developmental approach.* Upper Saddle River, NJ: Prentice Hall.

Goleman, D. (1997). *Emotional intelligence: Why it can matter more than IQ.* (2nd ed.) New York: Bantam Dell Publishing Company.

Goleman, D., Boyatzis, R., & McKee, A. (2002). *Primal leadership: Realizing the power of emotional intelligence.* Boston, MA: Harvard Business School Press.

Maxwell, J. (1998). *The 21 irrefutable laws of leadership.* Nashville, TN: Thomas Nelson Inc.

Chapter 3

Despain, J., & Converse, J. (2001). *. . . And dignity for all.* Upper Saddle River, NJ: Prentice Hall.

Maxwell, J. C. (2005). *The 360° leader: Developing your influence from anywhere in the organization.* Nashville, TN: Thomas Nelson.

Chapter 4

Collins, J. (2001). *Good to great: Why some companies make the leap . . . and others don't.* New York: Harper Collins Publishers Inc.

DuFour, R., & Eaker, R. (1998). *Professional learning communities at work: Best practices for enhancing student achievement.* Bloomington, IN: National Educational Service.

Chapter 5

Ackerman, R., & Masln-Ostrowski, P. (2002). *The wounded leader: How real leadership emerges in times of crisis*. San Francisco: Jossey-Bass.

Feinberg, W., & Soltis, J. (2004). *School and society*. New York: Teachers College Press.

Hoy, W., and Sweetland, S. (2001). Designing better schools. The meaning and measure of enabling school structures. *Educational Administrative Quarterly, 37*, 296–321.

Chapter 6

DuFour, R. (2007) Professional learning communities: A bandwagon, an idea worth considering, our best hope for high levels of learning. *Middle School Journal, 39*(1), 4–8.

Glickman, C. D. (2002). *Leadership for learning: How to help teachers succeed.* Alexandria, VA: Institute for Schools, Education, and Democracy.

Marzano, R., Walters, T., & McNulty. B. (2005). *School leadership that works: From research to results*. Alexandria VA: Association for Supervision and Curriculum Development.

Mink, O., Owen, K., & Mink, B. (1993). *Developing high-performing people: The art of coaching*. Cambridge, MA: Perseus Books.

Zachary, L. J. (2000). *The mentor's guide: Facilitating effective learning relationships*. San Francisco: Jossey-Bass.

Chapter 7

Ciancutti, A., & Steding, T. (2001*). Built on trust: Gaining competitive advantage in an organization*. Chicago: Contemporary Books.

Grant, R. (1996). *The ethics of talk: Classroom conversations and democratic politics, fearless cause. Teacher College Record, 97*(3), 470–482.

Mink, O., Owen, K., & Mink, B. (1993). *Developing high-performing people: The art of coaching*. Cambridge, MA: Perseus Books.

Chapter 8

Bossidy, L., & Charan, R. (2002). *Execution: The discipline of getting things done*. New York: Crown Business.

Elmore, R. (2003). *Knowing the right thing to do: School improvement and performance based accountability*. Washington, D.C.: NGA Center for Best Practices.

Gladwell, M. (2002). *The tipping point: How little things can make a difference*. Boston, MA: Little Brown and Company.

Chapter 9

Blankstein, A. (2004). *Failure is not an option: Six principles that guide achievement in high performing schools*. Thousand Oaks, CA: Corwin Press.

Fullan, M. (2001). *The new meaning of educational change*. (3rd ed.) New York: Teachers College Press.

Green, R. L. (2009). *Practicing the art of leadership: A problem-based approach to implementing the ISLLC Standards.* (3rd ed.) Upper Saddle River, NJ: Prentice Hall.

Marzano, R. J., Waters, T., & McNulty, B. A. (2005). *School leadership that works.* Alexandria, VA: ASCD Publications.

National Association of Secondary School Principals. (2004). *Breaking ranks II: Strategies leading high school reform.* Reston, VA: Author.

APPENDIX C

Roles and Responsibilities of the Principal

The principal serves as the lead learner in the school with responsibility for managing resources, leading the instructional program, and providing educational services for students and staff, consistent with established standards.

INSTRUCTIONAL RESPONSIBILITIES

The general instructional responsibilities of the principal include the following:

- planning, implementing, monitoring, and evaluating the instructional program in a manner that addresses the needs of all students in attendance.
- communicating to all stakeholders the vision, mission, and expectations of the school.
- facilitating leadership for the proactive, comprehensive planning and implementation of a curriculum that addresses the needs of a diverse and multi-cultural student population.
- working collaboratively with all stakeholders to ensure vision, mission, and goal attainment.
- holding all students to a standard of excellence that is aligned with local, state, and national standards.
- facilitating the school's engagement in an ongoing school improvement plan.

MANAGERIAL RESPONSIBILITIES

The general managerial responsibilities of the principal include:

- managing the school building to ensure a warm, wholesome, and safe school environment.
- preparing and managing the school's budget.
- maintaining records and reports, as required by local, state, and national agencies.
- supervising the use of all school facilities.
- assuming full accountability for school property, thus, maintaining an accurate inventory and securing storage facilities.

- operationalizing a system to secure resources for the school through establishing business partnerships, grant writing, and relationships with parents and community organizations.
- maintaining an effective system of student transportation.
- keeping central office administrators apprised of all school operations and needs.
- coordinating a program of food services with appropriate personnel.

PERSONNEL RESPONSIBILITIES

The general personnel responsibilities of the principals include:

- maintaining a quality-teaching faculty.
- participating in the recruitment, selection, and supervision of all school-level personnel.
- establishing and maintaining positive relationships with faculty, staff, students, parents, and community stakeholders.
- conducting a performance appraisal of all school-level personnel.
- providing a program of professional development activities that will address personnel needs as they surface for the expressed purpose of enhancing teaching and learning.
- practicing distributive leadership.
- facilitating the establishment of a school culture wherein everyone respects diversity and treats individuals with dignity and respect.
- establishing a positive relationship with all service providers and coordinating the delivery of services to students.

GENERAL RESPONSIBILITIES

In general, the responsibilities of the principal include:

- establishing a positive relationship with all central office personnel. Special consideration should be given to building relationships with individuals in the areas of: (1) curriculum; (2) instruction; (3) business services; (4) human relations; (5) plant management, and (6) pupil services.
- working collaboratively with the general public and establishing positive media relationships.
- maintaining high standards of behavior for students, faculty, staff, and other stakeholders.
- keeping the school in a positive light and in good standing with the local board, state, and national agencies.

APPENDIX D

The Key Elements of Impacting Schools

Over the last five years, we have prepared more than sixty (60) school leaders who are currently serving in school districts across West Tennessee. The preparation process included the involvement of stellar principals who served as mentors and coaches. During this five-year period, we have had various opportunities to observe schools that are making a positive impact in the lives of the students they serve. These principals and the schools they lead have some unique characteristics. In other instances, we have observed schools that are struggling, at best, simply addressing an onslaught of challenges on a daily basis. Quite interestingly, the schools that are not making an impact are failing in the implementation of the same characteristics that schools making an impact are succeeding in implementing. The characteristics that cause a school to make an impact in student achievement do not exist in schools that are not making an impact. Thus, a void in select characteristics is prohibiting some schools from making an impact. These characteristics are summarized below:

- *School leaders understand self and other individuals with whom they work and serve.* They know what they believe, what they value, and how their behavior influences the behavior of other individuals. In addition, they are knowledgeable of the beliefs and values of followers and how the behavior of followers influences the leaders' behavior. With this knowledge and understanding, school leaders are able to suspend assumptions, refrain from making broad generalizations, and balance the inward forces of their personal values and beliefs with the outward display of their behavior.

  School leaders who are making an impact on student achievement have built a capacity to lead. One approach to building that capacity is by developing a deep understanding of the individuals with whom they work and serve. This knowledge allows them to utilize the strengths and interests of individuals to effectively move the school organization toward its vision. With an understanding of self and others, there is a foundation for leadership. Once this foundation is built, individuals can strive to lead with confidence, embracing the skills and attributes of all stakeholders. School leaders who are not making an impact on student achievement do not have a foundation on which to lead. Thus, they use up human energies coping with problems, putting out fires, and justifying their behavior to the faculty, central administrators, and the community they are attempting to serve.

- *The collective faculty has deep knowledge of subject matter and is skilled in sharing that knowledge with students of diverse backgrounds and needs.* In impacting schools, the entire faculty assumes responsibility for every student in the schoolhouse, and they have created a system for the learning of all students to occur. They know the students, understand, respect, and appreciate them. Because they conduct inquiry into best practices and participate in extensive professional development programs, they are skilled in processes and procedures that can be used to teach students who lack background knowledge and are experiencing difficulty in reading and writing.

  In schools that are not impacting student achievement, the faculty complains about student discipline problems, their inability to read and write, their lack of background knowledge, and their fundamental problem-solving skills. They resist collaborating with one another, compete for high-test schools, and consistently engage in sidebar conversations about the school and the challenges the school is not able to address.

- *The school leader has a strong connection with central administrators and can influence them to support the needs of the physical plant and the instructional needs of students.* The bridge that makes these connections has been built through relationships. Success in the school organization has become a reality because relationships are built between the school leadership and central administration. There is power in the school leader's ability to influence central administrators to behave in a manner that fosters school goal attainment.

- *The faculty understands that schools are multifaceted social systems, and there has to be a solid connection between and among all of the parts.* They have come to terms with the need to develop an array of positive connections among themselves, their students, and their colleagues, as well as with various members of the external community.

  They realize that schools are social systems comprised of a large number of individuals employed to perform specific functions. Because functions in the schoolhouse are interdependent and interrelated, there has to be an interconnection. The extent to which one individual is able to complete a task in an effective manner is dependent on the cooperation, collaboration, and, often, the extent to which other individuals complete assigned tasks. Because of the interdependency of the work, individuals have to build relationships sufficient to make strong connections with other individuals in the organization. This connection causes the organization to function effectively. The stronger the connection between principals and teachers; teachers and teachers; teachers and students, and the school and community, the greater the impact the school is able to make in the area of student achievement.

When the connection is strong between teachers and students, teachers understand their students, provide a safe, supportive, challenging environment, and establish meaningful learning partnerships. Students view their teachers as being objective and not displaying cynical behavior. In schools that are not making an impact, that is less likely to be true.

Teachers in impacting schools view their peers as professionals who know their craft. Teachers in schools not making an impact are not so positive in their views of others, tending more to question the professionalism of their peers, provoking conflict of a competitive nature. Principals in impacting schools take a positive view of teachers, viewing them as professional and involving them in leadership roles and the decision-making process. Conversely, principals in schools not making a positive impact in the academic achievement of students frequently perceive the teachers as the major problem and avoid placing them in leadership roles or involving them in the decision-making process.

In schools that are impacting student achievement, there is a strong connection with the community. Parents are a part of the teaching and learning process. They are aware of school programs and activities, know their children's teacher(s), and are frequently engaged in collaborative dialogue with them.

Consequently, it is not beneficial for individuals to function in isolation. Rather, to effectively complete tasks and perform their assigned roles, individuals must function as a part of the larger system, connecting with other individuals and elements in both the internal and external environments of the schoolhouse.

- *The school leader, faculty, and community stakeholders develop and sustain a school culture that manufactures positive energy that they utilize to address school challenges with a focus on instruction.* A school leader who is making a positive impact on the lives of students is aware of the culture of the school and the impact that culture has on teaching and learning. Individuals understand that the culture of the school contributes to relationship building, commitment of individuals, establishment of policies and procedures, program development, and the level of trust that exists among organizational members.

  Conversely, if the school is not making an impact, it is likely because individuals inside of the schoolhouse are unaware of the nature and magnitude of their dissatisfaction. They fail to acquire answers to pertinent questions about the culture of the school and how it affects organizational life. They function as if all schools are the same, failing to realize that all schools are unique and different and when a positive school culture does not exist, academic achievement of students is negatively impacted.

- *The school is structured in a manner that facilitates the distribution of leadership, enabling the skills, attributes, and talents of everyone to be fully utilized. If programs, activities, and/or events are educationally sound, they are administratively possible.* There is a predetermined means of directing behavior, making decisions, communicating, and coordinating roles and functions, taking into consideration the critical need to establish interpersonal relationships. In schools that are making a positive impact on student achievement, the faculty and staff are aware of these means, have participated in developing them, embrace them, and utilize them to foster student achievement.

This scenario can be reversed in schools that are not impacting student achievement in a significant manner. There is little regard for the establishment of positive interpersonal relationships; the faculty is afforded little flexibility, and power and authority are invested in a few people at the top of the organization. In addition, little supervision occurs; there is a void in directions and little, if any, accountability for the actions of individuals.

- *The school community has collectively established a standard of excellence, and individuals in the community accept that standard.* That standard of excellence is in agreement with external standards established by educational centers at the district, state, and national levels. The daily focus is on programs and projects that the faculty and staff can implement to reach the established standard. The faculty, individually and collectively, has identified and accepted the role they must play in reaching the standard. They collaborate with others to acquire any needed assistance in fulfilling their role. Everyone has a voice and feels that his/her voice is accepted, valued, and appreciated.

Student achievement is the primary concern, and data regarding student achievement drive curriculum and instructional decisions. Teachers in impacting schools are conscious of the importance of quality teaching, and they conduct inquiry into best practices and discuss those practices with colleagues with the intent of addressing the needs of underachieving students.

Students in impacting schools appear to be more in harmony with teachers' efforts to have them learn than are students in schools that are not positively impacting their academic lives. Many students in non-impacting schools tend to resent the fact that they are not receiving an education that will serve them well in the future.

- *Self-reflection is common practice among faculty members, as they consistently reflect on past behavior to improve current conditions. Having reflected, they conduct inquiry into best practices to use in addressing the needs of their students.* In impacting schools, reflection of the leadership, as well as the faculty, builds the capacity of the faculty and staff to identify what works, what does not work, and how they can make improvements in their performance. They use reflection to build a better self.

The above list of elements is sufficient for the point that we would like to make regarding schools that are positively impacting student achievement.

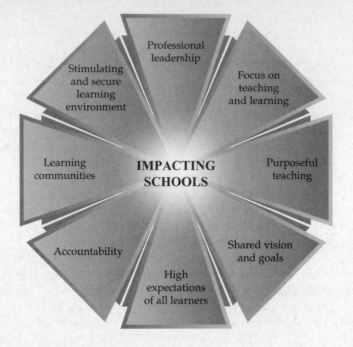

Individuals interested in educational renewal with the intent of making all schools impacting schools should give consideration to how we begin to establish standards, make connections, develop programs, and train a new "breed of teachers and school leaders" to seve a new "breed of students." The suggestions that we make center around the four dimensions: understanding self and others; understanding the complexity of organizational life; building bridges through relations, and utilizing best practices. These practices are the heart and soul of education. Practicing them, school leaders must balance the bureaucratic side of the school organization with the humanistic side, lest the acquisition of academic success for some students will remain a challenge.

APPENDIX E

Twelve Educational Postulates

An Agenda for 21st-Century Educational Leaders

POSTULATE 1

In order for educators to truly reform schools for the 21st century, they must first develop a deep understanding and appreciation for the needs of each individual who enters the schoolhouse doors.

Educators must refrain from the desire to continue to tinker with the system in the name of true educational reform. Schools are not significantly different today than they were one hundred (100) years ago. Educators must refrain from the compelling desire to teach subjects, replacing that desire with the imperative need to teach students.

POSTULATE 2

For schools to truly be effective, they must operate through partnerships, inclusive of universities, parents, community leaders, and governmental agencies.

The challenge of meeting the needs of today's students is more than anyone individual or institution can address.

POSTULATE 3

Every child who enters kindergarten must have at least six peak experiences to propel them out of Grade 12.

School administrators must consider the provision of peak experiences for every child a moral imperative. A peak experience must be sufficient to sustain interest at a particular level and bridge the gap between one level and another level-primary, intermediate, middle, and secondary.

POSTULATE 4

For ethnic minorities to perform exceptionally well on a grand scale in American public education, we must remove two barriers that inhibit academic achievement—the overt and covert manner in which we address cultural diversity.

In a diverse society, competing values are a natural phenomenon that must be respected and embraced.

POSTULATE 5

The conditions in American society that disenfranchise African-American males must be systematically removed.

With the existence of these conditions, it is unconscionable to believe that African-American males can negotiate the rungs of the ladder that lead to success.

POSTULATE 6

The American society rewards individuals who read well, write well, and speak well. An individual may effectively negotiate the rungs of the ladder that lead to success without reading well, without writing well, and without speaking well, but it will be a chance happening at best. Therefore, we must put a system in place that will assist all students to learn to read with comprehension before they exit third-grade.

If students are not reading with comprehension by the time they exit third-grade, they are likely to be challenged for the remainder of their K-12 schooling.

POSTULATE 7

American educators must not only refrain from using terms that categorize and label students, but they must express strong resistance to their use in society.

Terms such as at-risk, underachiever, disabled, etc., are red flags that do not target students for success; rather, they program students for failure. I contend that students may be at risk of failure at one point, and poised to achieve success at another. Then, the question must become, "What yardstick is accurate enough to use in predicting the terminal outcome of any individual, regardless of his/her circumstances? Is change an event or a process?"

POSTULATE 8

Dropping out of school is not an event; rather, it is a process that occurs over a period of time.

As some students interact with elements in the school environment (people, events, and activities), they are pushed to the margin. A dual phenomenon occurs. In some instances, there is an underreaction by individuals who administer the system; in other instances, there is an overreaction. Problems have two sides: the manifestation of an individual's fixed personality and responses to how that student is being treated in social interaction.

POSTULATE 9

Today's schools that are structured in a bureaucratic manner, using bureaucratic practices, are harmful to poor and minority students.

Schools must be structured in a manner that allows academicians to exhibit an expectation that all students will reach an established standard of excellence. In addition, schools must become places where students are viewed as individuals—where people understand and respect their needs and adjust the academic curriculum in a manner that recognizes their experiences.

POSTULATE 10

In American public education, there appears to be a real disconnect between central office administrators and school-based leadership personnel.

Central office administrators must come to realize they are in a supportive role, enabling and supporting school personnel as they seek to find and implement solutions to the challenges they face. We can no longer afford to use a cookie-cutter pattern that is developed in central administration and disseminated to all schools with the expectation that it will be effective for all students.

POSTULATE 11

Educators have established an unrealistic instructional time frame that inhibits the academic achievement for a large number of students.

For schools to be effective in addressing the needs of all students, we must remove this artificial system-imposed time frame that presupposes that all students learn at the same time, at the same rate, under the same conditions.

POSTULATE 12

To truly reform American public education, we must address the issues of assessment, equity, and excellence with the intent of removing barriers to access and achievement.

We can begin the process by providing students who have not met established standards with the best instructors our public school systems have to offer.

INDEX